MADE
IN WHITTINGHAM
STREET

A Memoir

by

GAIL J NEWSHAM

ISBN 978-1-78792-049-1

Book design, layout and production management by Into Print
www.intoprint.net
+44 (0) 1604 832140

CONTENTS

HELLO

Several times over the years, people have suggested I should write my own story, they say I have led an interesting life. I've never really thought that anyone would be particularly interested in anything I had done, and never gave it much consideration, until I started researching my family tree. The thing that struck me when you find out who your ancestors were, in most cases, they are just a name on a census, and pretty much all you can discover about them is their occupation, where they were born, and the names of their siblings and children, but nothing about the real person behind the name. Who were they really, and what did they do with their lives?

I was then inspired by a post I'd seen on social media that said; in a hundred years from now, someone else will live in my house and they won't know that I, or my family ever existed. I also came across a list of how many ancestors we all need to be here in the moment where we are today. In order to be born you needed:

2 parents, 4 grandparents, 8 great grandparents, 16 second great grandparents, 32 third great grandparents, 64 fourth great grandparents, 128 fifth great grandparents, 256 sixth great grandparents, 512 seventh great grandparents, 1024 eighth great grandparents, 2048 ninth great grandparents. For you to be born today from 12 previous generations, you needed a total of 4096 ancestors over the last 400 years. Just imagine all those people – How many struggles in their lives? How many battles did they have? How many difficulties did they overcome? How much sadness? How much joy? How many love stories? How many dreams of a better life for their future?

I am just very tiny dot in the great scheme of things, to be granted the gift of life. I hope I have used the opportunity well and hope my time here mattered. If, in a hundred years from now, my future relatives might be interested to know more of their ancestors, and if these memoirs survive, it might give them a bit of an insight about me, my precious and much-loved family, and my wonderful friends. It's a simple tale of family life, family love, family loss, and a few other events along the way. Courage, injustice and reconciliation. We came, we lived and we died. This is a small part of our life and times. If everyone who has a copy of these memoirs passes it on to the next generation, and each generation after that does the same, rather than simply being a name on a census, we might have a chance of being remembered.

For Sadie, Joe, and our Pat

Till we meet again

WHITTINGHAM STREET

Whittingham Street was situated off Ashton Street, in the Fylde Road area of Preston, nestling in the shadow of St Walburges Church, with its huge white spire that dominates the skyline, and St Marks Church, that has stood almost by its side for generations. Coming up from Fylde Road, Ashton Street ran up to the top of the start of Wellfield Road, and it was the artery of our neighbourhood, with all the shops necessary to keep every family fed and watered. We were a close-knit community, people looked out for each other, and you could leave your front door open and feel safe.

Ashton Street from Fylde Road (Images during demolitions)

To give you an idea of the geography of the area, there were five streets on either side of Ashton Street, all consisting of small terraced houses, and they were; Fleetwood Street, Whittingham Street, Mona Street, Priory Street, and Abbey Street. Pedder Street was the last street on the left. Each home mainly consisted of two bedrooms, a living room, a kitchen, a back yard, and some had a lobby between two houses for access to the yard. There were the odd exceptions for some corner houses who may have had more rooms. In the back yard there was a big wall separating your house from the one in the next street, we backed on to the opposite property on Mona Street. We lived at the top end of

Whittingham Street, which was second left if you were coming up Ashton Street from Fylde Road, and there were three other blocks going all the way down to Newsham Street, which is quite a coincidence, given our family name. Before you reached Newsham Street, there were Carlton Street and Bath Street. There was a ginnel between the houses on Carlton Street, Bath Street, Fleetwood Street and Whittingham Street, built in a kind of square. These properties had access to the ginnel from their back yard. As did those between Mona Street and Whittingham Street. Most of the houses were demolished many years ago, and now only memories remain.

The Ginnel between Whittingham St on left & Fleetwood St on right
Carlton St backs behind camera, Bath St at far end

I was born in Sharoe Green Hospital on 17 July 1953, and grew up at 42 Whittingham Street. I was christened at St Walburges Church, of Roman Catholic faith, but was brought up Church of England. Religion was a bit complicated in our family. Mum was a Scottish Catholic and Dad was C of E. Grandma was an Irish Catholic, born in Dublin, and Grandad was C of E. Dad was christened C of E, but his older sister Kath, was christened RC. Given that complicated little scenario, religion was something that was never forced on me or my sister Pat, and we all just came to our own conclusions.

My christening day outside St Walburges. Our Pat, Mum, Dad and me

We lived in a two-up-two-down terraced house, and like most of us who grew up round our end, as we often say in Lancashire, '*we had nowt, but we wanted for nowt.*' Even though our house may have lacked most modern-day amenities, I still have very fond memories of living there. And although there were periods of domestic upset and worry, I still look back on my life at 42 with great affection. It shaped me into being who I am, and no matter what, it was home. But looking back now, I think our house may have been in a slightly worse condition than some of our friends and neighbours.

It was rented from Charles Parker Bennett, and Mum and Dad did the best they could with what they had. When they moved in, in the late 1940s, there was no electricity in the house, just gas mantles on the walls; there was a big black fire place in the living room and stone flag floors in both downstairs rooms. They had electricity installed as soon as they could afford it, but throughout all our years of living there, it only ever consisted of ceiling lights upstairs and down, and just one plug socket in the whole house. It was a round pin socket situated in the living room, and you wouldn't believe how many electrical appliances ran off that one little socket, it's a wonder we didn't get electrocuted; the television, tele lamp, record player, standard lamp, hoover, and when we eventually got a washing machine, a long extension lead that ran to the back kitchen to power a twin tub. It wasn't plumbed in, and when in use, it had to be moved closer to the sink to be self-filled, and for the pipes to reach to enable the water to drain out. To avoid any leakages, we also needed a bucket to collect the remainder of the water from the lower pipe.

Monday was always wash day, and before we had the luxury of the twin tub, some of our clothes would be washed in a big round tub called a 'dolly tub', and then put through a mangle to squeeze out all the excess water before hanging them on the line, or occasionally in the lobby if it was raining. Mum would sometimes leave big items like bedding to be collected and taken away to be cleaned; in winter it wasn't as easy to get things dried. I can remember our clothes being all stiff and frozen up on the washing line. I'm not certain, but I think the laundry was run from Mrs Blissett's shop on Ashton Street, and we collected the clean laundry a few days later. Mrs Blissett was also the local seamstress who made clothes for those who could afford it, and also provided an alteration service for shop bought items needing a nip or a tuck.

The gas and electric meters, where we had to put our shillings in the slot, were in the living room in a cupboard to the left side of the chimney breast and someone would come round to empty them on a regular basis. It was horrible inside that cupboard; the walls were still unfinished rough brickwork with a touch of whitewash to try to make it look a bit better, and I remember lots of cobwebs and the smell of damp. There was a bigger cupboard on the other side of the chimney breast and it went right up to the ceiling with three big drawers at the bottom, but it was eventually taken out to make a kind of alcove where the bureau lived.

There was never any hot running water plumbed in at 42, and I have a vague memory of a shallow stone sink and a cold water tap in the corner of the back kitchen to the left of the window, before we progressed to a more modern unit with an enamel sink fitted under the window. The hot water we did have, came from a gas geyser on the wall which just about supplied enough hot water for one washing up bowl at a time. We didn't have a bathroom either and only had an outside toilet at the bottom of the back yard, which would often freeze up during the winter. My Dad would put a paraffin lamp next to the cistern to try to prevent the inevitable, and we had newspaper cut into squares to use as toilet roll. If we needed the toilet during the night, we had a bucket on the landing at the top of the stairs, only for number ones though. My sister Pat always blamed her constipation on having an outside loo, no one wanted to go down there in the middle of the night.

When I was born, my Dad was working on Ribble buses, in fact my Mum was a clippie there too, but left when she was pregnant with me. Dad was a driver, and he used to drive coaches to Scotland as well as doing local runs. When I was a toddler, I always wanted to play with the badge he wore on his uniform, *'Daddy's red badge,'* he could never get away from me. Mum always said I was a Daddy's girl and he was quite a 'hands on' Dad really, which I suppose was a bit unusual for a man in those days. Happen it was because he was away during the war and missed having those times with our Pat. He told me he used to wash my nappies, and when he was driving round the countryside in his double decker bus, he would often see nappies on washing lines as he drove through small villages, and he used to say to himself, *'they're not as white as mine'*!

Me, Dad in his Ribble uniform, and Mum

When I was only a few months old, Mums' brother, Uncle Phil, bought me a small teddy bear, he was called Sooty, and Mum used to make up a squeaky little voice for him, it was wonderful, I loved that bear so much. I think he must be one of the first original Sooty bears from the early 1950s, not a glove puppet, but a proper teddy bear. I remember one time we lost him, couldn't find him in the house anywhere, and I was inconsolable. But much to everyone's relief, Sooty was eventually found under the settee. He went everywhere with me and I still have him today.

When I was young, I shared the bedroom with my sister Pat, she was a war

10

baby, and ten years older than me, born on 12 February 1943. I always looked up to her and she was always the boss. I have no recollection of this but she told a tale about having me balanced on her feet while she was laid on her back on our bed, she was holding my hands pretending I was flying or something. I didn't have a nappy on during this particular play session and she was laughing and saying 'ahhh' as she waved me about, until apparently, I started to wee and it went in her mouth. Revenge was sweet though as when I was a bit older, and I do remember this, she used to make me walk round the bed and then hit me with a pillow at the back of my knees so that I fell into a heap, with her in fits of laughter as my legs buckled under me. And then she made me do it all over again. According to my Mum, I was walking at about ten months old.

Pat and me in 1954

There was another sister between Pat and me, our June, she was born on 2 June 1947. She was a blue baby and only lived two days. I don't really know what that was, but Mum said if she had been born just six months later, they could have saved her. It really upset me when she told me about all the baby clothes they had neatly folded in the drawers ready for her to wear when she came home, and how heart-breaking it was that she never did. Pat was so excited to be getting a new baby sister, and I can't begin to imagine how sad and upset she must have been. She was only four, but I'm sure she would still have felt the loss. My Dad told me he carried her little white coffin at the funeral and she is buried in Preston Cemetery with his auntie, Emily Edith Newsham. He never forgot baby June.

I think one of my earliest memories of our Pat was when I was about eighteen months old, possibly younger, and being sat on her knee. She was wearing a full skirt and was saying, '*Gail sits on Pats' knee; one, two, three, weeeee*,' and as she parted her legs I would giggle as I fell through her knees to where her skirt saved me from hitting the floor. I also remember my favourite item of clothing from round about the same time, it was a Siren Suit, a brown/fawn coloured onesie type garment with a zip up the front, I called it my teddy bear suit. I can still recall searching through the sideboard to find it because I always wanted to wear it. I also have vague memories of our Pat being a bridesmaid for Auntie Patsy, our Mum's sister, and I recall shouting to her as they walked down the aisle, while I was wearing my favourite suit. It was my absolute pride and joy; I loved that suit and was most upset when I grew out of it.

Our Pat left of bride and groom, Neville and Patsy 1954
Uncle Phil and Auntie May far right

At Patsy's wedding. Mum and me centre, in my favourite teddy bear suit, with her family 1954
Auntie Theresa, Julia, Uncle John, Auntie Ina, Uncle Sam, Auntie Nan

Grandma and Grandad lived just round the corner from us at 4 Ashton Street, on the corner of Fleetwood Street, where they ran a fruit shop together. Mary Kathleen, nee Toohey, and Robert Matthew Newsham, aka Kath and Bob, and they were married in 1911. There was a cellar in their house with stone steps going down to it from behind a door in the living room. I was always scared of that cellar, it gave me the creeps, probably because they told me there was a *bogey man* hiding in it to stop me going down and hurting myself. They had a black grate fire place in the front room and a small galley sort of kitchen at the back. Grandma used to make a delicious rice pudding and it was always a favourite when I went to see her. It was thick and creamy and I used to love the skin on the top and the burnt bits around the edges, I would ask my Dad to get it off for me, '*peel it Daddy*', and he used to scrape it off with a spoon. Grandma loved cats and she had a beautiful ginger tabby, he was a big cat who I called Chiddy. It wasn't his proper name, but it's what I called him. I think it was because I couldn't say the 'ch ch ch', sound you make when calling a cat to you. I'd visit her quite often and always came away with an apple or an orange from the shop.

13

Grandma and me, backyard Whittingham Street, August 1954

Dad would sometimes take us swimming in the River Ribble at Church Deeps in Walton le Dale. Our Pat and my Dad were good swimmers, and Pat used to go to Saul Street Baths with her friends as often as she could. There were also some 'Slipper Baths' available for families who didn't have their own facilities, and Mum sometimes took me there so we could have a proper bath. I caused her a bit of embarrassment one time when I said quite loudly, *'are you weeing in the bath Mummy.'* She wasn't too happy with me that day. There was also a clinic on Saul Street and I recall our Pat taking me for some childhood vaccinations. I cried all the way there and begged her not to take me in, but there was no escape. We also went swimming at Haslam Park Open Air Baths. The pool was always really cold and it would take ages to brave it and get in. The best thing to do was jump straight in and get it over with. There was a slide in the shallow end, and one time, my Dad took me up the slide while our Pat was waiting at the bottom, and I thought the plan was for her to catch me when I came down, but she deliberately let me go under the water. They were laughing when I came up coughing and spluttering and I said to her disgustingly, '**You**'!

Me, Our Pat and Mum at Church Deeps

Dad would take me out for walks when I was a toddler. They had a push chair for me, with small wheels and a red and white canvas seat, but I often wanted to push it myself, no doubt testing his patience going too slow. We'd go under the old canal bridge, which was just wide enough to allow one vehicle through at a time, to near where the Lime Kiln pub used to be. At the back of my mind, I seem to recall there being an old public toilet outside there, I might be wrong, but I do recall a green iron type construction, I think it was a gentlemen's only loo. There was some land on the other side of Aqueduct Street which had a bit of an incline going up towards the canal. For whatever reason, Dad called it '*the Cadley,*' and I used to love going to the top of it then running down into his arms as he caught me and swung me round. Simple pleasures but such fond memories. I had a pair of brown lace up ankle boots with fawn fur round the top which I probably wore running up and down the Cadley, or my red Jumping Jacks sandals, when the weather was better. I remember them both with the same fondness as my teddy bear suit.

Sat on the sideboard wearing my favourite boots

I don't know how old I must have been, but I was only very young when we had vinyl tiled floors put in the house. It must have been when they were covering the flag floors, because I can still recall the smell of the asphalt from the wagon outside. We had a gas fridge in the kitchen, a free-standing gas cooker, and a kitchenette unit housing crockery in the top compartment, some food stuff in the middle, and pans at the bottom. There was also a wooden rack up towards the ceiling, where we hung our clothes to dry and air. The rack was held up with rope and lowered by a pully. Imagine airing your clothes in a room where all the cooking was done, all our 'clean' clothes would have ended up smelling of chip fat and all sorts. But I suppose everyone was in the same boat, so maybe no one really noticed. As a young child, our Pat used to wash me in the kitchen sink, and I remember being sat on the draining board naked and shivering, asking her to swill warm water over me to help keep me warm. It was always cold in there especially when trying to have a 'bath', someone always wanted to go out to the toilet causing an icy blast of cold air while in a state of undress. It was bloody cold in the winter; especially upstairs, we had no heating at all up there and I can remember ice forming on the inside of the single glazed bedroom window. We often had to put coats on the bed for extra warmth, Dad's old army greatcoat and Mums beaver lamb coat, are two that spring to mind, and hot water bottles were a must.

When I was about four years old, I caught Scarlet Fever and had to go to the Isolation Hospital at Deepdale. I wasn't allowed any visitors in the ward which meant Mum and Dad were only able to talk to me through the window. I wasn't allowed to take Sooty with me either, whatever you took had to be incinerated when you left, so I had to take a scruffy old pot doll with no clothes and matted hair, I was a bit embarrassed about the state of her and she was nowhere near as comforting as Sooty. I was in a room with another girl called Lindsay and I was jealous because she had a lovely soft teddy bear to cuddle up to. We got into trouble when we ripped up a comic of hers and stuck it on our legs with our spit, pretending the bits of paper were plasters. When the nurse came round and saw all the mess she wasn't best pleased, but it was me who copped the blame and made to clean it up. I remember clearly the day I was going home, and can even recall the dress I was wearing, it was white with green stars, a green collar and trim. I got my knee stuck behind the radiator by the window trying to climb up, eagerly looking out for my Mum and Dad to come for me, and a nurse had to help me get free. We went home in a taxi, and when I went in the house, Mum said all my Easter Eggs were waiting for me in the big cupboard in the living room. I was so excited, I climbed up on her chair and opened the cupboard door so that I could see them all, it was a wonderful sight and I couldn't wait to get stuck in. I was glad to be home.

Our Pat used to play with me a lot, when I was younger, and when I was about five years old, she would teach me to jive. We had a small record player, and we'd play the old 78 records and be bopping along to songs like 'All shook up' and 'Rock around the Clock.' She always loved rock and roll; my favourite was 'Everyday' by Buddy Holly. As I got a bit older, we would sing 'If you were the only girl in the world', with our lips together. It made us both laugh as certain words made your lips tingle, probably the 'you's' and the 'world'. Try it, and you'll know what I mean.

Back yard at Whittingham St – me aged 5, with Sooty and my football

We had a coal fire in the living room and the back kitchen. Dad would some-times put the coal shovel up to the fire and cover it with newspaper so that it would 'draw' the heat and make the coal burn more quickly. If you didn't keep an eye on it though, the newspaper could catch fire. The coal-hole used to be under the stairs in the back kitchen and what a mess it was under there, a bit like that cupboard in the living room, only worse. I remember us having a toasting fork and Mum and Dad used to make toast straight from the fire. We eventually progressed to gas fires which made life a lot easier and the coal-hole was subse-quently given a bit of a make-over, but the toast never tasted the same. However, we eventually got a new cooker, a Flavel Equerry, if memory serves, it was white with red control knobs, and had a posh eye level grill. Much easier to make the toast on that.

Like most kids of my generation, I had head lice. We called them 'nits' or 'biddies', that were often discovered by a nurse who went round to schools inspecting children's heads. '*Nitty Nora, the biddy explorer,*' as we called her. My Mum used to make me sit on the floor in front of her while she looked through my hair trying to get them out. In her efforts to make me sit still, she used to tell me stories about one of the 'biddies' who she named 'little Derek,' but for some reason she called them Mowdies. I have no idea why, it might be a Scottish thing, but little Derek had lots of adventures and he always survived when she washed my hair with the special soap used to kill them off. I don't know if this haircut below, is a result of my Mum's attempt to rid me of the mowdies. I can't think of another reason why she would let me walk about looking like that.

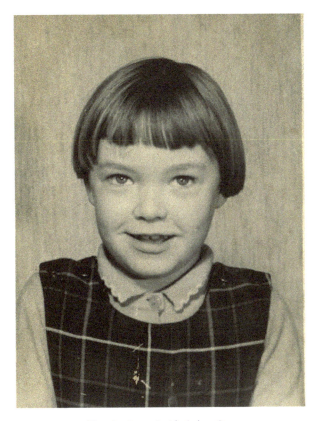

Mum's attempt at hairdressing

I do remember her singing the song, '*All I want for Christmas is my two front teeth*,' and this could be from around that time as mine just seem to be growing back. Mum used to enjoy singing, and being a Glaswegian, she would sing Scottish songs, *Bonnie Scotland* and *I Belong to Glasgow*, were two of her favourites and I would sing along with her. She would also sing some sad songs that made me cry. They'd be about kids who'd lost their Mum, or another who didn't get any toys at Christmas, I'd be sobbing my heart out saying '*sing it again Mum*'. I wanted to let those kids have all my toys when she'd sung these. See over for lyrics.

The bells they rang out, they were partners for life,
Then back to their homestead as man and wife,
When out of the room came a sad little lad,
And these were the words that he heard from his Dad,
This lady has come, just to look after you,
And there's one thing my darling that I want you to do.
To call this lady mother, to love her you must try
The same as the other, but the boy said with a sigh,
To call this lady mother, for your sake Daddy I'll try,
But to love her, no I could never, the same as the other,
Dear mother that I once had.

Why doesn't Santa Claus bring something to me, why does he never ever call?
Other girls and boys have got plenty of toys, but I've got nothing at all.
I have heard of Christmas Carols, I have seen a Christmas tree,
But I must have been a very naughty little girl, coz he never brings nothing to me.

Like every kid, I used to get so excited about Father Christmas coming down the chimney and bringing me all my presents. I was out in the street one Christmas Eve, just outside our house, trying to pass on the time till bed time, when Mr Sandman would come to put sand in my eyes and make me go to sleep before Santa came. There had been some work going on outside the Co-op. They'd been digging up the pavement on the opposite side of the street and I was jumping about on the rubble from one side to the other. Call it childhood imagination, but as I looked up to the heavens I saw an outline of Father Christmas on his Sleigh, with all the reindeers, just like we expect it to look, as clear as anything, travelling across the night sky. Must have been a dream eh; can't explain it, but that's definitely what I saw.

When I was a bit older, we got our first television. It was a small black and white portable, housed on the cupboard above where the gas and electric meters were. I used to love watching *Torchy the Battery Boy* and *Four Feather Falls*. We also used to watch wrestling and me and my Dad would wrestle on the floor together, and I'd get mad at him if I thought he'd let me win. When Mum and Dad were getting ready to go out on a Sunday night, '*Sing Something Simple*' was always on the wireless. Dad would be in the back kitchen singing along while he was having a shave. We had a tatty rectangular mirror with a wooden frame, leant up against the window for our vanity purposes, and as he was shaving the soap off his face, water always dripped off his elbow and wet the floor. I expect Mum would have shouted at him making a mess, so he put newspaper down to protect the tiles from being damaged. I always wanted to comb his hair when he had rubbed Brylcreem into it. He used to part it in the middle in those days and then put his fingers on each side to shape it and give it a wavy look.

Me and my Dad

We would sometimes go to the Savoy Cinema on Ashton Street, just across the road from Grandma and Grandads' fruit shop. It was reputedly the only cinema in Preston where the screen was behind you when you walked into the auditorium. I remember watching *the Three Stooges* and cowboy films there. We also went to the Star Cinema situated on the corner of Fylde Road and Maudland Road, opposite where Café Majorca used to be, and where the University of Central Lancashire Campus is today. This was another unique picture house due to the building being rounded rather than having corners. My Dad enjoyed going to the pictures and he would sometimes take me to the cinemas in town, the Gaumont, Palladium and Ritz were regular haunts. Two films that immediately spring to mind are '*Sergeants Three*', with Dean Martin, Frank Sinatra, and Sammy Davis Jnr, and '*Zulu*' with Michael Caine and Stanley Baker. I've seen Zulu so many times over the years and I always think of my Dad whenever it's on the tele. It's a great film. When I was six years old, our Pat took me to the Gaumont, to see a stage performance of the musical Oklahoma.

Pat used to do a lot of the cleaning around the house in those days, and an example of the older sister definitely being boss, was when my Dad came home one day to find me tied to the bed so she could get on with her chores without any further interference from me. Pat did the best she could to keep it clean, she always wanted it to look the best it possibly could.

Our Pat outside 42, just out of picture on right

The neighbours on our side of the street were Sally & Hughie Curran at 43, who we shared the lobby with, and Mrs Johnson on the other side at number 41. She used to bang on the wall if ever we were making too much noise. At number 40 was Tom & Celia Hastie and their son Frank, Mr & Mrs Dawson at 39, and Mr & Mrs Butterworth at the top in 38. On the other side of the street from the bottom were, Annie Taylor at 32, Bert & Annie Yeulett and their son Mick at 33, Mr & Mrs Ribchester at 34, Bill & Nellie Moss and their family at 35, Mr & Mrs Higham at 36, and a strange lady who always dressed in black at the top in 37. Mick Yeulett still lived at 33 with his own family after his Mum and Dad moved away, and it was he who made us the long extension for the twin tub. I used to babysit for him and his wife when I was older.

At the top of our street was Weston Street where my friend Diane Moore lived, and to the left was Farington Street which led up to the railway lines, there was some kind of scrap yard on the left, and houses on the right. The McCartan family lived at the top end and Doris McCartan was good friends with my Mum. They had three girls called Pat, June and Gail, which was another coincidence, and a son Keith. On the other side of Weston Street was Leyland Street. The photo below of me and my friends is taken on the corner of Farington St.

Back row: Diane Moore, Anne Kelly, Vic Woodburn
Front: Sharon Kelly and me

We used to have bonfires on the corner Farington Street, close to Weston Street. There wasn't a lot of room between the houses and health a safety would have a field day with it today. I don't know who organised them there, it was before my own bonfire building adventures. Looking back, it must have been a bit risky, and I do recall the lady in the corner house being concerned, but everyone had a good time and I don't recall any accidents or damage to property.

After my Dad left Ribble Buses, he worked as a milkman for Preston Dairies on Bow Lane, and I'd often go with him on his round at weekends or in the school holidays. I would sit on the crossbar of his bike as we cycled to the dairy together. I used to love leaving the milk bottles on the doorsteps and collecting the empties, especially the little half pint bottles. His round was in the Maudland Bank area, down Dunderdale Street, Bentick Street, Cobden Street, Tuson

Street, and Peel Street, then we would go up Tulketh Brow, Stocks Road, and all the streets off there. There used to be a chocolate flavoured milk called '*Micky*', and it was always a special treat. It was fascinating seeing all the electric milk floats being charged up in the yard, and pouring the left-over milk into big churns when we got back to the depot. I learned a lot from my Dad during those times, watching and listening how he dealt with the customers. I said to him one time, '*you awlas crack on you're grateful*', which I suppose was my early understanding of 'flannel'. He was good at flannel was my Dad, there's an art to doing it well, so the one being 'flannelled' doesn't realise. Dad was a master.

Mum often took us to buy new clothes from Wynn's dress shop, on the corner of Fylde Road and Maudland Bank. There was always a good selection to choose from and Wynn would allow customers to pay weekly, which was a great help to many families in those days. I would sometimes take the five or ten bob for Mum to pay an instalment off the slate, while pushing Sooty in my little toy pram. Mum also used to take me to Mary Hills Outfitters, which was a bit further up Fylde Rd on the other side of the road. I remember her getting me a blue blazer from there, it had white piping round the collar and cuffs, I thought it was really smart. We used to get some of our furniture from Mathers which was also on Fylde Road, just a bit further down from the Syntax. No flat pack stuff in those days, it was always delivered ready assembled.

Weekend treats were the eagerly awaited parched peas from Greenwood's newsagents. Annie and Winnie ran the shop, and they always put a billboard sign outside, '*Parched Peas Now Ready*'. They were thruppence (one and a half pence today) for a small triangular bag, or a tanner (sixpence) for a bigger bag, and they were delicious. If I went with my Dad for them, we would play Cowboys and Indians as we went down Ashton Street, pretending to be shooting at the Indians on the roof tops. When the Whitsuntide fair came to town, Dad would take us in the 'Pea Saloon'. The parched peas there came in a cup with some stock from the pan. I thought it was a great treat to be able to sit down on the wooden benches while we ate them with a plastic spoon, with all the smells and sounds of the fair going on around us. Mum used to love going on the Waltzer, especially when the guy would spin you round so it went faster, and pinned you to the back of the seat. The louder you scream, the faster we go!

Like most young kids, I wanted a dog and kept pestering Mum and Dad to let me have one. I was seven years old when Dad brought home a puppy. He had this little ball of fluff under his jacket, he was a mongrel with all white fur and a pink and black nose; we called him Tinker. I used to play with him on Farington Street near to the railway wall, chasing round on some wild grass at the top end, I really loved that dog. Our neighbours, Mr & Mrs Higham from further up the street, had a Lancashire Heeler and he used to come barking at our front door for Tinker to come out to play, they played together quite a lot. I came home from school one day and Mum and Dad were both sat in the living room and my Dad was waiting to tell me some bad news. Tinker had been killed in accident, he was just outside our house on the other side of the street, still under an old sack where the tragedy occurred. I ran out to see him, it was awful, poor Tinker lay there lifeless in a pool of blood, he was only nine months old. Apparently, a wagon had run over him while they were delivering meat to the butchers on Ashton Street. He was just laying outside in the sun, the driver didn't see him and ran over him as he was reversing, he was really upset about it, and said he could hear him yelping. I was heartbroken. My Dad wrote something in his diary, and I still remember it all these years later. *Tinker passed away today, killed by a motor. May he never know hunger nor thirst in the happy hunting grounds. From his Dad. 29 May 1961.* Coincidentally, his Dad had written in his 1945 diary, a tribute to his dog, also named Tinker. *He was a much beloved dog, the family's best friend. He served them well right to the very end. He was as nearly human as an animal can be, and he is mourned as one who leaves a lovely memory. Sweet of temper, fond of heart, and gentle in his ways, but human life, though brief, is not as short as canine days. And if there is a heaven for men, their dogs will find it too, and walk beside their masters in the way they used to do. To, Little Tinker, Dada's Baby.* Like father, like son.

Pat went to St Marks Junior School until it closed and then she moved to Christ Church on Bow Lane. She passed her eleven plus and went to the Park School, but she was very unhappy there. Some of the girls looked down on her because of where we lived and our Dad being 'just a milkman'. They all had big houses and Daddy would drop them off in their car, but Pat went to school on her pushbike. I'm sure this period of her life had a lasting effect on her. She couldn't wait to get away and left at fifteen without sitting any more exams. She went to work at the Lancashire Evening Post (LEP) and worked on the counter, front of house, and I would often call in to see my big sister when I went to town. Looking back, it must have been hard for her, me frequently coming in with my friends while she was trying to do her job, it could have got her into bother. I remember being told quite firmly, not to go too often, especially if I wasn't dressed up. Mum wasn't too happy. Pat used to get a day off in the week due to working on a Saturday. One time, I didn't want to go to school because I wanted a day off like our Pat. I was at St Marks Infants when this occurred, so I was only very young, and I think it was Diane Moore, who was a bit older than me, who was taking me when I decided I didn't want to go. I was wandering the streets and the teachers must have been wondering where

I was and it caused a bit of a panic. I'd walked all the way down St Marks Road and on to Water Lane. When I was found and asked why I wasn't at school, I just said, '*it's my day off.*'

I don't remember much more of life with our Pat at 42, but I do recall her not being very patient with me when she was teaching me how to tell the time. I had a children's Cinderella watch, it had a cartoon image of Cinderella on the face, and she would try to explain it all to me, quarter past, half past, quarter to, but I don't think I was picking it up as fast as she would have liked. My Dad helped me grasp it a bit better. I once went to a birthday party for my friend Steven Shaw, and it was our Pat who had to take me. I can imagine her not being best pleased when she would probably have rather been elsewhere. It can be a bit of a drawback when you're a teenager and you have a sister so much younger. I think I might have been a bit of a nuisance for her during those years, when she perhaps wanted to go out with her friends instead. I do remember a teddy boy coming round asking to see her. Dad answered the door and told him she wasn't at home and words were exchanged. I don't think he believed our Pat wasn't in and was quite insistent on seeing her. It all got quite heated and a bit of an altercation developed. I must have gone to the door because of the raised voices to find them fighting in the street, and I was saying, '*go on Dad, hit him*'. It all concluded with Dad pushing the teddy boy through the living room window of Mr & Mrs Yeulett, who lived opposite us. It must have been quite a shock for them and I don't suppose it went down very well at all. Dad was very apologetic though, he was acting under provocation, and did pay for the window to be replaced. Although a more recent image below, the house with the black door is where the incident occurred.

Cousin Una outside 42

26

Our Pat was working at the LEP when she first met Andrew (Andy) Hoyle. She was fifteen and he was ten years older than her. He was 6'2" and I'd never met anyone as tall as him before. I saw him for the first time with my Mum when I was five years old. I remember saying, *'Mum, he's a giant'!* I remember Andy coming to our house when they were courting and I must have been a bit of a pain because I was always wanting his attention and draping myself all over him on the settee. And when I was put to bed, I frequently came down stairs with the excuse of 'being thirsty.' It obviously didn't put Andy off, as he did pop the question and asked Dad for Pats hand in marriage. It was an exciting prospect for me being one of her bridesmaids, and she often made me practice walking up and down at the back of the settee to learn how to walk properly down the aisle on her big day, but when I got fed up, she'd threaten me with not being a bridesmaid if I didn't get it right. Andy once bought me some roller skates for my birthday and I remember risking life and limb skating hell for leather down Bath Street, towards Fylde Road. We'd roller skate down that side because the pavement had been resurfaced and it was lovely and smooth which meant you could roll a lot faster. We would be heading towards the main road but turn round just in time at the cigarette machine outside the newsagents shop and then do it all over again.

Pat and Andy got married at St Marks Church on 18 March 1961, and I remember her getting washed in our bedroom on her wedding day, with our red washing up bowl placed on the bedside cabinet. She was relieved that this would be the last time she would ever have to do that, she was glad to be leaving 42.

Andy and Pat

27

Me, Pat Atkinson, Stephen Sherlow   Me aged 7

After they were married, Pat went to live with Andy and his Mum at Holme Slack and they had a bathroom. I would go and stay with them every Saturday, even sleeping with them both in a three-quarter bed. Pat suggested I sleep with Andy's Mum, Mrs Hoyle, but I didn't fancy that idea, I'd always slept with Pat at 42. Andy must have been very understanding putting up with me every week, but eventually my visits were cut down to once a month. But Pat would still play games with me even then. They lived on the corner of Holme Slack Lane and Daisy Lane which had quite a big garden, and she would play tig with me and chase me round the flower beds, which was much better than the back yard at Whittingham Street. I was only about eight/nine years old, but I'd get the bus on my own to go over to see her, one bus into town from either Ashton Street by Molly's pie shop, or the bus stop on Fylde Road, outside the Grove pub, and then the Holme Slack bus all the way to the last stop before the terminus. Mrs Hoyle used to bake a lot and I always loved the sponge cake she made. She would cook the mixture in an oblong tin and cut it into slices and I always liked the crispy well done bits at the edges the best. It felt special going there, like being a proper visitor, she would get out china cups and saucers and we sat at a table to eat. Whittingham Street wasn't big enough to use a dining table every day, ours was just for Christmas. For breakfast we would have jam on toast, and Pat would put the toast back under the grill until the jam started 'bubbling', it was delicious.

After our Pat left home, when it was bedtime, I always asked my Dad to come and tuck me in, I suppose it helped with getting used to being in the room on my own, but it became the routine. When it was cold, it was like getting in between two sheets of ice and I'd be curled up in a tight ball, it took ages to inch my feet down to straighten my legs for the bed to be warm enough. He used to pull the covers up over me and say *'keep out of that wind'*, and he would tell me stories about soldiers who had been lost out in the snow and would dig a hole to protect themselves from the wind, and they survived. He said it was the wind that did the damage and he always made me feel toasty warm when he was tucking me in. Keep out of that wind was later abbreviated to KOOTW when he used to write to me when he was working away. It was something that always stuck.

A few months after our Pat got married, Mum's cousin, Maureen Harkins, was getting married in Glasgow, and we were all invited. It was a real adventure travelling up together and we had a great time. This is probably one of my first proper memories of my Scottish cousins. Theresa McCabe, daughter of Mum's brother John, was the flower girl for Maureen, she was about five years old and I was just eight. I can vividly remember the two of us running and sliding on the slippery dance floor having a whale of a time like kids do, and probably driving the adults mad with our antics. When Maureen was preparing to leave the reception to go off on honeymoon, her Mum, Auntie Jean, was crying. I went over to comfort her and said, *'don't cry Auntie Jean, they come back, our Pat did'.*

Auntie May, Gran, our Pat, Auntie Ina, Mum

When my Gran (Mums Mum) came to visit us from Glasgow, I think she must have stayed with Auntie Nan or Auntie Patsy because they had a spare room and a bathroom, we didn't have either. Gran would often bring periwinkles when she came to see us, and I always thought they were a Scottish thing she had brought down with her, we only seemed to have them when she called to see us. When I was a bit older I realised she had actually bought them on Preston fish market. I could eat them when I was a kid, but not sure I could manage them now.

Gran McCabe and me, Ribble bus station passage

The first school I went to was St Marks Infants until it closed down, and then I went to Christ Church Infants on Fitzroy Street. I remember being taught our times tables and we wrote them all down with chalk on a small blackboard as the teacher Miss Halliwell, recited them to us. One time we were putting on a concert for a parent's night. My part was skipping into the hall with some of the girls from my class singing *Polly put the kettle on*. My dad came to watch me and he was the only male in the audience. Poor Joe, the things you do for love.

My next school was Christ Church on Bow Lane. This school was for juniors and seniors, and I was following in our Pats footsteps. One of the teachers was Mrs Bishop, and she still fondly remembered my big sister as one of her star pupils. I always felt I was a bit of a disappointment to Mrs Bishop because I was never as clever as our Pat, and try as I might, I couldn't match up in Mrs Bishops eyes. I remember her teaching us a history lesson where we had to draw some prehistoric animals, and I could sense her disappointment in my lack of drawing ability. She also took us for PE, and I faired a bit better with that. In another lesson she was teaching us some spelling, and artificial was the word we had to learn and practice at home. I spent ages learning how to spell that word and could recite it quite fast. When we were in class, she asked for a show of hands for who could spell artificial. Mine shot up straight away, miss, miss, miss; but I wasn't chosen and I was so disappointed, my efforts were in vain. I always wanted to please her and I still look back on Mrs Bishop as one of the teachers who had the most influence on my life. She was quite strict and I did get hit by her with a ruler, and some slaps at the back of my legs, she didn't stand for any messing. One time, some other pupil was getting the leg treatment and she leant over too far on her chair and fell on the floor. It was quite embarrassing for her, funny for the class, but I actually felt sorry for her. She got the same bus home as I did, and one particular time the bus was full. When we arrived at the next stop, more people got on and Mrs Bishop told me to stand up to let someone sit down, and I did exactly as I was told. On another occasion, I stood up to give my seat to a man, but he said he was ok and told me to sit back down. Mrs Bishop said to him, '*she won't sit down while you're standing,*' and it's something I still do to this day. If I'm on a bus and other people are standing, I always get up and offer my seat, and I always think of Mrs Bishop. My Dad used to deliver milk to her, and on one particular occasion, she was going on to him about me. He said to her, '*Have you ever thought she might be frightened of you Mrs Bishop*'? I don't know what the outcome was but Mrs Bishop seemed to mellow a little, and became a bit kinder I suppose. I remember visiting her at her home on Tomlinson Road many years later. She seemed genuinely pleased to see me, like it really meant something to her. I went to visit her a few more times after that and she made me feel very welcome. I didn't realise but she was quite poorly and she passed away a short while later, I think she had lung cancer. I was sad to learn she was gone, but so glad I had the chance to make my peace with Mrs Bishop.

Teachers at Christ Church School
Back row: Mr Armstrong, Mr Halliwell, unknown, Mr Hopkins
Front: Mrs Morgan, Miss Beamish, Mr Hayes, Miss Barton, Mrs Bishop

Another good lesson I learned at Christ Church School was timekeeping. In the hall, they had what was called 'the line', it was an imaginary line, where if you were naughty, you had to go and stand on the line, which was basically just facing the wall in the hall, and your name was written in a book. If your name went in the book twice in one week, you got the cane from the headmaster. If you were late for school, you had to stand on the line, so if you were late twice in a week, you got the cane. I never got the cane for being late I am pleased to say. However, I was stood outside the headmasters' office one time, waiting for the cane, when Mr Hopkins came along and asked what I was doing there. *'I'm for the cane sir.'* He went in to the heads office and had a word in his ear, came out and told me to go back to my class. Thankfully I escaped the cane on that occasion. Dad also delivered milk to Mr Hopkins, and I think it might just have saved me that day, but I did get the cane another time.

I was made monitor for a short while with another girl in our class, we'd go in early to put books out on each desk, and make sure everyone had a pen. There was a free-standing double-sided blackboard in the classroom, it was fixed on to a standing frame with wheels at the bottom, and it could be turned over. I once had the daft idea of trying to balance on it while trying to keep it in a horizontal position. It ended in complete disaster; I fell off and grazed my left shin rather badly. I didn't get any sympathy from the teacher and was taken off monitor duties. I suppose I got off lightly really but I still have the scar today. Another injury occurred when we were learning to sew. We had those old-fashioned Singer sewing machines, the ones where you used your feet to pedal to make the needle move up and down. I somehow managed to get my finger in the way ending up with the needle going right through the nail on my middle finger and coming out at the other side. When I showed Miss Beamish, our teacher, she just pulled the needle out, put a plaster on my fingertip and told me to get on with it.

Christ Church School class photo – Junior 1
Back row: Miss Isaacs, Robert Holland, Ken Simmons, Steven Godkin, Peter? Keith Robinson, David Topping, Andrew ?, ?, Gordon Marsden, Mr Hayes Headmaster
Middle: Johnny ? Richard Howarth, Catherine Parr, Enid Davidson, Margaret Hornby, Sandra Thomson, Bill Nickson, Richard Coyle
Front: Elaine Utting, Susan McCourt, Janice Atkinson, Susan Townsend, Jennifer Whittaker, Wendy Nicholson, June Howarth, Mandy McGowan, Carol Woodburn, me, Sandra Jones

Corporal punishment was the norm in those days, not just at school, but at home too. I remember getting hit with Mum's blue slipper, and the occasional belt. Our Pat got the belt as well when she was younger. I never thought of it as abuse, or that I wasn't loved, it's just how it was back then. Maybe there was a trigger, or a short fuse, I don't know, but it's not done me any harm. Dad only ever hit me once, and it was just a slap on the backside. I asked him for some money, I wanted sixpence for some sweets or something, but he only had a three-penny bit. I threw it back at him in a tantrum, so he slapped me on my backside and told me to get in the house. I thoroughly deserved it too, I bet he was livid.

My first ever best friend was Marilyn Dawson. We called her Lynn back then, but she's known as Mal now. She found me in the street when we were about three and a half years old. She took me to her house in Fleetwood Street and said to her Mum, '*Mum, look what I've found*', and from then on, we became inseparable.

Me and Mal

We often got into lots of bother, and it was always me who got the blame; '*you're not playing with that bloody Gail Newsham anymore*', was uttered by Mals' Mum Doreen, on many occasions. It was the worst punishment ever not being able to play with my best friend. We were once taken home in a Police car for playing hopscotch on the zebra crossing outside Greenwoods on Fylde Road. And we used to play on the railway lines; the West Coast main line was just at the top of our street, on what we called 'Cock Robin'. I have no idea why it was called that, just one of those childhood mysteries still remaining unsolved. I remember once picking some of those purple flower things that grow on railway embankments, and giving them to Doreen. They were probably weeds really, but I was hoping a bit of an apology might do the trick, '*please can your Lynn play with me again?*' Happen a bit of flannel I had learned from my Dad.

Mal and I often reminisce about our childhood, it's a very special gift still

34

having someone in your life after so many years, and she shared a few of her recollections to paint a picture of some our exploits. Over to Mal. *'My Mum once sent me to the co-op on Ashton Street for a quarter of corned beef. She said she was really hard up and gave me her last half crown (23p today). I asked her, if there's any change, can me and Gail have some toffees. She said, 'I suppose so.' So, we took this half crown and went to the co-op. My Mum was waiting and waiting for us to come back with the corned beef but we never turned up, and she came out looking for us. We were playing at the bottom of our street and she shouted, 'Lynn, where's the corned beef,' and I said, oh, they didn't have any. So she asked me where the money was, and I said I haven't got any. She wanted to know why I didn't have it, and I said, I bought me and Gail some toffees coz you said we could have some. She was blazing. I'd spent my Mum's last half crown on two boxes of jelly babies for us both, and my poor Dad didn't get any tea!'*

'Another eventful shopping trip was when my Mum sent us for half a dozen eggs to Cross's grocers shop on the corner of Ashton Street and Mona Street. We went in the shop, got the eggs, and when we came out, there were some bananas on display on a shelf, and we fancied one. And you said to me, 'let's get one'. But there was a grid underneath the display and as I leaned over and stood on it, it gave way and I fell through and cut my legs to shreds. So, I cut my legs, got done for nicking bananas, and broke all the eggs. And that was another night my Dad didn't get any tea.'

'Another time, we made a trolley out of and old coach-built pram, the ones with big frames and great big wheels. We were sat on it and you were at the front driving and I was at the back. My Mum had just had this beautiful lemon and white check dress made for me, it was all smocked at the top and flared from the waist. So, we're driving this trolley and my dress got caught in the wheel and completely ripped the skirt off and I had to go home with my frock like that showing my knickers. I can't remember what my Mum said, but I can imagine.' So can I, and I probably got the blame; again.

We often played on Cock Robin, and would climb over the wall on to the embankment down to the railway lines. When I was there with the lads, we would often play 'chicken' when a train was coming under the bridge towards us. We would lay down with our head on the tracks, feeling the vibration of the steam engine approaching, and see who would be the last one to get up before the train reached us. I'll bet we nearly gave the drivers a heart attack. You could walk along the embankment all the way up to the bridge at Pedder Street, and those of us who were brave enough, or daft enough, would go down on to the tracks, walk under the bridge and play over that side, it's a wonder we never got caught, or injured. There were lots of bushes growing on the embankments and we would collect what we called sticklebacks. They were a bit like a small thistle, purple in colour at the top and prickly, apparently part of the Burdock family. We would pick them until they were all stuck together in a big ball and throw them on our friends' woolly jumpers or in their hair, and they would stick on you. They were a bugger to get off, especially out of your hair, but it was another source of mischievous amusement for us.

Just across the tracks at the top of Cock Robin, was a big water tower with a long metal ladder fastened to the wall, going up to the top. I once climbed up there with some of the lads, and once was enough, I discovered I didn't really care for heights. Near to the water tower at ground level, was an oblong shaped construction made of concrete and sunk into the ground like a swimming pool would be, but with dirty looking water in it. It had a railing around it and there seemed to be what was like a metal drum floating in the water, attached to some kind of pipework at one corner. You couldn't see the bottom to tell how deep it was, but there was a small metal ladder going down to near the water level, and there was also a concrete type of girder going across the middle, which we would sometimes balance on to walk across from one side to the other. We never knew what it was for, it was just somewhere to play. But we had a lucky escape on one particular occasion. Over to Mal for another of our escapades.

'We came home one day and asked my Mum if we could put our swimming costumes on, you'd got your cozzy and a towel, and I went to get mine. Then we went up to Cock Robin, climbed over the railway wall, went down the banking, and crossed over the railway lines. We were going to go swimming in the water. Thankfully my Mum came to the rescue in the nick of time, shouting across the railway lines telling us not to get in because it was a lime pit. It's a good job she realised what we were up to before disaster struck.'

The terrible twosome! Mal and me

Mals' sister Wendy was born in 1959 and we always thought the midwife had brought her in a basket on the back of her motor scooter. Mal remembers her Dad saying, *'come down stairs and meet your new baby sister,'* and her Mum told her Wendy had been found under a gooseberry bush. Our childhood logic figured it must have been the midwife who found her under the bush and brought her home in the basket on her scooter. Here's another recollection from Mal. *'We asked my Mum if we could take Wendy a walk in her pram down the canal to Haslam Park, she must have only been about eighteen months old at the time, which made us both about eight. We pushed her all the way along the canal, as far as the park, and when we got to where the little stream is, we parked her up and went off playing, probably for about two hours. When we remembered Wendy, we came back and she had gone, the pram was empty. I was frantic, thinking, oh my God, where has she gone, and I was running all over asking everybody, have you seen a little girl in a white dress with little blue velvet spots on, and a woman said, 'there's a little girl just like that sat on the bridge.' When we found her, she was sat holding the railings and dangling her legs into the pond watching the ducks. When I got hold of her, I pasted the bloody living daylights out of her, I was mad at her for wandering off but so relieved to find her. She could have been kidnapped, she could have drowned, or anything couldn't she. What was my Mum thinking of letting two eight years old take out an 18-month-old baby?'* But what were we thinking of going off and leaving her.

Mal and Wendy

On another occasion, I had two railway sleepers in our back yard at 42. The biggest one was propped up on the wall near the toilet at the far end. Mal came round and we thought it would be a good idea to use the sleeper as a slide, but Mal cut the top of her leg quite badly on a splinter as she was sliding down, it was quite deep and there was a lot of blood. So that was another occasion for her Mum to utter those famous words, '*you're not playing with that bloody Gail Newsham anymore.*' The plan for the sleepers was to make a big cross for a procession at Easter. My Dad got me some six inch nails from Holderness' hardware shop and I worked really hard hammering away in our back yard putting it together. I had some blocks of wood and made a little step to stand on, and even made an INRI sign for the top. One of the lads was going to play Jesus and drag the cross around the streets and up to Cock Robin, where he would stand on it like in the crucifixion. We'd put notices in Gerties shop on Ashton Street, Targett's shop and Turner's chippy on Carlton Street, to let everyone know about our procession so they could watch as we passed by. But come the big day, the lad in question chickened out of dragging the cross, so I had to do it myself. We couldn't let our public down, could we? We had a Roman soldier, dressed in one of those plastic outfits they had back then, and Mary Magdalene was wearing our Pats wedding dress. I dragged that big cross down our street, across Ashton Street, turned right at Carlton Street, which was cobbled in those days, right at Fleetwood Street and all the way up till we arrived at Cock Robin. What we looked like I dread to think, and I'm sure the neighbours had a bloody good laugh at us, but we meant well paying tribute to Jesus at Easter time.

Many happy hours were spent on Cock Robin and we always had our bonfires there on 5th November. The houses on Weston Street, Farington Street and Leyland Street had been demolished, so there was all the spare land available to build bigger bonfires than before. Wendy remembers the potatoes we used to throw in the embers of the bonfire and picking them out when we thought they were cooked. They were charcoal black, and half raw, but we still ate them thinking they were delicious. Wendy said she remembers me as 'the queen of the bonfire' because I was always organising collection of all the wood. We'd go knocking on people's doors asking if they had any bits of wood they didn't want, and we'd store it in a den area on Cock Robin. They would give us old doors and all sorts of stuff they wanted rid of. We wanted our 'bommy' to be bigger than the one on Abbey Street, or any other in the area for that matter. It was a sense of pride knowing ours was the best, and all our hard work was worthwhile. We once had most of our wood nicked by the Abbey Street lot, so it was a mad rush running round trying to collect more. I'd often go home with grazed knees and elbows from our adventures on Cock Robin, in fact I took a big chunk out of my left knee one time, it probably should have had some stitches in it, but Mum always had plenty tins of Germolene on standby to make everything better.

Mal moved away, or did a flit, as we called it in those days, so we didn't see each other as often, and eventually lost touch. It was daft really, they'd only moved to Wellington Street, which is literally just the other side of St Mark's church, not far at all, but in those days, our world was a lot smaller I suppose. Another friend who moved away was Steven Shaw. He lived on the corner of Whittingham Street and Carlton Street and it was around the time that the new estates were being built in Ingol. Steve's Mum Barbara, was good friends with my Mum. What I remember most about Steve is a time when we were racing our bikes down Fleetwood Street, and somehow, he fell off his bike and his arm got caught in the front wheel of mine. What a mess it was, he had broken the ulna and radius, and his arm was literally flapping about. When he went home and showed his Mum, those immortal words were uttered once more, '*you're not playing with that bloody Gail Newsham anymore.*' After they moved away, we lost touch for many years.

The Miley Tunnel was another haunt that kids of our generation used to frequent. Nearly everyone who lived round our end remembers the Miley Tunnel, it has become part of the folklore of our childhood. The railway line was still operational in those days, the tunnel went from the Maudland area right through to Deepdale, and playing down there was a dangerous game, but many of us took the risk. Apart from the obvious danger of the trains, was the fear of being caught trespassing. There was a signal box just before the entrance, and how we managed to sneak past it without them spotting us, I'll never know. The tunnels were pitch black when you were in the middle. There was a bend in the tunnel and you couldn't see a thing, either in front of you, or behind you, and it was so still and quiet, you could hear the silence. But you had to be very careful if a train came along, or a railway man was walking through. There were safety alcoves to stand in, and if you were lucky, they wouldn't see you, but you had to stand ever so still and hold your breath till they passed by. And if you wanted to be in the 'gang', you had to go through it on your own, without a torch. The gang was called 'Preston Patrol' and the gang leader made us all a membership card. Our secret password was the name of that railway station in Wales. I'm just glad we didn't have to spell it. Llanfairpwllgwyngyllgogerychwyrndrobwllllantysiliogogogoch. Try saying that to get in the den in a hurry!

Miley Tunnel

We also used to go train spotting, and any serious train spotter had a book, known as a Combined Volume, from Sweetens book shop. It had a list of every class of steam, diesel, and electric trains, with all their names and numbers. We'd climb up and sit on the wall on Pedder Street just opposite St Walburges Church, where the west coast main line went to Scotland, and the local line to Blackpool, going to the right passing by St Marks Church and beyond. It was great waiting for the steam trains to go under the bridge with all the smoke billowing out. We sat there for ages noting all the numbers on the engines, and when we got home, we would carefully underline the numbers of all the ones we had seen, in our special book. Sounds a bit boring now, but I loved it back then. There were some train sheds on the other side of the line where the steam engines would go if they needed any maintenance or repairs. We used to sneak into the sheds from an area named '*The Piggy*.' The entrance was at the bottom of Pedder Street and the corner of Maudland Bank. It was called the piggy because there used to be a piggery, where pigs were brought and kept in pens before being taken away in goods trains, presumably to slaughter. Once inside the sheds, we would climb up into the cabs of the engines and I once managed to get in one of the bigger steam trains named *Sir Christopher Wren*. This train was one of the Britannia Class, and you didn't often get to see them. It was quite a feather in my cap at the time.

When I wasn't risking life and limb on the railway lines, or getting into trouble, more often than not, I was playing football with the lads. We'd regularly go on Ashton or Haslam Parks, and we'd also play in the street between Carlton Street, Fleetwood Street, and Whittingham Street, and there were loads of us. John Brooks, Fred Brooks, Russell Flanagan, Mike Turner, Ken Simmons, Tony Jenkins, Paul Mattin, Mick Walpole, Mick Cornall, Cliff Swindlehurst, Mick Whittle, Steve Shaw, Paul Targett, Jim Westhead, Richard Sterziker, and anyone else who wanted to join in. Mr Proctor, who had the garage on Carlton Street, was always coming out and moving us on, because we got too close to the cars he had parked in the street. I don't suppose his customers would be best pleased if their cars were damaged by us playing football, but we didn't really appreciate that back then. We also used to climb over the gates and sneak into his workshop for a look around when it was closed. We didn't take anything, we were just being mischievous. We'd also get into bother climbing over the boards at the bottom end of Mona Street where the railway lines were. I remember getting a good hiding for coming home late from playing down there. And Bulmer's scrap yard on Abbey Street was another source of our exploring where we got into bother if the owner caught us playing in there.

The Canteen grounds on Carlton Street and Mona Street, provided more adventures. The canteen was used by pupils from St Walburges for their school dinners, and when the building was closed it was a bit of a playground for us. It had railings all-round the perimeter and we would squeeze in between them to get in, or climb over the gate. The railings were flat on the top and we would balance on them and try to walk all the way round. I don't recall anyone making it the whole way, but it didn't stop us trying. It was a single storey building surrounded by grass, and we would climb up on the roof and hang down from the bottom of the apex and drop down to the grass below, or those of us who were daft enough, would jump off the lower roof over the entrance to the building. It was also another place for us to play football and we would practice for hours crossing the ball and heading it towards goal, each taking it in turn to be the one doing the crossing, perfecting our craft. Centre-ing and heading as we called it.

Clive Wareing was another of the lads I used to play football with. We would play on Weston Street just outside St Walburges School with John McCann and many of his other mates, including some from down Marsh Lane. Clive was a very good football player and was always team captain when we played our hotly contested street matches. We got back in touch a few years ago and he told me

41

I was always his first pick for his team because I was a better player than most of the lads. Clive played in many of the top amateur teams in Lancashire for a good number of years. Truth be told, he should have been professional really, he was certainly good enough, but family commitments got in the way.

I just want to take a moment here to remember Michael Allen. He was a good friend who lived on Pedder Street and played football with us on Weston Street, and also joined in with collecting wood for our bonfires on Cock Robin. He sadly passed away when he was just eleven years old after a battle with Leukaemia. It was a very sad time, he was very much part of our gang and he was greatly missed.

The canal was yet another adventure playground for us. There was a wooded area by the side of the canal, opposite the houses on Shelley Road, and we had a swing rigged high up in the trees. We also went fishing with our little nets and jam jars to see what we could catch and often came home with sticklebacks, tiddlers and newts. In the winter time, when the canal basin had frozen over, we would play on the ice, being oblivious to the danger. One time, one of the lads who lived further down Fleetwood Street pushed me in the canal and I landed feet first up to my waist in the water. I daren't tell my Mum and Dad I'd been on the canal again, so I called at my Grandma's on the way home to try to get my trousers dry and asked her not to tell them. Standing in front of the fire waiting for them to dry made me late, but they didn't dry and I got found out anyway. I daren't tell them I'd been pushed in, I just said I fell in. However, revenge came sometime down the line, when the lad in question was a bit too close to the edge, and one of my friends pushed him in for me; he didn't land on his feet like I did though and consequently got a bit wetter. His mother went to his house playing merry hell, carrying all his wet clothes to show his Mum and Dad, you could see the drip marks all the way up the street. We didn't knock about with him much after that, keeping out of the way of his mother.

The canal was drained in the early 1960s and we risked life and limb playing there during all the reconstruction work. With the canal bridge being demolished there was then a big drop going down to the road level and lots of sand was used for all the filling in. We would run and jump from the height of the bridge to the ground level, landing in the sand, without ever considering any dangerous consequences. The canal was drained parallel with Fylde Road, right the way up behind the Canning Factory and Thorn Lighting, under the road near Maudland Bank, past the Watering Trough pub, and down to towards Marsh Lane. The houses on Grove Street, Dewhurst Street, Goodier Street, and Flax Street also fell victim to the demolitions, and many of the shops on Fylde Road were also demolished during this period, including the Grove pub and the Brick Makers. One of my favourite shops to disappear was Bramwells. It was like a small temperance bar and we'd go in there for soft drinks like dandelion and burdock, it made us feel grown up. After the canal bridge went, the whole area was opened up as the canal then began from approximately the beginning of Shelley Road, and the road was widened going up to Aqueduct Street. A prefab Brick Makers pub was built on its original site that lasted a few years, and Lorries used to park on the waste land where the houses once were. That became yet another playground for us, the wagons were covered with tarpaulin and tied with rope to keep the load secure, and we would climb up on them and jump from one to the other until we got chased away by the drivers.

Grandma Newsham passed away in September 1962, she had been quite poorly and confined to bed. She had several things wrong with her but was also suffering from senility, as they called it then, but she still recognised my footsteps when I went round to see her. She heard me coming up the stairs and said, *'that's our Gail.'* My Dad was with her at the end and I remember him coming home late at night to tell Mum and me she was gone. In those days, they would have the coffin at home before the funeral, and Grandma was laying in repose in the shop, it was sad seeing her there like that. I was given her Rosary Beads and a necklace to remember her by. I still have them today.

After our Pat had left home, Mum and Dad got a new record player. It was called a Carousel. It had a reel-to-reel tape recorder and radio in the top compartment, and a record player in the bottom that actually played ten records at time. My Dad used to buy random batches of 45 singles from Preston market and we'd always wonder what he would be bringing home next. Mum used to take the micky out of him saying they saw him coming. One of the many records he bought was a piece of music called *Lost Patrol,* and he'd have me marching around the settee with him in military fashion while it was blaring away. *Help Yourself* by Tom Jones was another song he frequently played and always reminds me of him. Mum loved the song, *It's all in the Game,* by Tommy Edwards, and she used to play it on repeat over and over again. *Devil Woman* by Marty Robbins was another of her favourites. There are so many songs that bring back many happy memories of our days at Whittingham Street. This photo over the page, although taken some years later, shows the Carousel under the window, and you can just make out the only plug socket we ever had, to the left of the clock.

43

Auntie Nan, Patrick and Una

One night, I was woken up by some strange noises coming from the streets outside. It went on for quite some time and I couldn't get back to sleep, it was an eerie sound and I was quite scared. I eventually plucked up the courage to wake my Dad to tell him I was frightened of the noise. He sat up to listen and then he got up. He told me to get dressed and we'd go out and see what it was. He said the best way to lose your fear, was to confront it. We walked to the top of the street, round the corner to where the noise was coming from, and we saw a beautiful big white owl sat on top of the cross on the roof of St Walburges club. I'd never seen an owl before and it looked amazing. It was a clear moonlit night, and it sat there quite majestically, looking down and hooting at us. It was wonderful sight. I got back in bed feeling totally reassured and fell fast asleep. Dad did later confess to being a bit apprehensive because he wasn't sure what it was either, but he was absolutely right about confronting your fear, what a valuable life lesson.

I loved my Mum and Dad very much, and I was always telling them or leaving notes for them. I wrote on a wooden coat hanger, which still survives today, *I love my Mum and I hope she loves me too. She is the best Mum in the world,* and on the other side, *I love my Dad and I hope he loves me too. He is the best Dad in the world.* I always wanted to hold Mums hand and I remember sitting beside her on the floor as she sat on her chair in the front room, I said, '*Mummy, when you die, I'm going to cut off your hand and keep it on the mantel piece so that I can hold it whenever I want.*' My Dad seemed invincible and strong, but I would get quite distressed if my Mum was ever injured. She once scalded her hand quite badly when she was working at the Canning Factory, and it really upset me. And after she had her ears pierced at Ashton's jewellers on Fylde Road, they went a bit septic, and I was distraught. There was green matter and blood coming out of them, they looked really sore and I couldn't stop crying. I remember her gently bathing them with salt water and cotton wool and I was so relieved when they got better. Mum was very poorly in 1962, and I had to go and stay with my Gran and Aunty May in Glasgow, until she got better. I was too young to be told what was wrong with her, and after a few weeks away, I was very unhappy and started to fret; so much so, my Dad had to come for me and bring me home.

But, as in most families, it wasn't always domestic bliss at 42. Mum and Dad used to argue quite a bit in their younger days, and it was sometimes quite scary as a young child. I can look back now and perhaps understand why their relationship was sometimes so volatile, and I'm sure alcohol was a contributing factor, but as a kid I used to worry about Saturday nights when they were coming home from the pub. I could sometimes hear them arguing as they were walking up the street and I used to dread the fights when they came in. A child should never have to see their Mum and Dad at each other's throats, and our Pat said it was the same for her before I was born.

Mum had been sent down from Glasgow to work in munitions at the Royal Ordnance Factory at Euxton during the Second World War and would no doubt have expected to return home after the conflict was over. She met my Dad at the Empress Ballroom on 3 March 1941. While they were courting, she was renting a room at a house on Cardigan Street from a lady called Mary McConachie, (I think Mum later had a room at Mrs Walker's on Fleetwood St) and sometime down the line she found herself pregnant. She would never admit she was expecting when they got married and always maintained that Pat was born two months premature. They were both just weeks away from being twenty years old.

45

Joe and Sadie on their wedding day. 25 July 1942.
(Harold Sharples best man, Auntie Kath maid of honour)

It must have been devastating when Dad was drafted into the Army only a few months after their wedding, leaving Mum, who was expecting their first child, living with his Mum and Dad at the fruit shop on Ashton Street. I'm not sure exactly when he left, but he did send her a telegram in January 1943 saying he was being stationed in Dorset. I can't begin to imagine what it must have been like for them both being separated so soon. Mum must have felt very lonely and scared with a baby on the way, and the prospect of being a lone parent, and I don't know if anyone was with her when baby Pat was born.

It must have been extremely difficult coping with all of these things, while also worrying and wondering if her new husband would be safe and if he would return. Added to Mums situation was the death of her beloved father in September of 1943, only a few months after Pat was born. She was always very close to her Daddy and it must have been the most difficult period of her young life. Mum was his first born and he named her after his mother, Sarah Mulgrew McCabe. I can't begin to imagine how hard it must have been for her, coping with the grief of losing her Dad, and bringing up a child on her own in the middle of a war, miles away from the place she regarded as home. Paddy McCabe was only fifty two years old when he passed away and I don't know if he ever saw his first grandchild. I hope he did.

Mum, baby Pat, Dad 1943

Grandad, Patrick McCabe

But Dad had his own struggles to come to terms with. Unable to be there for the birth of his first child, and leaving behind his new wife and everything he knew. He was homesick, scared of what lay ahead, praying he would make it back, and I'm sure he was worried sick about how Mum was coping with all her heartache. It wasn't exactly an ideal start and I'm sure all of these things took their toll, probably more than they realised. And it's possible by the time he did come home, the years and distance apart had changed them both, and rebuilding their relationship may have taken some time. Looking at things from Mum's point of view, she was probably still grieving the loss of her Dad and hadn't had time for herself to be able to process and work through it all. And war does change people, they obviously had a lot to contend with emotionally after all they had been through. Pat didn't know her Daddy either, she only knew her Mummy, and now this strange man had come to live with them, so there could have been a lot of tension and possible resentment added to the mix.

Dad, Pat and Mum 1947

It can't have been an easy situation for either of them, and a lot of adjustments would have been necessary on all sides, which might explain the fights and the frustration. I don't know whether or not Mum thought she had made a mistake getting married, or felt she didn't have a choice, but she sometimes made him feel inadequate which fed into the inferiority complex he had rooted in his childhood, and it likely wouldn't have helped matters. He told me he had twice passed his Eleven Plus to go to grammar school but didn't want to go because he wore clogs and a jersey and had a slight stammer, all of which made him feel the other lads were better than him. Another incident he shared that likely fed into his lack of self-esteem, was a time when he wanted to go and play football with his mates, but wasn't allowed to go until he had cleaned and 'donkey stoned' the front steps. He could see his friends playing in the street while he was hurriedly scrubbing away and he thought they were laughing at him. And when he was a teenager, he was made to push a truck around the streets selling fruit and vegetables in all weathers. He absolutely hated it.

Dad with his truck, August 1937

These things had obviously troubled him for him to share them with me so many years later. So, I imagine being on the receiving end of some of Mum's verbal put downs, probably didn't help with his own self-worth and added to all the frustration. I'm sure he was no saint, but he certainly wasn't a bad man, and nobody is perfect, but I know he always loved her and just wanted her to love him back, and deep down I'm sure she did. I have read some letters they wrote to one another during the war and they are full of love, so it's all a bit of a puzzle.

49

To be fair to Mum, apart from the things already mentioned, she more than likely had more of her own stuff to deal with and wasn't able to talk about it, and sometimes things between them would just blow up.

All that said, life wasn't always turbulent, there were lots of happy times too. Being a proud Scot, Mum really enjoyed Hogmanay, she was very sociable and had a great sense of humour, and there were many happy nights with friends seeing in the New Year. I was sometimes allowed to stay up for these house parties, and my party piece was miming to Andy Stewarts *'Donald Where's Your Troosers'*. My makeshift mic was a Ewbank carpet sweeper, it was just the right size. Mum and Dad were good friends with the Atkinson family in Fleetwood Street, and many a good night was had round at their house too. Alice Atkinson gave my Dad a prayer book when he was going off to war and he kept it safe for the rest of his life. Their daughter Kathleen used to babysit me, and Pat Atkinson was our Pat's chief bridesmaid when she got married. Ray and Christine were family friends too. Also living on Fleetwood Street, was Mrs Whittle and her son Jimmy, who was another good mate of my Dads. They had a Mynah bird that could talk, and I can remember us kids shouting to it through the front door, *'where's Alec,'* and the bird would say, *'gone for a pint, E. L. I'.* I'm sure Mrs Whittle got a bit fed up of us, but we loved hearing that bird talk. My friend Pamela Jenkins, also had a Mynah bird. Her Mum would shout upstairs to get her up in the morning, *'Pamela, Pamela, Pamela.'* Well, the Mynah bird learned to shout for Pamela in her Mum's voice didn't it, and poor Pamela never got a lie in at weekends. The bloody bird kept shouting her name and she didn't get any peace. I bet she could have rung its little neck.

Patsy and Nan had followed their big sister Sadie, and also came to live in Preston, while her brother Phil lived in St Annes. My Dad had a lot of respect for Phil, he was badly beaten by Japanese soldiers during WW2, he was a very brave man and always welcome at 42. Everybody was. Nan couldn't have children of her own and adopted Una and Patrick, while Patsy had Stephen, Gary and Terri. It was great growing up with so many cousins close by and I'd often play football with Stephen. In the early years they all used to live on Richard Street, off North Road near where the Unicorn pub used to be, and Mum would take me with her when she visited them at weekends. We always knew when she was ready for home though, her get out of jail card was, *'I'll have to go now, I've left my meat in the oven.'* She didn't really have any meat in the oven, it was just her excuse to leave when she'd had enough, and it became a bit of a family saying in later years when we made fun of her, or when we jokingly used the same exit strategy between us.

We always had a proper Sunday dinner, and mum would send me to Mrs

Allen at the butchers with a ten-shilling note to get a piece of brisket. If there were any left overs, she would make, what she called rissoles, for Monday night's tea. These consisted of left over spuds and veg all mashed up together with a bit of onion added to the mix. Then she would take a handful, pat it into a round, coat in some flour, and fry them in the chip pan. They were delicious. A lot of our food was fried, either in a frying pan or the chip pan. Our roast potatoes were always done in the chip pan and fish on a Friday was cooked the same way. Mum would even put a meat and potato pie in the chip pan, but I think it must have been a Scottish thing. Another fried treat was scallops, sliced potatoes in batter, done in the chip pan, and they were really tasty, dipped in tomato sauce. Yummy. When I was a spotty teenager, I once asked if I could have something for tea that wasn't fried. When I came home, she had made me a tin of beans and sausage, with some sprouts. I ate a bit of the sausage, and moved the sprouts to the other side of the plate, and asked for normal services to be resumed. But she did make wonderful plated savoury mince or meat and potato pie, her fairy cakes were lovely and buttery and her parkin was the best. And I have to say I have never tasted a better roast onion or spring cabbage, than those made by my Mum. (I have tried to emulate them both, but mine don't quite cut it.) Her piece de resistance though, was her tablet, another Scottish thing. Tablet is a very sweet fudge like toffee, and Mum made hers with a pint of full cream milk, 2lbs of sugar and some vanilla essence for extra flavour. It took ages to get it thick enough to set in a tray, it had to be left simmering for ages, but it was very much worth the wait and I always wanted to scrape the pan, it was too good to waste any. I think it's one of those things you had to be brought up with to really enjoy it.

I left Christ Church in 1964, and went to Tulketh Secondary School. It was a brand- new school and we were the first pupils to go right through the years. My best friend there was Julie Greenhalgh, we sat next to one another in class and became lifelong friends. Funnily enough, her Mum and Dad knew mine. Dad was a good mate of Bill Masheter, Julie's Mum's brother, they used to play football together when they were younger. Julie's Mum was a really good baker and she used to make jam tarts for us when we walked home from school. They were delicious, probably the best jam tarts ever, but I think we often ate more than perhaps were intended for us. My other best friend at Tulketh was Pat Eames, we went on a school trip to Austria together. My Dad affectionately christened her '*Whispering Smith*', because of her very loud knock when she came to our house. We'd often go on the North End together, even to the reserve matches in the days of Ricky Heppolette, Ernie Hannigan, and Alan Spavin et al. I was bridesmaid for her at her first wedding in 1972. We are also still friends today.

After a few years of living with Mrs Hoyle, Pat and Andy had saved enough money to move into their own home. A new housing estate had been built on former farm land just up the road from Daisy Lane. All the roads on the estate were named after places in the Isle of Man, e.g. Ramsey Avenue and Oban Crescent, and they bought a three bedroomed semi-detached property on Ronaldsway. Soon after, in November of 1966, Pat gave birth to their first child, Ian Andrew Hoyle. It was wonderful becoming an auntie and having a new nephew and I would often stay with them at weekends. It was just one more stop on the bus, and unlike at Mrs Hoyle's, I had a spare room to myself and slept in a fold up divan bed.

I'd been pestering Mum and Dad to let me have another dog. Tinker was still only a puppy when he was killed, so we didn't have him very long. I was round about thirteen by this time and was due to go on a school skiing trip to Austria. They said they might see about a dog when I came back from Austria, so I said I didn't want to go, I'd rather stay at home and get the dog sooner. With a lot and a little, we did get the dog and I did go to Austria. Dad took me with him to the RSPCA at Ribbleton but I wasn't allowed into the kennels to choose one. He came out with a lovely sheep dog/collie sort of dog, with black and brown markings and a white chest. He was probably about four years old and we called him Rover. He was a good dog and settled in with us really well. He was great at playing football with me in the street, I could never dribble the ball past him, and if I threw it up for him, he would catch it between his paws, put in on the ground then wait for me to do it all over again. He was lovely and all was well for a time.

The Austria trip was a fabulous experience. We went by coach and train and it seemed to take ages to get there. We were picked up outside Isherwood's garage on Strand Road sometime after midnight, and travelled to Dover. I felt a bit sea sick going across the channel, and I remember having omelette for breakfast for the first time, and I didn't like it at all, it was a bit too sloppy for me. We then had an overnight train journey which took us to our destination in Austria. We stayed at the Hotel Drei Mohren near Oetz, in the Tyrol region. It was a beautiful place; I wish I would have had a proper camera in those days, we all had a wonderful time. The beginners ski slope wasn't too far from the hotel, we were right in the middle of the mountains and the typical Austrian chalets were very picturesque. I had taken Sooty with me in case I felt home sick, and this was the very first time I'd ever seen a continental quilt on a bed. I wondered if I would be warm enough without any blankets, but all was well. We must have been a bit of a handful for the teachers, but we all survived. We played table tennis at night in the hotel, and I tasted apricot brandy for the first time. The skiing experience was fun, but none of us would have become Olympians and there was lots of laughter at our ineptitude. It was while we were there we heard the news of Donald Campbell being killed on Coniston Water, it was front page in all the papers. We got the hovercraft across the channel on the way back and I brought home a cuckoo clock as a souvenir for Mum, and a cigarette lighter, made like a small hand gun, for Dad. And Rover was still there when I got back.

In those days, some of my mates were paper boys, earning their own spending money delivering newspapers for the local newsagent, and I quite liked the idea of having a paper round as well. You had to be thirteen years old before you were allowed to deliver papers back then, but that didn't appear to apply to girls. I couldn't understand why, I just knew it wasn't fair, so I wrote to the then prime minister, Harold Wilson, to tell him my plight and ask why I couldn't have a paper round when the boys did. Amazingly, I got a reply from his secretary in 10 Downing Street: *"The Prime Minister has asked me to thank you for your letter of March 10, 1967. If you have permission from your parents to deliver newspapers, Mr Wilson does not think there is any reason why you should not do this job. Both boys and girls are employed by newsagents."* Now armed with approval from the PM, I got a paper round for a week at Greenwoods newsagents as cover for one of the boys who was on holiday. My new nephew Ian, had been born only a few months earlier, and with my week's wages of 28 shillings, I bought him a teddy bear. He was called 'Talky Ted' and he was well loved throughout his teddy life time.

I was once looking after Ian while Pat went into town to do some shopping. She assured me when he woke up from his afternoon sleep, he normally only had a wet nappy. Unfortunately, fate was against me that day and the nappy gods decreed it to be a dirty one. I'd never changed a nappy before, let alone a dirty one, so this was a whole new experience for Auntie Gail. I had Ian laid on Pat and Andy's bed while I tried, very unsuccessfully, to change a dirty nappy for the first and only time in my life. Now let me explain; these were Terry nappies made from towel, with nappy pins to keep them in place, and plastic elasticated pants to cover them and prevent any leakages, not your easy disposable ones with Velcro that are so familiar today. So, picture the scene. I don't know how the poo got in the creases at the top of his legs, but there it was. I was doing the best I could, balking at the smell, while he was kicking his legs about and giggling away without a care in the world. *'It's alright,'* balk, *'won't be long,'* balk, as I tried to wipe it up while getting it all over my hands in the process. And, trying to get the pins back in the nappy without piercing his delicate little body, I was pricking my fingers for fun. Then our Pat walked in to survey the scene and rescue me from this unfolding disaster.

I was coming home from our Pat's one Saturday, and got on the Ashton A bus outside the Harris Museum in town. The bus was making its way down Fishergate when the driver suddenly put his foot on the brake outside Marks & Spencer to do an emergency stop, and all the passengers lurched forward. There was some screaming going on at the front of the bus and we got off to see what the commotion was all about. A very young boy had been run over by the bus, he was under the front wheel and the driver had to reverse to free him. He was with his Grandma and she was hysterical; *'my baby, my baby, you've killed my baby.'* I'll never forget seeing him lying there, a beautiful blond haired little boy, wearing blue shorts and a cricket cardigan, with his little wooden windmill and some jelly babies on the floor beside him. His Grandma was distraught and heart-broken. How she coped afterwards I'll never know. I had nightmares about it for quite some time myself. He was killed instantly, he was only about two years old; his name was Lee Baverstock. I've never forgotten him.

After some time, Mum said she didn't want a dog in the house and if I wanted to keep him, he had to live in a kennel in the back yard. So I thought, ok then, I'll build him one, I'll show you. I'd had practice making that cross for Easter a few years back, so I knew what to do with a hammer and nails. Don't ask me where I got them, I think it might have been in the attic at the Syntax when Auntie Kath was landlady, but I made this kennel out of old doors. There was a full-size door for the floor, two half doors for the sides, another door for the roof, and some hardboard for the back and front. It was massive; I could have lived in it with him. But it didn't work out because Mum wasn't really a dog person and Rover had to go. Dad took him to a lady over Aqueduct Street way, and she gave him a good home. He would ask about him whenever he saw her, so we knew he was being well looked after. I can't remember what happened to the kennel though. Happen it went on the bonfire.

Mum worked at the Firelight shop on Ingot Street for a number of years, auntie Kath was there for a while too. Mum was quite well thought of there by the boss, I think she was a supervisor. I once worked with her for a week during the school holidays to earn some spending money, helping wrap and pack the firelights into boxes. She got to know a bloke called Syd Lewis, during her time there. I met him too, he was a nice chap. He was friendly with the boss at the fire-light place and I think between them, they were converting the corner house on Ingot Street and Wellfield Road into flats. He was a musician and lived further down Wellfield Road, he was quite well known back in the day. Mum and Dad would have a drink with him in the Ribble View pub from time to time. Sadly, the firelight shop met a tragic end when it was burned down in a fire, and Mum was out of work for a while.

Kash 2nd left and Mum 2nd right outside Firelight Shop

Dad also worked there at the same time as Mum, he'd do a shift making the firelights after he'd finished one of his other jobs. At one time he was doing three jobs at once. He would work on the milk round, which was a very early start, and also delivered newspapers for Abel Heywood's, based in the old school building on Croft Street. I would sometimes tag along with him and go round in the van dropping off the papers at various newsagents' shops. I was never short of comics when he worked there, *Topper, Beezer, Dandy, Beano, Judy, Bunty*, I had them all. After that, he would fit in a shift at the firelight shop. He certainly had a good work ethic, they both did. Mum worked all her life and I recall her working at the Canning Factory on Fylde Road, an evening cleaner at Goss, a Home Help, a canteen assistant at Lancashire County Council and various other cleaning jobs. They both worked hard and always did their best.

Sadie and Joe

Dad left Preston Dairies and got a job working away for quite some time, laying new gas pipe lines in various parts of the country. The pay must have been better but I know they were both unhappy being apart. We missed him very much and always looked forward to his letters. Mum and I went down to visit him one time to some place in Cheshire. He was staying in a kind of converted wooden hut, it was pretty basic but he made it as warm and homely as it could be. Mum stayed with him in there and I was in an old caravan. They had a watch dog called Rebel, an Alsatian cross, and Dad looked after him, he thought the world of that dog and Rebel would do anything for him. He was good with animals, very caring. He also worked in Reading for quite some time and had lodgings at a pub called the Jolly Anglers. He became good friends with Flo and Jack, who ran the place. They kept in contact for a number of years after he came home, in the days when people used to keep in touch by letter.

I left school in 1968. I left on a Friday, and celebrated my fifteenth birthday on the Monday. I had two weeks off for Preston Holiday fortnight and then I went to work at Tweedales Shoe Factory on Fylde Road. My first job was in the lasting room, and this involved assembling racks of different size lasts and boxes of uppers, to begin the shoe making process as they went along the production line. Each last had a different colour painted on the top to depict what size it was, red was size four, yellow size 5 and so on, and they were all kept in large wooden storage crates with the colour coded size painted on the front. All new workers were sent to the stores for a 'long stand', and this was part of my initiation to working life. '*Can I have a long stand please*', '*certainly love, wait there*', and there I stood for ages. When the storeman came back to the counter and asked why I was still there, I said, '*I've come for a long stand*,' and he said, '*you've just had one*.' I went back to the section all red faced and feeling stupid while everyone was laughing. I eventually learned quite a number of the different elements in making a pair of shoes, from shaping the heel of the uppers at the beginning of the process, to finally putting the soles on at the end to finish the shoe. That was one of the highest paid jobs for women and you had to be quick. Betty and Barbara were the main sole layers, and nobody was as quick at it as them. We were on piece work, which meant the more shoes you completed, the more money you made.

Me outside Tweedales with Jeannie Whittle, Anne Cuerden

I was allowed to keep my first week's wages and I bought Ian a small kiddie's three-wheeler bike from Chris Moss & Sons on Fylde Road. Pat and Andy had a garage base made in their back garden and there was at least a two foot drop at the end of it. Ian would pedal at full pelt down the drive heading towards the garage base at the bottom of the garden, and Pat always worried he would fall over the edge and hurt himself, but he never did, always skilfully turning at the last second. Later in the year our Pat gave birth to my beautiful niece Elaine Marie, and I was thrilled to be an auntie again. She was born at home and I remember seeing her for the first time, all pink and warm just a few hours later, with Pat sat up in bed having a cup of tea and a piece of butter madeira cake from

M&S. I bought Elaine a giant teddy which was just as well-loved as Talky Ted.

I had become quite interested in Tennis in the late 1960s and my favourite player was Billie Jean King. The first time I ever watched anything on a colour television, was at Sheila Berry's house in Carlton Street. Sheila was the sister of my friend Pamela, and she let me come in to watch a tennis match at Wimbledon. It was great to see it as it really was, the green grass of the court and all the different colours in the crowd, it was so much better than our black and white tele at 42, and quite exciting to actually see my favourite players in colour.

Many of my Saturday nights were spent staying with our Pat and Andy, seeing Ian and Elaine and watching *Rowan and Martin's Laugh In* and *Match of the Day*, and I could also have a proper bath. I was sharing the room with Elaine now; she was in a cot and I still had the fold up divan bed. Ian would sneak in the bedroom early on Sunday mornings to help Elaine climb out of her cot, and they would be playing and making a noise when I wanted a lay in after a hard weeks graft at the factory. One morning I put my head above the headboard and in an effort to get some more sleep I said, '*If you don't shut up, I'll give you a clout,*' and Ian whispered to her, '*that means a smack.*' I couldn't stop giggling under the covers and we laughed about it on many occasions over the years.

Ian and Elaine

We used to look forward to Cuffs ice cream van coming round on Sunday afternoons. It was one of the best ice creams in Preston, with a closely guarded secret homemade recipe, and there was always a long queue, but well worth the wait. When they got their first car, a silver Ford Cortina Mark 2, I often went with them when they were taking the kids out for picnics. We went to lots of places, but a particular venue that sticks in my mind is the Royal Umpire Museum at Croston. It's a touring caravan site now, but it was a great place to visit back then with lots of different mock ups of cabins depicting different historical periods and living conditions, and American cowboy settings. Fairhaven Lake was another favourite. For our picnics, Pat had her own special way of making the sandwiches. The tomato had to be placed between two slices of luncheon meat so that the bread didn't go soggy, but they had to be made early so they would be soft, and I have to say they always hit the spot. We would often have a run to Chipping for an ice cream and then go up Beacon Fell to blow away the cobwebs. On a clear day, you can see for miles across the Lancashire countryside and it was so peaceful with only the birdsong and the rustle of the trees to be heard. We did that little excursion many times and would often joke that all roads lead to Chipping.

We always took it in turns for who made Christmas dinner. One year it would be at Whittingham Street, then at our Pat's in Ronaldsway. It was Pat who introduced us to table wine with our dinner; Mateus Rosé with your Christmas dinner, how posh was that. We had lots of laughs getting things ready the night before and I would help Pat peeling the vegetables. We were never quite sure how much of everything to prepare, it's always a worry there won't be enough, and one time Pat said, '*if I put another parsnip in, do you think there'll be enough carrots?*' When she realised what she'd said, we were in fits of laughter and it became another of the many family sayings we would often recall. Pat had the kids well trained, they weren't allowed in the living room to see all their presents on Christmas morning until 9am. It was lovely watching them open everything. I can count on one hand the amount of Christmases I didn't spent with either Mum, Dad, or our Pat and Andy. Every Christmas Dad would recite, '*it was Christmas day in the workhouse, and the snow was falling fast, and up spake the workhouse master, you can shove your Christmas pudding up your ass*'. Where it comes from, I have no idea, but it's another of those things that's always with us.

Dad was a funny one with food, and that's probably where I get some of it from, but I don't think I'm as bad as he was. He would never eat anything unless Mum had made it, even when Pat or I made Christmas dinner, he would still struggle to eat it, only Mums cooking was ever good enough for him. He'd move things about a bit on his plate, eat a few spuds, and then say, '*I've enjoyed what I've had*', as his excuse for leaving the rest. He said the same thing every year, and yet another family saying was coined. He did love shellfish though. There was a shop at the bottom of Fleetwood Street, just on Water Lane, *Paul's Fish shop,* and he'd often bring home fresh cockles and mussels and cook them himself. It's because of him I can eat them. They're not the prettiest of things to look at, but I do enjoy them. He could also neck a fresh oyster straight from the shell, but I drew the line at that. Manx kippers were another of his favourites, they still had the heads and tails on when he brought them home, but he'd cut them off and then cook the kippers under the grill. They used to stink the house out. And yet, he never ate a boiled egg in all his life. How he got through the war, I'll never know.

I'd never been on a family holiday with Mum and Dad. When I was younger I would pester them to take me to Butlins having watched the adverts on television with free rides on everything, but it never happened. I didn't understand it then but they simply couldn't afford it. We'd go to Glasgow to visit Mum's family and it would take forever if we were travelling by coach, there were no motorways then. Gran and Auntie May, lived in Shettleston, Auntie Ina, lived at Easterhouse, and Uncle John was in Baillieston, other than that it was just days out to Blackpool or Cleveleys, but Dad did once take me to the top of Blackpool Tower. My first experience of going on a proper holiday was when I went away for a week with Pat and Andy to the Isle of Man when the kids were quite young. We flew from Blackpool airport, and stayed in a lovely hotel in Douglas on the sea front. It was a wonderful adventure flying for the very first time and actually staying in a real hotel. It wasn't during Preston Holidays though, I had to take a week off work from the factory without pay, but it was so worth it.

Me, Ian and Elaine, Douglas IOM

Dad's older sister, Auntie Kath (aka Kash), had been landlady of the Doctor Syntax pub on Fylde Road for a few years and I would sometimes help out behind the bar. We had lots of good times in the Syntax, and I have very fond memories of some of the regulars. I had a soft spot for Mrs Helvin, an elderly lady who lived just round the corner on Fleetwood Street, and I always used to buy her a Guinness when I saw her. Mum was good friends with Audrey Flynn, who lived further down Whittingham Street and they were drinking buddies, we had lots of laughs together, and Frank Loram used to wait on. Frank had a really bad stammer and I once had a joke with him asking if he fancied a game of snap. He took it in good spirit and said, *'n no thanks G Gail, I'm not v very good with my s.'* Like many pubs in those days, there was a piano in the main room. Kash was a good pianist and she often got the whole room singing along to all the old favourite songs. It's a very special memory of bygone times, singing with Kash playing the piano, she was a lovely lady, and I can seldom think of her without smiling. There was a piano at the fruit shop in Ashton Street, it must have belonged to her, and I remember trying to play chop sticks on it as a kid. I don't know where she learned to play, she may have been self-taught. Kash told me she wanted to study to be a music teacher, but her Dad wouldn't let her, she had to go to work in the cotton mill, which I found very sad, but it's just how it was in those days, money was always tight. Mum and Dad were going through a bad time in their relationship during the time Kash was at the Syntax, he left home for a while and went to stay with her there. I can't remember how long he was away, but I was very unhappy about it all and went to the pub to ask him to come home, and thankfully he did.

An Asian family moved in next door to us in the early 70s, I think they were Hindu. They were lovely neighbours and they invited us to a wedding. I couldn't go, but Mum and Dad went. Wally, as he was known, was the first Asian driver on Preston Corporation buses. When they moved away, we still saw him driving his bus. Kash bought the house from Wally when she gave up the Syntax and lived next door to us with her husband Hughie, and Grandad. They had the luxury of a bathroom at 41. She had looked after Grandad since he left Ashton Street, after Grandma died, and he went to live with her in Mona Street, on the block opposite the canteen. She took care of him for the rest of his life. Hughie wasn't a well man, he had a serious drink problem and living at the Syntax made it all too easy for him to have access to the whiskey; the temptation was just too great. He had some stays in Whittingham Hospital where I think he had electric shock treatment. I remember us visiting him there. Before Hughie died, my Dad told me about him deliberately burning Grandads war medals in a fire in the shed in their back yard and they were completely destroyed. Goodness knows why he did it, he was obviously not of sane mind, but what a sad loss. I'm sure Grandad, and my Dad, were devastated. You simply can't replace something as precious as those.

Sadly, I don't know a great deal about Grandad, I knew he had been in the First World War, and he used to go round selling fruit and veg from a horse and cart when they had the fruit shop. The horse was called Billy and was stabled at the back of the old Steamer pub on Fylde Road. My Dad used to talk about Billy and I have vague memories of being at the stables with Dad feeding him carrots, he was very fond of Billy. Grandad was still working in his early 80s as a night watchman at Shelley Road Mill, and he liked a drop of Lambs Navy Rum with his pint, and that was pretty much all I knew. Kash had a bed for him in the living room at Whittingham Street, he was pushing ninety by this time and couldn't get up and down the stairs. She would suggest he sat at the front door for a change, to get some fresh air. He wouldn't do though, he said only old folk did things like that. One morning when she came down stairs, he asked her who had come into the house during the night. She told him no one had, but he was adamant there was, he said, *'someone came in through the door and they were beckoning me.'* Grandad passed away peacefully only a few days later, he was ninety-one years old.

Grandad selling fruit and veg with Billy, the horse

In the early 70s I went to get my eyes tested; the optician said I was short sighted and needed glasses. Mum thought I only wanted to wear them because Billie Jean King did, but he assured her I really did need them. Being a working teenager now, I was starting to go out to local pubs with friends. The Princess

Alexandra on Fylde Road, more commonly known as *Ole in t' Wall*, was always popular, along with The Steamer and Fountain. The Watering Trough was handy for a Christmas drink as it was very close to Tweedales. For my eighteenth birthday in 1971, our Pat took me to The Villa at Wrea Green, near Kirkham. I'd never been to a proper restaurant before, I'd been with Mum to cafés in town or on the prom at Blackpool, but never dined out in the evening before, it just wasn't something we did in those days, we would just have a bag of chips on the way home. Pat came to pick me up in the car and it was really special, just the two of us. The Villa was quite posh, nothing like I was used to but it was a lovely experience. I ordered a mixed grill and couldn't eat it all, and asked Pat if it was ok to leave some. My introduction to the finer things in life.

I was still in touch with Julie from school, and we used to go round town at weekends. We would start off in the Bull & Royal, then go to Yates Wine Lodge for a glass of plonk, and on to the Boars Head. There were lots of pubs in town in those days, New Cock Inn and the Exchange were quite popular during that time. The Pig and Whistle is another old haunt where I would go with Julie and worth a mention, and there was also a disco on once a month at the Cricket Club down Broadgate. It was always packed.

Me and Julie – Bull & Royal

I was beginning to go to the occasional parties at friends' houses and this was something of an eye opener. They weren't terraced houses like ours, they had bathrooms, central heating and gardens, and seeing the kind of homes some of my friends lived in, I suppose it made me feel as though I wasn't as good as them. You just take for granted how you live, without realising everyone's circumstances aren't the same, and I sometimes felt embarrassed bringing people home to 42. Mum and Dad bought me a new teenage bedroom suite, and a blue fitted carpet to cover the lino on the floor, well I say a fitted carpet, it was patched up in several pieces down the side of the wall where my bed was, but it was a big improvement on the cold lino. There was still no heating upstairs though and my clothes would sometimes have mould on them when I took them out of the wardrobe. All these things added together gave me a bit of an inferiority complex, and no matter what I chose to wear, I never felt as good as my friends. Growing up can be really hard sometimes. You can't see it at the time, but when you get older and look back, you realise that in the great scheme of things, all of those issues weren't really that important, it's who you are that matters most. It was important at the time of course, it bothered me a great deal, you feel you get judged and I often felt inferior to my peers. One of my Mums favourite sayings was, *'you can't put an old head on young shoulders,'* and it's one of the wisest things she ever said. Looking back with an older head, no matter what the house was like, I never really wanted for anything, I never went to bed hungry, and I certainly never felt unloved. You can't put a price on that.

Despite the lack of home comforts at 42, we still often had visitors come to stay. Auntie Patsy had lived with Mum and Dad before I was born, and Mum's other brothers and sisters were often on the guest list, as well as some of Dad's old army mates from time to time who would kip on the settee. Mum's brother John, and his new wife Theresa, stayed during their honeymoon according to my Dad, and when they had their family of nine children, they would call on their way home from month-long camping holidays in Spain. They had a big van to accommodate all the kids, Julia, Agnes, Theresa, Patrick, John, Andy, Margaret, Michael, Kathleen, and all the camping equipment. It looked fantastic, and I was very envious of their adventures. They would arrive in Preston and distribute a few kids with Patsy, some with Nan and some with us, to kip on the floor overnight in their sleeping bags. It was great when they all descended on us. I spent a lot of time visiting them in Glasgow over the years, they will always be a special part of my life. I'd sometimes get the midnight coach from Preston to Glasgow on a Friday, arriving at their house around 7am, return home on the late bus on Sunday night and go to work at the factory on

Monday morning without any sleep. Uncle John and Auntie Theresa had a stall on the 'Barras' in Glasgow. Barrowlands is a very famous market where you can buy pretty much anything you want and I would sometimes help out when I was up visiting.

We occasionally went to a disco in Glasgow called 'Electric Gardens'. Both Theresa and I had dental crowns, and when we were all dancing, the ultra violet lights made our crowned teeth look green, it was a dead giveaway. Another time we all went to see the film *Love Story* starring Ryan O'Neil and Ali MacGraw. It was one of the biggest hits of 1970 and we sobbed our hearts out. Andy Williams sang the theme song, '*Where do I begin*', and our Pat bought me a musical revolving doll that played the tune. It hasn't played a note for years, but it is still a treasured keepsake. At the end of one of my visits, Theresa came to see me off at Glasgow Central Station and came on to the train to make sure I was settled. The guard blew his whistle for the train to depart, when we suddenly thought it would be a good idea for her to come back to Preston with me. Auntie Theresa and Uncle John went ballistic when she let them know where she was, and I don't think I was ever forgiven. Another one of those '*bloody Gail Newsham*' moments for sure. We both went back up the following week on a coach with Uncle Phil. He used to run a Blackpool/Preston Celtic Supporters Club, and they were going up for a match at Celtic Park, so we got a free trip back up the road. An icy reception awaited but I couldn't leave her to face the music on her own.

Theresa and me

65

Back at work, I heard about some of my friends at Tweedales who were playing football for Peter Craig Ladies and I asked if I could join in. A new women's league had been set up in Preston and I joined the team in 1971. I'd never really heard of there being any women's football teams before, apart from once seeing some girls playing on Moor Park, and a team called the Dick, Kerr Ladies who seemed quite well known in Preston, but I didn't know anything about them. I'd loved football all my life but girls were never allowed to play when I was growing up. I didn't know why; it was just one of those things you had to accept because that's how it was. The only football I ever played was with the lads, which I did for many happy years when I was younger. Learning there was actually a women's league in Preston was a revelation, and it was wonderful to have the opportunity to play in a proper football match every Sunday. I was in my element, and for me, it was the start of a lifetime love affair. Some of the older women I worked with at Tweedales used to organise concert parties to raise money for charity, and I got involved with them on numerous occasions. It was great fun dressing up and singing all the old songs. During the Preston Guild celebrations in 1972, I joined in with them doing a Morris Dance routine with the North Star pub on Hawkins Street. Connie was the landlady then; she was quite a familiar personality in the area and she made us all very welcome. It was a popular pub back in the day.

Preston Guild 1972

I worked through the three-day week in early 1974 when the electricity would go off suddenly due to the strikes during that period. I remember being in the shoe factory, and everything would just stop. The machines shut down, the lights went off and it was pitch black until someone turned up with a torch. At home, we'd have candles to light the way. It seemed like a bit of fun at the time, but I'm sure it was very difficult for families trying to keep things going and make ends meet. Wages were obviously affected and money was tight for everyone but I still had to give Mum the same board money every week, even though I only had three days' pay. I thought at the time she was being really tight fisted, taking most of my money when I didn't have a full wage. But tough love teaches us good lessons. What I learned from that period was not to be in debt, and that's pretty much how I've lived my life. Thanks to my Mum. She always said, *'neither a borrower nor a lender be'*.

Women's football was slowly taking off, and news had spread of Sue Lopez, a girl from Southampton, who had played semi-professional football in Italy. It seemed like a wonderful thing to be able to do, so I hatched a plot with a friend I knew from football, to see if we could do the same. In the spring of 1974, we set off to hitch hike to Italy in the hope of finding a team to play for. I gave up my job at Tweedales, my friend Linda had a car and dropped us off at the motorway slip road at Broughton, and off we went with our football boots in our rucksacks, and about £76 in our pockets. A lorry driver soon picked us up in Preston, and when he dropped us off somewhere much further down the M6, he told us to look out for rigs with TIR on them as they were the continental vehicles. We must have got a lift with a lorry driver on this side of the channel who was travelling through France, because I don't recall hitching it when the boat landed in Calais. We were driven the length of France, having never realised before just what a big country it is. By the time we were dropped off in Montpellier we were absolutely knackered. We booked into a small hotel, and slept like babies. As soon as my head hit the pillow I was out like a light. I think I woke up in the morning in the exact same position I'd been in when I crawled into bed. We got a lift next day, en route to Italy, from a guy called Luigi. He seemed like a nice chap and was stopping over somewhere in his rig for an overnight stay. He took us into a café and bought us something to eat, it was spaghetti and I didn't really care for it, but thought how kind he was. However, it transpired the meal wasn't for free after all and he expected payment in kind from my friend when we got back in his lorry. She wasn't having any of it, so we had to reimburse the cost of the meal and sit in the front of the cab all night while he slept in his bunk. It was a very long night but at least we were lucky he accepted the NO word.

We eventually reached Rimini in Italy and booked into a hotel for a few days.

But, there were no women's football teams to be found, it was close season and totally the wrong time to embark on what we hoped would be a life changing adventure. We wandered around somewhere near a beach and this guy came over to talk to us, he was driving a white soft top Mercedes and his name was Bibi. We chatted a while and he asked what we were doing in Italy, and we told him our plans. He told us he was involved in the film business and had worked with Charles Bronson and Claudia Cardinale. He invited us back to his apartment for something to eat and drove us there in his Merc. He showed us some pictures of himself with the two film stars he'd mentioned and then prepared us some lunch. After which, he went for his siesta while we washed the dishes. Decent bloke with no ulterior motives and when he woke up, he dropped us off back at our hotel. I think we stayed about three days in Rimini where I tasted pizza for the very first time, and like father, like daughter, I didn't really enjoy what I had. We had no luck searching for a football team to play for, so we decided to head for Spain and try our luck there. I don't recall all the details of how we got there, but there was a lift in a little Fiat car who dropped us off in the middle of nowhere, high up in the hills somewhere, but we did eventually get back to civilisation. Of all the lifts we did get, we never got one from anyone driving a Citroen, we knew when we were stood at the side of the road with our thumbs out, they would never stop for us. Another lorry driver picked us up and the coast run from Italy through France down to Spain was absolutely stunning. We travelled through Genoa, Savona, Menton, Monte Carlo, Monaco and Nice; it was spectacular, I'd never seen the sea looking so turquoise blue before, and we eventually ended up at Barcelona in Spain. I don't recall how, but we managed to get a lift from two Spanish guys in separate rigs. Looking back, it was an extremely risky thing to do, but fortune favours the brave as they say, and they were decent blokes who drove us all the way down to Valencia without any problems. We stopped somewhere on the way down and had some fresh oranges straight from the tree, they were the juiciest most delicious oranges I had ever tasted. It made a very welcome change from all the bread and pâté we had eaten. We eventually made our way to Benidorm, and realising we didn't have very much money left, didn't quite know what to do. We decided on a coin toss to choose to either go to Alicante, where my friend had once worked, to see if we could find something there and continue our adventure, or go to the British Consul to ask for help to get home. I'd had enough by this time to be honest and being the one flipping the coin, I made sure the latter won the toss. Our adventure was over after about two weeks, and I was ready for heading back to Blighty.

I have only vague memories of our meeting with the Consul, but I don't think they believed our cock and bull story of how we ended up with no money, but they did give us £46.00 each for our journey home. I don't recall exactly what mode of transport we took to get back to the UK, but I do remember being on a coach. When we arrived in Dover, the authorities were waiting for us and we had our passports impounded until we repaid the £46.00. When we eventually got to Victoria coach station, I made a reverse charge phone call to our Pat to let her know I was safe and on my way home, and asked her to let Mum and Dad know too. Looking back, they must have all been worried sick about me, I didn't have the means to contact them while I was away, and to be honest I don't think I ever even thought of it. When I got home and knocked on the door, my Dad opened it and just said, "*Is that it now Wacker.*" I reckon he was just relieved that I was safe and well. It was good to be back at 42.

Me and Mum soon after I'd got home

I got my job back at Tweedales, but it would only be a few months before I was off on another adventure, but first I had to repay the British Consul to get my passport returned. My friend Kath, who worked behind the bar in *Ole in t' Wall,* very kindly gave me the money, and my passport was duly despatched, still with the 'impounded' stamp on it, but new adventures were just around the corner.

YOU'RE IN THE ARMY NOW

After returning to Tweedales following the hitchhiking adventure to Italy, the wander lust reared its head again. I'd gone into town with my friend Linda from the football team, we were at a bit of a lose end and found ourselves outside the recruiting offices of the RAF and Army. We were looking in the windows and wondering about joining up, and I said, *'you go in the Air Force careers office, I'll go in the Army, and we'll compare notes when we come out.'* Well, it all happened so fast, the recruiting Sergeant, Carol Gibb, was a very nice lady, and when I came out, I'd made an appointment to start all the rigmarole of joining up. It sounded great. Then Linda went in and made an appointment as well. Having left school at fifteen without any formal qualifications, and not many prospects ahead of me to be perfectly honest, it seemed like a wonderful opportunity for a better life than the monotony of being on a factory production line making shoes from 8am-5pm day in day out. There were no opportunities for a career in football in those days, it was just a hobby and something we did for love, so all of that had to be left behind. We passed all the aptitude admission tests and medicals, went to Manchester to meet Captain Muldoon to swear the oath, take the Queen's shilling, and the date was set for our departure to Guildford. We had a bit of a farewell party at the *Ole in t' Wall,* and proprietors, Dick and Doreen, supplied us with a buffet. Dick was originally from around that area and was eager to come down to see us for a drink on our first weekend out, and we made plans to meet up in the town centre.

Then before we knew it, we were on the train to embark on our six weeks basic training in the Women's Royal Army Corps. On 17 September 1974 we arrived at the WRAC Training Centre, Queen Elizabeth Park, Guildford, in Surrey, to begin a new life. I don't think my Mum really wanted me to go, she was a bit backward at coming forward helping with things I needed to take with me, and some friends stepped in to help out, but I think my Dad was quietly pleased that his young lass was going to be a soldier, if I could handle Army life that is. I'm sure there were some who thought I'd never hack it. It's not easy is it, or everyone would do it wouldn't they?

We weren't allowed out of camp for the first three weeks, which were full of learning all about army life, how to keep things clean, and how to look after our kit. Bulling shoes, starching shirts, learning how to march, and what seemed like endless injections, it was full on. Every morning before breakfast, we had to strip our beds and then re-make them army style, not a crease allowed to be seen anywhere. Everything had to be pin sharp. There were four of us to a room, each with our own bed space consisting of a small single bed, a wardrobe, a chest of drawers with a mirror attached, and a cork display board above the bed to pin pictures on, or messages from home if you were feeling homesick. We also had a table and chairs by the window. Every morning the Duty Officer would come in to inspect you. The command from the Corporal (NCO) would echo down the corridor, '*Stand by your Beds*,' and as they approached your room to enter, the NCO (Non-Commissioned Officer) would say in a loud voice, '*room, room, shun*', (short for attention) and you had to stand to attention while the officer looked you up and down. Once she had finished with the front, you had to do an about turn for her to inspect the back of you. At first, I couldn't get the about turn right without losing my balance and wobbling over, but I mastered it eventually.

We had to learn how to 'bull' our shoes to get a mirror shine on them. This was achieved with black Kiwi polish, a yellow duster, and some water in the lid of the polish tin. The method was to put some polish on the duster with your finger, dip it in the water, and rub it on your shoes in small circular movements. Eventually, you would have a pair of shoes fit for the Parade Square. I remember spending well over an hour and a half bulling my shoes and feeling quite chuffed with my efforts, but when I took them to the Corporals' office for inspection, she said they weren't good enough and I had to do them all over again. It was the same routine with our shirts. The size of the pleats in the sleeves, and darts coming down from the yoke at the back, had to be seen to be believed. We had to iron them with Robin Starch until there were no creases to be seen and the pleats neatly flat. A near impossible task in my opinion, but they had to pass the muster. There was so much starch in them, they almost stood up on their own, and as soon as you put them on, they got creased anyway. Then we had to attach the collar with collar studs, and learn how to get used to wearing them all day. It took a while, but eventually became second nature.

Keeping our uniform smart was another must. We weren't allowed to have creases in the sleeves of our jacket, and we had to roll up a towel to put inside the sleeve and iron it with a pressing cloth. It was a wonderful feeling being in uniform, it gave you such a sense of pride, almost made you feel taller. When wearing Number 2 Dress Uniform on parade, we wore a Forage Cap, a beret was worn at other times. Our beret had to be shaped properly though, otherwise it would look like a big saucer on your head. To achieve the correct shape, you had to dampen the beret and place it on your head. With your cap badge above your left eye, you had to press and pull the beret over your head and shape it towards your right ear, then take it off and leave it to dry in that position. It took numerous attempts before finally getting the finished look. We also had to practice our saluting technique in the mirror above the chest of drawers. Longest way up, and shortest way down. Our room had to be spic and span every morning for Officers inspection, but Monday nights were what they called, In Night. This was when we had to clean the whole block, as well as our room, and everyone was allotted a 'block job'. The baths and toilets, (ablutions) ironing room, sitting room, corridors, stairs, you name it, it all had to be cleaned to within an inch of its life, and be ready for OC's inspection (Officer Commanding) on Tuesday morning. If it didn't come up to scratch, it had to been done again until it was to the standard they required. I can remember once having to clean the stairs with a toothbrush. It was all character building, to see what we were made of, and getting us familiar with Army discipline, but this would consist of our daily and weekly routine.

During the day we would be in the classroom learning all about the Army. Ranks and Badges of Officers and Non-Commissioned Officers, history of the Corps, rules and regulations, protocols, and everything in between. Then there were the jabs in the medical centre. I can't remember how many we had, but our childhood vaccinations were updated and blood samples taken to ascertain our blood group. In order for the sample to be taken, we had to stand in a queue rubbing our ear lobes to make them a bit numb, and then they would prick it with a needle to get a blood sample. This seemed to be rather enjoyed by the Corporals, and for some reason, my ear seemed to be the one they wanted to puncture. I could see them gleefully rubbing their hands as I got closer to the head of the queue. Seemed like another case of *'that bloody Gail Newsham'* expression following me to the Army.

Learning to march with your platoon was a great sense of pride when we got it right. We had to learn to 'take our dressing' when in squad, so that we were all lined up with each other. Keeping the correct distance between you and your comrades was crucial, and precision was key. Once we were brought to attention, the command would be, *'squad will dress to the right, right dress'*, this involved turning your head to the right and lifting up your arm to be just touching the shoulder of the person next to you with your fist to ensure the correct distance, then you shuffled about a bit until you were all perfectly in line with the those in front of you, and to the side. Then the order came, *'eyes front,'* and everyone put their arm back down exactly at the same time as turning to face the front. The next order was, *'squad will move to the right in threes,'* which meant right turn, and you were then facing the correct direction to march off in squad. For our first efforts we would sometimes go out of step until we got the hang of things. We had a girl in our platoon who struggled with coordination and she 'camel marched.' Rather than swinging her left arm in step with her right leg, she was swinging her left arm while stepping with her left leg, or vice versa. We tried helping her in the block at night having her marching up and down the corridor, but she couldn't quite get it, and we knew we weren't going to win the drill cup. I was shouted at one day when we were marching along and I fell down a grid and started laughing. The Corporal shouted, *'Private Newsham, are you deaf as well as daft.'* I did get better at it though. Practice makes perfect, as they say.

Another part of becoming a soldier was NBC training. Nuclear, Biological and Chemical Warfare, to give it its full title. We had to learn how to use a gas mask and get it on quickly in the event of a gas attack. The Corporals would shout *'Gas, gas, gas,'* and we had to get our mask out of its case and covering our faces within a certain number of seconds in order to be safe. I struggled to get mine on in time before the count was up, so would probably have perished in a real gas attack. The other aspect of NBC training, was to walk through a gas chamber filled with tear gas, while wearing your mask and a special suit, which was nicknamed a *'Noddy Suit.'* It was made of special materials to protect you from being contaminated by biological or chemical weapons, and we also had to practice de-contaminating ourselves with a special powder like substance. Walking through the gas chamber wearing all this equipment initially appeared like a fun experience until you had to take off your gas mask and tell the Corporal your number, rank and name, before leaving the smoke-filled chamber. The tear gas got you straight away, stinging your eyes and it really made you cough and splutter. I came out with my eyes streaming and my arms out in front of me saying, *'I can't see, I can't see.'* There was a lot of tears and snot flying around during this little exercise I don't mind telling you, but we all laughed about it later when the effects had worn off.

Pay Parade was nerve wracking procedure we had to go through. We were all lined up in the corridor and the Platoon Officer was in a room sat behind a desk with our pay in front of her. One at a time we had to march into the room and up to the desk, salute her, check our pay and say, *'pay and pay book correct Ma'am,'* salute again, about turn and march out. I was so nervous the first time I had to do it, I'm sure my hands were shaking as I tried to count my pay, but it was another part of the process of teaching you Army discipline. Time keeping was also something that had to be strictly adhered to. The mantra was, *'to be early is to be on time, to be on time is to be late,'* and woe betide if you were ever late for anything. If you had an appointment for 1200 hours, you had to be there for 1150 hours.

At night we could relax in the NAAFI, and meet up with girls from other platoons who were in different accommodation blocks. We were all in the same boat, and being raw recruits, by sharing all our days' experiences and getting to know each other, friendships and bonds were very quickly made. Some of the girls were only just seventeen years old, having never been away from home before, feeling home sick and out of their depth, but everyone rallied round to lift them and keep their spirits up. We all had our moments. It was hard sometimes coming to terms with all the discipline and trying to get things right, it would have been easy to throw in the towel, but we soldiered on, as they say. I was a bit older than many of the girls, and a bit of a joker, so I tried to make light of it all and make a joke to help them not feel so overwhelmed. A good night in the NAAFI having a few drinks and a laugh was a great tonic. I got on quite well with a lass in our platoon, her name was Sheena; she came from up Carlisle way. We often used to sing together and harmonise to some of the old Jim Reeves songs, and others of the same genre. The girls seemed to enjoy it, as did we. I could hold a tune a lot better in those days though. *Kung Foo Fighting*, by Carl Douglas, was the song that used to echo around the camp during that time, and I get transported back whenever I hear it.

2 Platoon, Guildford 1974 – me front row 2nd right

On 5 October 1974 we had made it to the half way point in our training and three weeks of being confined to barracks. Everyone was getting excited and looking forward to a bit of freedom and seeing Guildford for the first time. It was Saturday night and it would be packed with young trainee soldiers letting their hair down without any NCOs breathing down their necks. It was the busiest weekend in the town for military personnel, and we were making plans to go out with the girls in our platoon. Linda and I had heard from Dick, the landlord of the *Ole in t' Wall*, to tell us he unfortunately couldn't make it for our planned meet up, which was perhaps for the best as Linda wasn't feeling too well and wanted to stay local, so we went for a couple of drinks to the Wooden Bridge pub just down the road. We hadn't been there long, just got a round in and sat down enjoying the night, when someone came over and told us there was a bomb scare and advised everyone to evacuate the premises. We took our drinks with us and went outside with the other customers and stood around on the car park waiting for the all clear to go back inside, when someone came over and said they were closing early. They said two pubs had been blown up in the town centre and there were some fatalities.

It's a bit of a blur how we made our way back to camp in the panic, we initially set off in the wrong direction, but managed to flag down a taxi, and eventually got back safely. The news was being reported on the television and it was pandemonium in the guardroom. The phones were ringing non-stop with people trying to find out if their loved ones were safe. We didn't know exactly what had happened at this stage, or who was responsible, it was all a bit chaotic waiting for things to unfold. We were told to go back to our rooms and wait, and we weren't allowed to use the phone to call home. There were no mobile phones in those days, we only had the one phone box near the NAAFI, and we couldn't let our families know we were ok until we were given permission. I suppose they needed to get as much Intel as possible first. We went back to the block as instructed and waited with baited breath and hoped those who had gone into town would return safely. We had gone out on the same bus as Sue Scott from our platoon and we were extremely worried about her. We knew she was heading for the pubs and we were waiting for what seemed like ages for some news of her. We asked the first few girls who returned safely if they had seen her, but no one had, we were getting more concerned and anxious as time went by. Several more girls came back to the block and then finally, Sue arrived and our relief was overwhelming. Thankfully, due to missing the earlier buses she hadn't actually been caught up in the explosion, and what no doubt saved her from serious injury or worse, was her choice of clothes. She wasn't happy with the dress she was wearing and decided to nip back for a quick change, but it made her late. Otherwise, she would almost certainly have been in the thick of it when the bombs went off. She definitely had a guardian angel watching over her that night, and maybe we did too. If Dick had come down from Preston as we had planned, we would have certainly been in the pubs in town, and with Linda being unwell, it likely saved our bacon.

It was a long night; I don't think many of us got much sleep. Thankfully, the majority of the girls from our platoon did return safely, but unfortunately there were some who had been injured and taken to hospital. We didn't know how badly hurt they were, but hoped they would be ok. I vividly remember Jane, a girl from our platoon, who had been in town with her friend Caroline, and a few other girls from another platoon. They were in one of the pubs when the bomb exploded. Jane made it back to camp with some minor lacerations but was completely dishevelled, shocked, and traumatised by what she had witnessed. Fortunately for her, she was in the toilets when the bomb went off, and escaped some of the devastation, but came out into the carnage to discover her friend Caroline had been fatally injured in the blast. Jane saw her being put on to a stretcher in a very bad way. It was obviously deeply distressing for her. She just kept saying, '*She's dead, she's dead, I know she's dead.*'

That weekend was the first milestone in our journey to becoming proper soldiers. We had completed the first three weeks of our basic training, and this was the first time the new WRAC recruits were allowed out of camp, and the pubs were all packed. Everyone went out in high spirits but returned devastated and traumatised by the night's events. Two of Guildford's most popular pubs with servicemen and women, Seven Stars and The Horse & Groom, were blown up by the IRA in their terror campaign. Five people were killed and sixty-five were injured. Anne Hamilton aged 19 from Crewe, and Caroline Slater aged 18 from Cannock, were both in the Horse & Groom. Caroline was sat near the jukebox, where the bomb had been hidden behind, and she took most of the blast, with Anne sitting close by. Two young teenage girls with their whole lives ahead of them, brutally murdered, their lives cut tragically short on a night when they had so much to live for and so much to look forward to.

At 7am the next morning, I went to the phone box near the NAAFI, to ring our Pat and let her know I was ok, Mum and Dad didn't have a phone at home back then. Pat had seen it on the news while she was doing some ironing, and was gripped with panic, thinking I was certain to have been in the pubs, which under normal circumstances, I would have. She rang the camp immediately to see if there was any news about me, and was told I had returned safely. She let Mum know, but for some reason Dad didn't find out until the morning after. We were all spoken to by the top brass, as they tried to return calm to everyone on camp. Company Sergeant Major Jeffries, even let us play football on the parade square on the Sunday afternoon, and that was a huge gesture in those days. The Parade Square was considered an almost sacred place, you were never allowed to just walk on it, risk it at your peril, you could only march on it in regimental order, so being allowed to play football on it was a really, really big deal.

The next few days were taken up with interviews by the CID, police, and security forces. We had to give a statement of our whereabouts on the Saturday night, and to see if anyone saw anything that could possibly identify those responsible for the atrocities. There was a bomb scare on camp which thankfully turned out to be a hoax, probably by some nutter who thought it was funny. We also learned which of our platoon members had been caught up in the explosion and what their injuries were. Ranging from perforated ear drums, to badly lacerated limbs and other wounds, they got off reasonably lightly, but they were still hospitalised and unable to take part in our passing out parade a few weeks later. Sadly, they would have to take their place in a later intake and pass out with another platoon.

My Mum, Dad, and our Pat, came to my Passing out Parade. I booked a family room for them in a small hotel in Guildford close to the train station. Our Pat said she didn't get much sleep with being in the same room as Mum and Dad. It was quite funny really and I don't think any of them slept particularly well. But for years after we'd laugh when Pat told the tale of my Dad asking Mum during the night what time it was. She couldn't see properly without her glasses and said, *'it's either quarter past two, quarter past three, or quarter past four.'* I don't recall my Dad's reply, but Pat was killing herself laughing under the bed clothes.

Our Passing out Parade was a very emotional day with injured girls and ambulances on the parade square. A stark reminder of the danger we faced, but we all tried to put on a good show for our injured comrades and for our families who had travelled so far to share in our big day. My Dad loved hearing our platoon Corporals shouting their orders at us, *'swing those arms, they won't fall off,'* which no doubt took him back to his own Army training. I think we marched off the parade square with the band playing *British Grenadiers*. It was a very proud day becoming a proper soldier in front of my family.

Marching off the Parade Square – me 2nd left

With Dad and Mum   with our Pat

With our basic training now complete, it was time to leave Guildford and say goodbye to everyone as we were sent off to different camps to learn our new trades. I wrote a poem of the whole experience.

ARMY TRAINING

I joined the Army for a career, to see the world and have some fun,
They sent me down to Surrey, so I waved goodbye to our Pat, my Dad & Mum.
I felt really apprehensive the day that I arrived,
But I was in the Army, and glad to be alive.
The Army did a lot for me; they taught me how to march,
And how to iron a shirt with the help of Robin Starch!
They put me a Uniform; they made me look quite smart,
And gave what I was looking for; I now had a fresh start.
I had injections by the score and sugar lumps as well,
Are they making me a Soldier? Only time will tell.
You think six weeks will never end and can't wait to get away,
You're sick of scrubbing, cleaning and ironing every single day.
But when you leave you realise, it really wasn't all that bad,
You want to go back forever and keep the friends you had.
The Army gave me many things, but took away so much,

The friends I made while training, I hope will keep in touch.
I made many friends at Guildford, as we were all put to the test,
And one thing is for certain, we all gave our very best.
Those six weeks basic training, weren't really very long
We learned to work together, and together we were strong.
We forged a special bond and we are soldiers now together
I feel sure I will remember those days, always and forever.

Gail J Newsham – 1974

Linda went to Catterick to work in Signals, while I had chosen to be a Staff Clerk and was posted to Blackdown Barracks in Deepcut, along with Sue Scott from our platoon. I liked Sue, she was good fun, a party girl. She went out one night wearing a gold lamé dress, but couldn't wear a bra because the straps were showing. She needed something to give her boobs a bit of a lift, so she used sellotape to do the job. She used to ask me to sing to her when we were in the ablutions having a bath. We'd chat from each cubicle and I'd be singing away to her. I quite enjoyed my time at Blackdown and learning all the new skills required for my Army career. It was still pretty strict during the trade training period. We had to be back in camp by 2359 hours or suffer the consequences, even being one minute late got you in bother, and the cleaning regime was much the same as in Guildford. Apparently, once you were posted to a working unit, it was a little more relaxed, but it all had to be adhered to. The RSM (Regimental Sergeant Major) Agnes Doig, kept us all in check and she used to scare the pants off me. The cook house was a different experience at first because unlike the WRAC Centre, this was a mixed unit, but I soon got used to it. Army food was pretty good really and I loved the compo sausages, they were delicious. Compo rations were tinned foods used when on exercise or in war situations, some had been left over from WW2, and the sausages were great. There was a disco every Monday night, and once we had completed all our duties for 'in night', we all went down to the NAAFI to enjoy the disco. Many a sore head was brought back to the block from those nights I can tell you.

It was while I was at Blackdown I started getting some pains on the left side of my chest. When I was breathing in, it became quite painful. I went down to the guardroom to tell them my plight and they sent for an ambulance to take me to the Cambridge Military Hospital in Aldershot, to get checked out. I was being examined by a young doctor, I think he was a 2nd Lieutenant, still learning the ropes, and he was listening to my chest with his stethoscope, asking me to breathe in. I was rather uncomfortable and wincing with every inhalation, when he said, 'well you're trying hard, but I can't find anything.' The cheeky bastard, I was struggling to breathe properly and he comes out with rubbish like that. I was admitted to a ward and kept in for almost a week and was propped up with pillows because I couldn't lay down. Another doctor said I had pleuritic pains and thought I had pleurisy. They decided I should have an endoscopy and was given a general anaesthetic for the procedure. The pre-med injection made me quite drowsy and giddy, and I do recall singing my head off behind the curtains around my bed. The diagnosis for their findings was that somehow, an air pocket had burst in my lung and this was the cause of the pain. They advised me to rest for a while and I was sent back to camp once all was well.

After our trade training was completed, and we were now fully-fledged B3 Staff Clerks, it was time to move on again. Sue was posted to Rheindahlen in Germany, and I was sad to see her go, we'd had some fun times going to the disco, and singing in the bath, and I wondered if our paths would ever cross again, but that's Army life, you're never in one place for very long. I was later posted to the WRAC Officer Cadet Training College in Camberley with Val Mahoney, a cockney lass from Streatham in London. We ended up sharing a room together and Val was in the opposite bed space to me. As we were now at a working unit, we had a bit extra room to display personal mementos on a shelf above our beds, and we could also make our own bedside table out of a cardboard box and cover it with fancy paper. Pictures were permitted on the wall, but only with blue tac. Val and I worked together in the same office, with Cathy Evans from Wales, and Terri Allen from Ipswich. Our new job at Camberley was in Training Wing, which was the hub of the training centre for Officer Cadets. Among other duties, we were responsible for typing and duplicating (printing) all the training schedules for the Cadets, and were often asked to take part in 'Demonstration Orderly Room,' where the Cadets were faced with lots of different scenarios with unruly soldiers. It was fun acting out being a bolshie private, giving them a hard time. I think we did a good job. I got on well with most of the Cadets, but one in particular seemed right down to earth, she was from up North, and we'd chat from time to time. We weren't allowed to mix, it was just in passing in the corridor, or round about the place. I'd seen them come and go over time, and hoped it wouldn't go to their heads once they got their commission and moved on. I once said to her I hoped she wouldn't change when she had a few pips on her shoulder. She said, 'can you imagine me ever changing?' and assured me she wouldn't.

The College was also a training unit where Warrant Officers (WO) and NCO's came for training courses if they were being promoted. There were Corporals, Sergeants, and Warrant Officers courses, and there was a special accommodation block for them known as WO/NCO block. When our block was being deco-rated and improved, we had to move into WONCO block while the work took place, which meant we all had the luxury of a small bunk to ourselves. The floors were best described as bare shiny asphalt, and we had to polish it with an elec-tric buffer on in night. It was difficult not to leave any marks from the buffer, or footprints on the floor, for OC's inspection, but it had to be done. Being able to levitate would have come in very handy. We were glad to get back to our own block when the work was completed where the floors had square vinyl tiles and weren't as much of a faff to keep clean.

In our office, we all had to take a turn at being Duty Clerk, and this included several tasks; being there early to open up, taking important paper work over to HQ which always had to be exactly on time, and brewing up for all the officers in the wing. There were about fifteen brews to be made several times a day, and you sometimes had to cater for their pet dogs. Major Hodgkinson had a snappy little Jack Russell called Scuttle, who wasn't always very welcoming, and a bit territorial when you went in her office with a brew for him, which was specially made in an old margarine tub. None of us particularly cared for Scuttle, and it was sometimes a rush to get out before he got you if he was in a bad mood. Captain Lobban had a beautiful Red Setter called Abigail, and Captain Hanlon had a lovely black Labrador called Snoopy, and they always got a lot of attention from us. I had a big soft spot for Abigail, she was a stunner. One time, when Terri was duty clerk, she went into Major Hodgkinson's office and didn't realise she was there. Terri was a lovely lass with a really funny dry sense of humour, and a slight endearing lisp. She put the Major's cup of tea on her desk and went to bend down to give Scuttle his brew, and said, *'here you are Scuttle, and if you go for me again, it'll be the last thing you ever do,'* or words to that effect, only to hear the Major's voice from behind the cupboard door, *'oh, poor Scuttle.'* Terri was mortified and we were all in fits of laughter when she came back to the office and told us the tale.

I was picking up quite a nice accent being at the College with so many officers. Many of them spoke as though they had a plumb in their mouth, and I found my Lancashire accent softening slightly, you can't help but pick up how other folk speak when you're with them for any length of time. Our Pat was particularly pleased when I went home on leave and I was speaking a little less *'Lankysher'* and even sounding my aitches. It didn't last long though. Camberley was a good posting, I loved my job, and for the most part, I enjoyed my time there and I look back on it with great affection. After in night on Monday, they put on transport for us to go to the disco at Blackdown, which was always eagerly looked forward to. I used to have quite bushy eyebrows in those days, but Terri and Val thought they could do with a bit of attention. They pinned me down to pluck them one time before we were going to Blackdown, and just left me with quite a thin line. When we got there and I was dancing, my eyebrows were throbbing like mad and beads of sweat were dripping down from my forehead, but my new eyebrows were too thin to stop it from running into my eyes. And they never did grow back. Other disco trips were to Bordon, at the REME Depot where I once got my purse stolen and it had my Army ID card in it. It was a chargeable offence if you ever lost your ID card, so that was me in bother on a 252 (Charge Report Form Number) because someone nicked my purse, and all my money, while I was having a boogie.

Princess Anne was living at Sandhurst with her husband, Captain Mark Phillips, during my posting to Camberley, it was just down the road from the WRAC College. We had to go to Sandhurst for dental treatment and the like, and the girls would often come back saying they had seen her, but I never caught sight of her once. I always used to hope the Queen might attend a commissioning ceremony for the Officer Cadets, in those days I would have been excited to see her, but she never came. We did go to the Sovereigns Parade at Sandhurst though. It was a really big event, all pomp and ceremony and good to see it firsthand. Farnborough Air Show was another great day out during my time in leafy Surrey.

I went on a camping trip to Inverness with Terri, Cathy, and Val, the four of us had become good mates, and we each got a travel warrant and went up on the train. It seemed to take forever to get there but we had a good laugh on the way. There were some lads in the compartment next to us and there was a girl with them. There was quite a bit of alcohol being consumed, we could hear lots of laughter and they seemed to be having a good time. The guard came round checking our tickets and when he went into their carriage, the girl was there alone, barely conscious, and naked from the waist down. It looked very much like she had been raped by all those lads, who were now nowhere to be seen. The guard pulled the chain and stopped the train, but the lads had jumped off and got away. I don't know what ever happened to the young girl, but hope she got through life ok after her ordeal. We arrived at the campsite in Inverness and eventually got the tent up. It was quite a cold and windy night, we had no electric hook up or any heating and were feeling a bit miserable, so we all decided to go back south and packed everything up again the next day and went back to Camberley. We then decided to go to Portsmouth, heaven knows why because we didn't have enough money for an overnight stay, but we plucked up the courage to ask at one bed and breakfast place if we could all share the same room. Surprisingly the owner agreed, and two of us kipped on the floor, so we had one night in Portsmouth, wandered around a bit, had a look round HMS Victory and then went back to camp the next day. What a waste of time.

The four of us went on a six-week dry skiing course together at Aldershot, travelling over in the evening once a week. We weren't very good at it but we had to keep going until all the sessions were finished. The long ski slope came to a level once you reached the bottom, but unusually, there was a small drop at the end, a bit like a gully. They were teaching us to do the snow plough, I'd remembered a bit of it from when I went to Austria with the school, but still couldn't master it very well. We set off down the slope one after the other with Cathy at the rear, and when we got near the bottom, we were to do the snow plough to slow us down and stop. This meant placing your skis pointing inwards, as if you were pigeon toed, and leaning on your left leg to enable you to turn right, or vice versa. Three of us just about managed to stop on the level, but Cathy was finding it more difficult. We could hear her coming up behind us saying, '*I can't stop, I can't stop,*' as she approached the drop. We couldn't do anything to help her, and she ended up falling into the gully at the end. It was so funny watching her fall, legs akimbo and skis pointing skywards as she ended up laying on her back on the floor. We all literally peed our pants laughing at poor Cathy, but she saw the funny side too, and it was only her pride that was hurt. Our skiing skills didn't really improve and we were glad when the sessions ended. I never skied again.

The girls in the office all got posted away pretty much at the same time. Val went to Northern Ireland; Cathy went to Cyprus and Terri married a guardsman from Pirbright. I was sorry to see them go; we'd had some really good times together and I felt a bit lost and lonely for a while. But new roomies were soon posted in, and more friendships were made with Sue Bailey, Karen Latham and Sue Jackson. Sue Bailey worked at Sandhurst, while Karen and Sue worked in the office with me in training wing. The officer Sue worked for at Sandhurst called her Bailey, instead of Private Bailey. We all thought it was quite funny and it stuck. Bailey was in the bed space opposite me, the one vacated by Val. I'll never forget her teddy bear called Eric, the name really suited him and she had him on display on the shelf above her bed, while I had Sooty on the shelf in my bed space. I don't know why, but she once rubbed Sootys' nose with the sand paper on a match box. It made a scuff mark on his little snout and I wasn't best pleased. Sooty came everywhere with me. The other Sue was into heavy rock, while I was pretty much a Motown fan, so our music choices in the room varied quite a bit, but I always think of Sue whenever I hear *Bohemian Rhapsody*. I think Karen and I were more on the same music wavelength. Tubular Bells was very popular around that time, and I always associate it with Camberley. It reminds me of the ironing room and the smell of robin starch.

I played table tennis for the unit and was entered in the Army Championships at Aldershot. I wasn't really a great table tennis player but you got roped in to these things sometimes. I'd been to Preston Barracks in Brighton to play against their unit, and I'd lost there, but our PTI, WO2 Battison, cajoled me into playing in Aldershot. I was just making up the numbers really and was coincidentally beaten again by the lass I'd played against in Brighton, but proud to say I did take part. I also had a very short spell in the hockey team, but it was never my forte. They made me play in goal against Guildford, who were the best team around. They said I wouldn't get hurt wearing the protective goalkeeping pads, but they lied. I kicked the ball on one occasion and bruised my foot, it was quite painful. We got absolutely slaughtered, something like 16-1, but I did save one shot when I instinctively put up my right hand and caught the ball, thus preventing another certain goal. This was my last encounter with hockey.

I went on a four-day Tennis course to Aldershot. I loved tennis and it was a wonderful opportunity to go and learn more about the game. The Officer who took us for the course, Lt Moles, reminded me very much of Virginia Wade, she was definitely her doppelganger. After a strenuous PT session in the morning, we then played tennis all day. I had blisters on my hand from the tennis racket, and during the night, I had terrible cramp pains in my lower right arm, my muscles were shot. But it was a great experience nonetheless. When I returned to my unit, I had to visit the OC (Officer Commanding) to sign the report from the officer in charge of the course. In her summary she said it was a pleasure to have me on the course. The OC said she had never seen anyone say that about a participant before. I was really chuffed, and it made a pleasant change from *that bloody Gail Newsham*. I played tennis for the unit for a while, but I wasn't very good and never won a game, but my forehand improved and I enjoyed practicing on the courts just outside our accommodation block.

While at Camberley I went on two Adventure Training Exercises, with 2nd Lt Alison Trehern in charge. The first was a camping trip to Wales, *Exercise Mountain Goat*, where we took part in numerous outdoor activities. The rock climbing was particularly scary and I was somewhat relieved when it was over, but it was all leading up to the finale of the week; climbing Mount Snowden via Crib Gogh, a 3000-foot high crag with a narrow path at the top and a sheer drop on either side. We weren't taken by a path to walk up the crag, it was a scramble climb, and quite a test for us. One of the girls had a panic attack and needed help to go back down. Being young I was quite blasé about the height of it and was running about on the top with no fear at all, but when I see pictures of Crib Gogh today, I can't believe I actually did it. The second, *Exercise Mountain Goat II*, was another trip to Wales, this time to walk the Brecon Beacons where we stayed in a youth hostel. The weather wasn't all that brilliant, quite misty on the walk, but it was a great few days away and at least we weren't under canvas this time.

Camberley – Remembrance Day 1975

I did go through a bit of a down time when I was at Camberley. There was a girl in our block called Frances, she was a stewardess, always had a smile, she seemed a happy soul and at peace. Where everyone else had pictures of their favourite singer or film star on the wall in their bed space, Frances had religious pictures and prayers on display. I did believe in God, but wasn't really a church goer, I don't really care for organised religion. I did go from time to time of my own volition, but was never forced to go every Sunday like other people I knew growing up. Religion was never a big thing in my family and I don't really know where my faith came from, it was just something I always felt. One night, I'd gone to bed and couldn't sleep. I was tossing and turning, trying to work out what was wrong with me, why was I feeling so down. Then it dawned on me, I sat up and said to myself, *I know what it is, I'm without God*; so I got up, got dressed and went outside. It was a cold November night, crisp and clear, and I sat on a bench on the green just outside the block. I was talking to God telling him I realised I'd let him slip away, I knew it was my fault and told him I was sorry. I asked, if he was listening, could he give me a sign to let me know he'd heard me. Just as I said that, a shooting star went right across the sky, and I burst into tears. I know many would say it was just coincidence; while others would say there's no such thing; but I took it to be my sign and I started to feel better. I wrote this poem.

I BELIEVE

In this world full of trouble and strife
It's important for God to be part of your life
If He is with you there's nothing to fear
He'll carry on helping you year after year
Always there to help you, waiting for your call
If you acknowledge His presence, you will never fall.
I remember life without Him, I felt so empty deep inside,
But when He listened to my plea, I was so happy I just cried
He took away my doubts and made my belief so strong
And He helped me to see where I was going wrong.
He gave me peace of mind and a contentment in my soul,
He made my life complete – I was half, then I was whole
I gave to Him my trust and He knows that I believe
Even though there are many things my mind cannot conceive.
All I did was have faith in Him and I'm not ashamed to say
That when I go to bed at night, I oft times sit and pray.
All I did was believe in Him, look what He has done for me
And He would do it for everyone if only they could see
That with faith and trust in God and a simple little prayer
He is waiting if you need Him
And if you need Him, He'll be there.

Gail J Newsham – 1975

The cook house was just opposite our block, so it wasn't far to traipse for our meals. Sergeant Jackson used to make a corned beef and tomato pie, which was surprisingly quite tasty, and her egg beanos, which I think are peculiar to the Army, were a treat. It's just a fancy name for fried egg and beans on toast, but they were always very popular. On the menu on one occasion, was what we thought was chicken pie. I opted for something else, but Karen chose the pie. It wasn't until she had eaten it, we discovered it was in fact rabbit pie; Karen was mortified, and kept saying, '*I ate a bunny, I ate a bunny*,' she was really quite upset. I think she went vegetarian after that.

At Christmas time the officers would serve us our Christmas dinner, which was a welcome role reversal after all the cups of tea and coffee we had made for them, it was lovely festive cheer and much appreciated. The NAAFI was always on hand if you wanted more to eat later on, or if we wanted something different, we would sometimes cycle round to the chippy on the Old Dean housing estate for a curry pie and chips. Miss Colbert, the NAAFI manageress, used to make really good ham and tomato toasties, which were my favourite. Our side of the NAAFI was separate from the Corporals because we weren't allowed to mix, and it was good to be able to let your hair down a bit without being told off. In those days you could get three tunes on the juke box for 10p, and we always kept ourselves entertained. If there was a lull in the music, I would start singing, which was a good way to get someone to put more money in the juke box; worked every time. The College was predominantly WRAC, made up of clerks, cooks, stewardesses, drivers, PTIs, medics, and a hairdresser, but there were a handful of soldiers from the Pioneer Corps who were there to undertake maintenance and light engineering tasks. There was one chap from Liverpool, he was a quiet lad, never had much to say, and maybe a bit introverted, but he was brilliant at playing draughts. I would often have a game with him in the NAAFI, but I could never beat him, it was fun trying though.

Having spent a year at the WRAC College, I was posted with a promotion to Lance Corporal, to Dusseldorf in Germany in early 1976, and I took a typing speed test to be made up to a B2 Staff Clerk. I was called in to the OCs office for her to give me the news about my promotion and posting. It was exciting and scary all at the same time. I can't recall the full conversation I had with Major Heath, but she said something that remained with me throughout my life. She said, '*Private Newsham, you are far more important than I am, you are the one who does the work.*' I have never forgotten those words and how she made me feel valued. It showed what a true leader is, how to motivate and inspire. Its people like her who you would put your head above the parapet for. You can't teach that on any management course, you've either got it or you haven't. I was really chuffed at being promoted, but it was an unwritten rule that you didn't sew your own stripes on your uniform. Karen, Sue and Bailey very kindly sorted it for me, but I wasn't a Lance Corporal until I touched down in Germany. I was really sorry to leave Camberley and so sad to say goodbye to my roomies, lots of tears were shed and I wondered would our paths ever cross again. I wrote this poem for them all.

TRIBUTE TO TRAINING WING STAFF WRAC COLLEGE, CAMBERLEY, 1976

Here is a small goodbye note, just from me to all of you,
Present friends and past ones, everyone I knew.
I'd like to say a special thankyou in the best way that I know,
And this is with a poem: Hanky's out and here we go.
It's been a pleasure to know you all, it's really been great fun,
And I'll remember my happy days at Camberley for many years to come.
Thanks for putting up with me; it must have been a trial,
But through all my blunders, you still managed to smile.
Sincerely, I will miss you all when I am gone from here,
And just between the few of us, I'll even shed a tear.
Thank you CSM Brooker for sorting out our leave,
One of the best of those I know with rank upon her sleeve.
To the 'regal' Captain Lobban and Abigail as well,
Thanks a lot for everything, I think you're both just swell.
To the Northern Captain Spencer, thanks just for being you,
And thanks for all the 'burning' you helped me to get through.
Good luck and thanks to Captain Fisher, it really was a treat,
To meet a real live Yankee, your accent's really 'neat'.
Thanks to Captain Cannon for 'Demonstration Orderly Room',
I'm just glad it was in fun, and not to meet my doom!
Thanks to Major Blueman, my complex soon did go,
Even if my tea was horrible, you never let it show!
Thanks to Major Roulstone, of you what can I say?
Other than when you smile, you help to brighten up the day.
Thanks to SGT's Russell and Reed for Parade States bang on time,
They helped to save a precious neck; of course that neck was mine.
Many thanks to Captain Laing-Morton for all of your support,
In upholding the name of the TTLFS in all aspects of sport.
Good luck and thanks to Captain Hanlon, and to cuddly old Snoopy,
Your husband's sexy voice really sends me loopy!
Thanks to the girls in the office, for being such good friends,

I hope all your success goes on and never ends.
And now the big Finale, my final tribute to you all,
In my up's and down's in Training Wing, I've really had a ball.
So here's a gigantic thank you, my appreciation's really over-flowing,
And I can't help but feel quite sad now that I am going.
I wouldn't be where I am without the help from All of You.
So Thanks a lot and Good Luck in everything you do.

Gail J Newsham

I was flown out to Dusseldorf from Luton airport and had to take care of a young girl on the flight who was travelling alone going to meet up with her parents. She had some kind of medical impairment issues, and we had reserved seats at the front of the plane and the journey passed without incident. It took a little while to settle to my new life in Germany, I was quite sad for the first few weeks, but once I got used to the new surroundings, and new people, I started to really enjoy it.

My bed space in Dusseldorf

I was working at Carnarvon Barracks, HQ Rhine Area, and part of my job involved typing Standing Orders for distribution to the whole of BAOR,

(British Army of the Rhine) so they had to be perfect every time. Major Soffe was the senior officer, and I had to do a lot of typing for him. His writing was quite spidery and rather difficult to decipher, but I did eventually get used to it. My Staff Captain was Captain Erskine, we had a good working relationship and I had a lot of respect for her. Some of the girls thought she was rather strict, but I got on quite well with her. To illustrate the kind of relationship we had, when you saw an officer outside, you had to salute them, to honour their commission. I saw Captain Erskine on one occasion, just outside HQ, I was on the other side of the square and I saluted her, but she just waved back at me in acknowledgement. She also let me have an afternoon off one time so I could watch an important tennis match at Wimbledon on the television. I like to think she saw some potential in me, I'd only been there a short time when she was recommending me for promotion to full Corporal. It would mean going back to Camberley to do the Corporals Course, and I was eagerly looking forward to re-visiting my old posting and maybe catching up with some familiar faces. I knew you had to give a presentation as part of the course, and I was tentatively planning mine. The Human Kidney. I remembered some things we were taught at school and I thought dissecting one and explaining how it worked, would be an interesting, if unusual, topic.

We didn't have 'stand by your beds' inspections in Dusseldorf, it was a working unit and a little more relaxed than being in training, but we still had to be well turned out, keeping our uniform clean and pressed, and our shoes bulled. We would have a parade outside the block at regular intervals and an NCO would be appointed to take the parade, which I was tasked to do. The girls would be lined up, stood at ease, and as the OC approached, the NCO would bring the girls to attention by saying, '*Parade, Parade, shun*', and everyone stood to attention. The NCO then marched towards the officer, saluted her and said, '*X soldiers on parade and ready for inspection, Ma'am.*' She then inspected the girls, and once she had concluded the inspection, and made any comments, the NCO saluted her again and dismissed the parade.

While I was posted in Germany, my Mum and Dad were on a coach trip travelling through Europe. My Dad asked the tour guide if he could contact my OC to get permission for me to meet up with them in Cologne. It was a wonderful surprise to be allowed to go and I had an unexpected lovely day out with my Mum and Dad. We had some lunch near Cologne Cathedral, and my Dad thought I could speak proper German because I could ask for three beers. *Drei biers bitte*. Bless him. What a special day that was.

Mum and Dad at Cologne Cathedral 1976   Mum and me

It was a hot summer in Germany in 1976 and we certainly packed a lot in to that year. We went camping down the Rhine, and Mosel River, with CSM Wynne Pickard in charge of the trip. We had a great time seeing places like Koblenz and Boppard, it really is a beautiful part of the world. I always said I'd go back one day. I also recall German wine being about the equivalent of 50p a bottle, my first introduction to Liebfraumilch and Hock. There were many photos taken of me singing on tables during this trip following that little discovery. Another camping trip was to Austria. In those days, you could get a travel warrant to take you fifty miles across the border of Germany, so we made plans to go to a camp site named Natterer See, not far from Innsbruck. We borrowed the tent and equipment from the stores on camp and dragged it on luggage trollies when we got off the train. It was a beautiful campsite, surrounded by mountains, and the weather was lovely, lots of sunshine, blue skies and fluffy clouds over the mountain tops all week, it was stunning. Everything was very expensive though and we mostly lived on tins of goulash soup the whole time we were there. We went to Innsbruck for a day trip and saw the Golden Roof. I'd seen it before when I was on the skiing trip with the school, it was lovely to see it again, and the cuckoo clocks in the souvenir shops reminded me of the one I took home for Mum and Dad. We decided to treat ourselves to a cake at one of the many cafes, the Austrians were famous for their delicious pastries and it was too good an opportunity to miss. It cost a fortune, but made a welcome change from the goulash soup.

In those days, we were still living through the 'Cold War' period, and with Germany being close to what was known as the *Iron Curtain*, we had to be prepared for anything. Everyone was afraid the Russians would be coming, I don't know why really, it's just what had been fed to us over time. We had a week-long exercise in the cellars below HQ where we had to act out having been involved in an NBC attack. We had to wear our gas mask and Noddy suit while trying to perform office duties. I thought it was all a bit of a faff to tell you the truth, and I typed a letter to our Pat, telling her exactly what I was wearing, gas mask on, the lot. I'm not sure she could picture the scene, it had to be seen to be believed.

In combat gear during the exercise below HQ

The camp were asking for volunteers to help out at the Nijmegen Marches in Holland. These marches are an event of International Four Days Marches, and is the largest multiple day marching event in the world. Its origins began in sporting events for army units held all over the Netherlands between 1904 and 1908. The goal was to improve the physical condition of conscripted soldiers by walking 40km distances over the four consecutive days. It is organised every year in mid-July as a means of promoting sport and exercise. We were to act as stewardesses providing drinks and refreshments to participants and it was another great experience to be part of.

Sandy & me, Stewardesses at Nijmegen Marches 1976

Me, Nijmegen 1976

We also went on an weeks Adventure Training Exercise to the Ardennes in Belgium, under the guidance of one of the Belgian Army's most famous regiments, the Chasseurs Ardennais. We stayed in the accommodation where the Belgian conscripted soldiers did their training. It was very basic with old iron beds and metal lockers. There were about eight of us in a dorm. The showers also left a lot to be desired. It must have been miserable for the local soldiers in winter time, it was bad enough for us and it was only for a short stay. The food wasn't up to much either and someone told us there was horsemeat on the menu. We tried to eat out as much as we could after hearing that. Mushrooms on toast at a local café was much more palatable. We did all sorts of activities during the week, I took part in abseiling and orienteering for the first time, and had a couple of mishaps. During the abseil training, we were getting to grips with the method on a steep embankment. Once you had the safety harness and ropes attached, you walked down leaning backwards, until you felt confident enough to jump out and land again a bit further down. It was all going swimmingly until we moved on to a bigger embankment. Somehow, I had my harness on wrong and when I was walking down and jumped out, it pulled me back in towards the rocky embankment. I was ok, but a bit bruised where the harness fits under the tops of the legs. The second mishap was during the orienteering, I managed to get my hand caught on a barbed wire fence and was stuck until Captain Erskine came to my rescue.

Captain Erskine abseiling down the first embankment

The abseil training was all leading up to the big finale of abseiling down some rocks with an eighty-foot overhang to jump out from, and land at the bottom. I did try, but I'm afraid fear got the better of me on that occasion. But I wasn't alone, I was sat in the woods watching from a distance with a lot of squaddies who felt exactly the same as I did.

Watching the brave abseilers   and even got in some football

We went through a phase in the block when morale was pretty low. It happens from time to time; everyone would have been through it at one period or another. We'd had some bad reports from the OC (Captain Pierce) after our in-night duties, we weren't up to scratch and she wasn't happy. A few of us decided to try to turn things around and get the block gleaming. We made lists for all the block jobs with everything itemised so that everyone understood what tasks were required, and we set to. Everyone pulled together and we left nothing to chance cleaning absolutely everything in sight, and then we waited. When the OC came round to do her inspection, she wrote her comments in the book which simply said, '*Excellent*'. We had never known there to be no faults found in an OCs inspection before, and we were rather chuffed that all our hard work had paid off. Just shows what can be done when everyone works together. After our glowing inspection report, we went to see her to ask if we could have a party in the block to further raise morale. We wanted her to trust us and promised everything would be ok. She thought about it for a while and eventually agreed, and everyone got together to make the arrangements. She was away in Rhinedhalen over the weekend of the party, and put her trust in us in her

95

absence. We had a disco in the downstairs communal area and the laundry room was the bar. It was a huge success and morale was greatly improved. Everyone was happy she had trusted us to be responsible and we didn't let her down, not one of us. It was a great night, and once we cleaned everything up, you'd never know we'd been there.

It was during my posting to Dusseldorf that I met and fell in love with Martha, (not her real name) another female soldier, she was a Corporal and was actually the lass who beat me at table tennis when I played at Brighton and the Army Championships in Aldershot. This is not an easy time for me to write about; first and foremost because it is deeply personal; it isn't easy to bare your soul when the whole experience of coming to terms with 'being different' was a very painful and difficult chapter in my life. Things were very different back then, attitudes were sometimes very cruel and hurtful things were said. Secondly, and equally important, because of the emotional and psychological scars that still remain from what I am about to share. We both knew we couldn't be together in the Army, so we put in our notice, which was a period of eighteen months, and were intending to leave and set up home together. We were excited about it and already buying bits and pieces for a 'bottom drawer.' We had just bought a new car together, a blue Mazda 1000. Neither of us had passed our driving test, but the plan was to learn with the Army so we would have our own transport when we were back in civvy street. Martha was intent on being a recruiting Sergeant, and retaining connections with the Army were important to both of us. Everyone knew we were together; we weren't the only gays in the village, and no one was bothered. Well, I say no one.

One day, out of the blue, I was sent for to go to the SIB block (Special Investigation Branch) for what turned out to be a very lengthy and prolonged interrogation. I didn't know initially, but the same fate was happening to Martha. Someone had reported us because of our relationship, and so the witch hunt went into full throttle. I can't remember how long the interrogation lasted but it was brutal, we were put under extreme pressure and it was exhausting. They went through all my personal belongings, scrutinising letters from family and friends, making the most ridiculous suggestions and implying things out of absolutely nothing. They made you feel dirty. I can't remember many of the details, perhaps its nature's way of protecting you by making you forget, but I do remember one particular letter I had received from Kash. I had written to her keeping in touch and asking how she was, she was a widow living alone. We always had a joke with each other, and I'd said something to her like, *'make sure you don't get pregnant'* in my previous letter. She replied to my comment quoting a line from an old music hall song saying, *'nobody loves a fairy after she's forty'* and they even wanted to make something out of that. She was my auntie for Christ's sake, what kind of minds do these people have? In the end, I'd had enough and just told them yes, I was having a relationship with Martha. But it didn't stop there. To inflict yet more torment, we were made to see a psychiatrist so they could pick through everything all over again to make sure we weren't trying to 'work our ticket.' The way they treated us was absolutely despicable, I'd even say barbaric. For our punishment, they said we could be separated and accept a posting to different units, but what good would it have done? Would it have changed or solved anything? We were already scared, disillusioned, and totally broken by everything they had put us through, it would have been the final straw that broke our hearts completely. I didn't want to be part of something that could treat you so cruelly and inhumanely. The only option was to leave.

So, what brought all of this about? In our block, an NCO was put in charge of a room to give the girls someone to turn to in the first instance if they had any problems. I was NCO in charge of a particular room with two young girls, one of whom (BG) wasn't pulling her weight. The other girl (KJ) was left to do all the work on her own on in night, while BG wasn't bothered about the rules, leaving her clothes over the radiators and other belongings strewn all over the place, and this had been going on for some time. KJ came to me because she was upset at how she was being taken advantage of. The truth of the matter was, and this is in no way fabrication, BG often didn't sleep in her own room, she was well known for being rather familiar with numerous RMPs (Royal Military Police) in their block. And that was fine if that was her calling, no one reported her for it. But it wasn't fair to leave KJ to repeatedly pick up the slack on in night. I advised KJ to leave BG's things where she had left them for the inspection, and brought this to the OCs attention. The matter resulted in a re-inspection where BG had to make sure her side of the room was up to standard. It was because of this that BG reported us to SIB, for nothing more than a cold and calculating act of revenge for having to clean her room properly, just like the rest of us did, every week.

The girls in the block were shocked and absolutely disgusted at what had unfolded and they didn't want us to leave. Whether it's true or not, some thought that if Captain Erskine had been our OC, it would never have happened because she was stronger. They even got up a petition to let us stay. I think that might be why it took them so long to let us go. It was a really tough time waiting for the axe to fall and the future was very uncertain. We were worried about selling the car, we still had all the finance to sort out and without a salary to meet any payments, we didn't really know what we would do.

I had to write to my Mum and Dad to tell them the devastating news. Not only about my relationship with Martha, but I was also losing my job because of it. I didn't want them to be ashamed of me and told them I wouldn't come home anymore if they didn't want me to. My Dad was heartbroken, not necessarily as much about me and Martha, although it did take him time to come to terms with, but also because I had to leave the Army. He had been so proud of me, so very proud, and I was about to let him down, massively. He had served during WW2, and his Dad in WW1, so we had a family military history to share. He went to see our Pat to ask her what was going on, he was really upset, and I know at first my Mum didn't really understand, but when push came to shove, they were always very supportive of me. I know it wasn't easy for any of them, and we sometimes said things that hurt each other, but when the chips were down, they were there when I needed them most, and I am so grateful for their love and support. They sent me a telegram just saying, *'it doesn't matter, we love you'*.

Our Pat was equally supportive, and the funny thing is, I'd already written to her only the month before any of this happened, to pour my heart out and tell her about me, about my own struggles coming to terms with things, and all about Martha and our plans. I didn't want to be a disappointment and an embarrassment to her, and again said I wouldn't come home anymore if she didn't want me to, and how much I would miss Ian and Elaine. But she also said that she loved me no matter what, and just wanted me to be happy. She wrote, *'I only know I love you and want the best in life for you, and if you mention not coming home any more, I'll throttle you! I hope you don't mind, but I showed Pauline your letter, I needed to talk to another female, and she cried as she read it. In fact, it took her a few minutes to compose herself and then she said, "You should be proud of her, I defy anyone to read that letter and not be touched by it." And if you need any more proof of how much we all love you, Ian said to me only yesterday', "I wish aunty Gail hadn't joined the Army, we hardly ever see her. I think it's a waste of time."* After all the struggles and heartache, I had the support of my family. Who could ask for more? What anyone else thought simply paled into insignificance.

While we were waiting for our discharge, The Carpenters were appearing at Philipshalle in Dusseldorf. We both liked them and thought it would be a bit of light relief from all the uncertainty. We managed to get tickets to the show and they were amazing. The German audience were a little bit more reserved than we expected, and we made a tad more noise that they did, it was wonderful to actually see them perform live. Karen Carpenter playing the drums was absolutely incredible, and more than lived up to everything that had been said about her ability. I bought their new album, *'There's a Kind of Hush'*, and wanted to get their autographs if at all possible, so we waited for ages outside the stage door. It was a chilly November night, but eventually they came out and obliged all the fans who had braved the cold. Karen Carpenter was really tiny, much smaller that I imagined, and I'm only 5'2". It was an unforgettable night for sure.

So, we went home for Christmas, still in limbo waiting for the axe to fall. Everyone got to meet us as a couple, and everything went well, they liked Martha as I knew they would. They all took her to their hearts, as she did in return, and it was just the same with her family. We were going to be ok. I'd asked my friend Kath to help find us a bed sit in Preston, the same lass who gave me the money to get my passport returned, and that worked out well too. When we got back to camp after the festivities, our discharge date was up on standing orders for the middle of January 1977, and we started preparations to leave the Army and say goodbye to all our friends. We were told that BG was supposedly sorry for what she had done. She apparently never meant for this to happen, she just wanted to pay me back for the room nonsense. Pity she didn't think of the consequences beforehand.

Before we left, I met Captain Erskine as I was walking up the stairs in HQ, she told me she was being posted to Camberley. You couldn't make it up, could you? I asked her if I could put her down as a referee if I got an interview for a job. She said yes. What an absolute star. I don't know what I would have done without her support. CSM Pickard in Dusseldorf, was also very supportive in helping with the sale of the car we had just bought. We lost quite a lot of money on it but she attended to the sale for us and sorted out what was left. It was all a bit messy with the finance company, but we couldn't have managed without her help.

Captain Erskine at Camberley 1976

99

I received a glowing reference from the OC in Dusseldorf, and it makes you wonder exactly what the whole thing was about. *'LCpl Newsham has been employed as a clerk during her career in the WRAC, and throughout this period has proved to be extremely efficient and reliable and very willing to accept responsibility. A bright, cheerful and quick-witted young woman whose general enthusiastic approach to life is an asset to any office and makes her a popular member of the team. She has a very pleasant personality, is extremely smart, and thoroughly honest and trustworthy. There is no hesitation in recommending LCpl Newsham to any future employer'.* A reference to be proud of, but I could never show it to anyone, in the box that noted reason for discharge, it said, Services no longer required. Thank heaven for Captain Erskine.

These witch hunts happened quite often in the Army, when from time to time they would have a 'clear out' and destroy people's lives and career. They simply didn't care, and the truth about it all is, many of those responsible for ruining young soldiers' lives, were just as guilty of the same 'crime' themselves. How they ever managed to sleep at night is beyond me. While I was stationed at Camberley, I overheard a conversation between the CSM (Company Sergeant Major) and one of the Officers in Training Wing. They were discussing the relationship between two of the female Sergeants on camp, but not in a 'we must report them' kind of way, simply discussing their particular situation, they obviously didn't see it as an issue. But as always, it's one rule for them and a different one for us. Funnily enough, I bumped into that particular Officer when we were going through Guildford finalising our discharge. She was surprised to see me and asked why I was there, I told her the Army didn't want me anymore. She looked quite sad. Another Officer I saw again while we were sat in Guildford HQ waiting for the paper work to be completed, was that young Cadet from Camberley, the one who said she would never change. I don't think she recognised me, or perhaps she did and didn't want to acknowledge me because she knew what I would be thinking. She was so full of her own self-importance, I found it quite nauseating. The three pips on her shoulder had most certainly gone to her head. I hope they kept her company in times of need. Many years later, I heard they had a 'clear out' at Camberley, not too long after I had been posted out apparently, and it made me sad and angry. I knew some of those girls who ended up losing everything, they were dedicated and good at their job, and weren't causing any harm to anyone. But they weren't Sergeants you see, and that seemingly, made all the difference.

It's really not easy to talk about this period in my life. The events in Dusseldorf left huge scars, and for over forty years I lived with a sense of rejection, of not being good enough, and worst of all, a sense of shame. From time to time, I did have regrets at not being allowed to see it through, and I used to have recurring dreams where I was back in the Army but having to go through the same scenario every time. I was a good soldier, we both were, and I think I could have been successful given the chance. I always watched the Festival of Remembrance with a pang of sadness, wondering if I would see anyone I knew, and wishing I could have taken part in something so prestigious, it would have been such an honour. But I do believe that everything happens for a reason, and in time, I would come to realise why I believe this whole sorry episode had to happen.

LIFE AFTER 42

When we came back to Preston in 1977, we initially lived in a bedsit on Deepdale Road. It had one room to live in, which comprised of a bed, two arm chairs, a wardrobe, a sideboard, an electric fire with two elements, and a small table with two stools. We made it as nice as it could be and cleaned it from top to bottom. We shared the kitchen and bathroom with two Greek guys, and it wasn't exactly a harmonious experience sharing with them. We were both Army trained in cleanliness and hygiene, and it didn't really gel with two blokes who left dirty plates all over the kitchen and always left the bathroom in a mess. We were eventually able to move next door to the flat the landlord vacated, where we were all self-contained. Thankfully, after about a year on the housing waiting list, we were allocated a newly built first floor council flat on Dovedale Avenue in Ingol, on the other side of town. I saw an advert in the paper for a local ladies football team who were looking for new players, and I went along to sign for Ingol Belles in 1978 rekindling my love affair with women's football.

Mum was diagnosed with oral cancer in early 1978 and it was an extremely traumatic and devastating time for all of us. We were absolutely terrified of losing her, I can't put into words the depth of the fear, the gut-wrenching anguish and desperation that manifests as a physical pain inside your whole being, but she was a tough little soul and bravely fought her way back. What she went through was beyond words, and I can't revisit those memories without feeling a deep sorrow for the pain and suffering she had to endure. Her courage throughout all her ordeal, was a testament to her inner strength, and I am immensely proud that she is my Mum. It hurt very deeply watching her go through those times and it rocked me to the core, feeling desperately helpless and unable to change anything to take away her pain. I was so scared of losing her, I didn't want my Mum to die, I didn't know how I would get through life without her. I prayed so hard every single day, and my prayers were answered. Mum bravely battled on.

Dad was working at BAC on Strand Road during this time. He was a fitter's mate on Maintenance, working with Tommy Gill. They would have open days at the works and I went round with him so he could show me his domain and see what his job entailed. He was proud of working there and told me he used to write his name on pipes and gantries on jobs they had done all over the building, Joe Newsham was here. He was a good mate to Tommy and they got on well. Sadly, Tommy was tragically killed at work when he put his head through a hatch into a large metal container, unaware it was full of some sort of toxic gas. Dad thought Tommy was just acting the fool when he was half inside the tank and not moving, but Tommy had died instantly. Dad took it really hard, he was devastated and in shock, it was some time before he came to terms with what had happened. There were some long strikes at BAC during Dad's time there, some of the shop stewards were quite militant in those days and there was no money coming in during these periods. Dad had to go to a money lender to keep things ticking over, and I know Kash gave him some money to help out. They were hard times.

I passed my driving test in 1980, at the second attempt, and got a bank loan of £400 to buy our first car, a blue mini with customised gold markings down the side, on the roof, and bonnet. It looked quite cool, but it was a bit of a rust bucket letting in loads of water. But it was my first car and I loved it.

Mum, me and our Pat outside her house at Dukes Meadow

By this time, I was working at Peter Craig's Catalogue Mail Order, in Tulketh Mill, off Blackpool Road. It was part of the Littlewoods Empire and I worked there about eight years, processing customers' orders on the VDU section. They were a great bunch of girls to work with, and very kind and supportive when my Mum was ill. One time, I organised a trip for us to be in the audience for the television programme, *The Price is Right*, hosted by Leslie Crowther. They told us to wear bright clothing and be ready to *'come on down*,' if any of us were chosen to take part. Lady luck was on our side when one of our girls, Margaret, was given the call and went on to win the star prize. Another adventure with a happy ending and I took this picture below of us celebrating on the coach on our way home.

Celebrating on the coach

We also went to see Diana Ross at the NEC in Birmingham. We hired a mini bus and I drove us all there and back. It was a fantastic night and it might even have been the time I managed to hold hands with Diana Ross when she came down into the audience singing *'Reach out and Touch'*. I was a big fan of hers back in the day, but went off her a bit when I heard that she expected people to address her as Miss Ross. What's all that about, eh? Our annual Christmas party nights at the lovely Waterwheel restaurant in Chipping, were always eagerly looked forward to, and definitely worth a mention for the memory box. We would meet up at the Crest Hotel in Preston and hire a coach to take us to the Talbot pub in Chipping, before crossing the road to the restaurant, where we had some rather, shall we say, high spirited after dinner festive cheer. The staff were very good putting up with our good-humoured antics and always let us return again the following year, I think they enjoyed it really. Many of the girls also came on the treasure hunts I used to organise for the football team. They were always very generous and supportive of all my fund-raising efforts. They were great days to look back on.

Kash got married for the fifth time in 1979 to Luke Lawson. She had never had any children and we never really thought anything about it, just assuming she couldn't. It was only when our Pat was taking her to a hospital appointment, she told her she had previously had three miscarriages, all baby boys. Poor Kash, we never knew.

Kash and Luke on their wedding day

We moved from Ingol to Fulwood in 1980/81. The introduction of the Shared Ownership Scheme gave us the opportunity to get on the property ladder and buy a flat. It was a new build, with a brown bathroom suite and no central heating. We didn't have much money after getting enough together for the deposit, and couldn't afford any floor covering for the kitchen, so our Pat offered to pay us to do some cleaning for her at Dukes Meadow and it enabled us to get it done. We did eventually get central heating installed which added value for any future sale.

In 1981, we were going on holiday to the South of France to stay in a caravan

105

at Port Grimaud, not too far from St Tropez. It was a train ride to London, and an extremely long coach journey through the length of France, we didn't have much money and this was the cheapest way we could do it. I asked our Pat if we could take Ian and Elaine with us for their first trip abroad. The kids were keen to come and Pat eventually agreed to let Auntie Gail be in charge and saw us off in tears at Preston station, having never been apart from her two babies before. But by the time we got home two weeks later, she said she had enjoyed the house being just as she left it while they were away. It was a great trip enjoyed by us all.

Me, Ian and Elaine, South of France

We went on holiday with Pat, Andy, Ian and Elaine, to Wadebridge in Cornwall, and when the kids had left home while furthering their education, we went with Pat and Andy to Menorca, Corfu and Rhodes, and many more family sayings were coined on these trips. One of our favourites was for directions in the car. Straight ahon was a combination of straight ahead and straight on, and that particular one stayed with us for all time. One of my all-time favourites originated when Pat and Andy were taking the kids to visit their Scottish relatives for their first trip over the border. They were only young, and Ian said to Andy, *'do people in Scotland talk different than us Daddy?'* Andy said they did, and Ian asked what things they would say. Andy thought for a minute, he wasn't very good at accents, and he just said in his normal voice, *'well, if they were going to say they liked your new car, they would say', "I like your new car, Jock."* As though putting Jock and the end of it, made it Scottish. It was a great source of amusement over the years, and even today, when we buy something new, we'll say, '*I like your new shoes*, or whatever, *Jock.*' Keeping the memories alive.

In the early 80s, the terraced houses in Whittingham Street, and the surrounding area, were being demolished, and Mum and Dad went to live in Hassett Close, off South Meadow Lane. It was a one bedroomed ground floor council flat, and they both loved it. Far removed from 42, it actually had central heating and a bathroom with plumbed in hot running water, and plug sockets in every room. Imagine that, after being without such basic every day amenities for most of your life, to finally have these luxuries was nothing more than they deserved. Dad thought it was a little palace.

It was while the demolitions were underway, I decided to drive through the area where I grew up, to hopefully take a look at my childhood home one last time, before it was gone forever. Thankfully, 42 was still standing, but the windows had been bricked up and other demolition work had taken place inside. The bulldozer was at the top of the street, near to Cock Robin, ready to do its worst. I managed to get access to the back yard and the kitchen door was open, so I gingerly crept inside to take a peek. As I stood inside the kitchen by the bottom of the stairs, the tears immediately began to fall, and I sobbed my heart out. So many memories fell on me like a ton of bricks, and the intensity of the emotion took me by surprise. The old kitchenette was still there, and other utensils Mum used to use were on the floor. There was even a note from Dad telling her about some shopping he'd done or something like that. It wasn't safe enough to go upstairs, or anywhere else, the ceiling had been taken down in the living room and it was too risky to venture further. I think, mixed up in all the emotion, were memories of all the years we had shared there together before Mum became ill, when life was 'normal' and everything was ok. It really is a moment in time I will never forget, and it struck me just how small our world was back then, when we were living off Ashton Street. It looked so tiny, yet so many people who had lived in that space, had been part of our lives. I was deeply moved by the whole experience and wrote a couple of poems about it all.

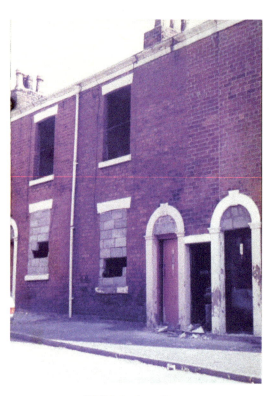

42 Whittingham Street

AN ODE TO 42

Standing among the rubble of a home that used to be
Lost in an avalanche of memories that came flooding back to me.
Standing in the ruins of what seems an empty shell,
Crying for the home we once knew and loved so well.
It hurt so much to see it in its sad state of decay
With so many happy memories of my childhood yesterday.
For in this House were Santa Claus and all my childhood joys,
Waking on Christmas morning and playing with my toys.
Remembering my Mum's love, and remembering my Dad's care,
Alone here in this rubble, those feelings still live there.
Nursing my cuts and bruises, making better all my ill's,
Stoking up the fire to chase away those winter chills.
The laughter and the tears, the happiness and pain,
All of these emotions came flooding back again.

But our House is lost to progress, it's now known as a Slum,
Yet for me it was our home, with Pat, my Dad, and Mum.
And no matter where I wander, no matter what I do,
I'll always remember with affection our days at 42.
Our times weren't always happy, and many times we cried,
But we are a close family, and I think of that with Pride.
For the love and the affection that grew within our home,
Will be treasured in my heart where ever I may roam.
For it was more than bricks and mortar, and I can't help but cry,
Because houses are like people: Now 42 must die.
It won't be long before it's gone, the Bulldozer lies in wait,
And soon our house will be no more. I guess it's down to fate.
I suppose it's evolution as the old makes way for new.
But I'm so glad we had those days, our days at 42.

Gail J Newsham – 1981

In the ruins of 42

ASHTON STREET

I walk along familiar streets now desolate and bare,
And remember the thriving community that once was living there,
I remember all my friends and the things we used to do,
And I sometimes stop and wonder if they're remembering me too.
We made castles on the pavements; we tried to float on a balloon,
We made ships from cardboard boxes and rockets to the moon.
We had a lot of fun with the games that children play,
But now those times are gone, they're just part of yesterday.
There was a shop on every corner where you could go and meet
Everyone you ever knew from each and every street.
Passing my Grans fruit shop, and Greenwoods selling papers,
And remembering with pleasure my impish childhood capers.
There was Gerties selling toffees, with that enormous 'penny tray'
And the 'pop shop' on the hill where we could sit all day.
Ruby in the cake shop who always had a smile,
Mrs Allen at the butchers, who seemed happy all the while.
There was Dorothy in the Co-op, she'd serve you in a sec,
Especially when I went in to claim our 'divvy cheque'.
Mrs Holderness at the Hardware, and that smell of Esso Blue,
And Freda at the chemist who made your prescription up for you.
There was Lily at the 'offy', she'd serve me my Mums' stout,
Mrs Blissett altered your clothes so you looked pretty going out.
Mrs Sumner at the chippy, made the best chips down our way,
And Molly's home-made pies were the order of the day.
There are so many friends and neighbours, too numerous to name,
But suffice to say without you all, my life wouldn't be the same.
You are tucked inside my memory, to be there my whole life through,
And truly it was a pleasure to have spent those years with you.
But where are all these people now? Where have they all gone?
I hope they all remember where they all came from.
So many people lived within the world of Ashton Street,
And I can't help but wonder if once more we all shall meet.

To talk about the good old days, and relive times from the past,
To cry and laugh for times gone by, life passes by so fast!
Some of them they are no more, they're in the community in the sky,
But I'll keep them in my memory as the years go rolling by.
And as I think and reminisce of the things I used to do,
I really hope from time to time, they'll be thinking of me too.

Gail J Newsham

Hassett Close was a good move for Mum and Dad, but especially for Dad. He joined the Middleforth Branch of the Royal British Legion and it enabled him to take part in the Remembrance Day Parades where he proudly wore his war time medals. He served with the Royal Engineers during the Second World War, in India, Burma, Malaya and Singapore, and he never forgot his comrades. When I asked him what it was like for him during those times, he said he '*had a good war*'. I don't know what having a good war really meant, other than perhaps many of his pals didn't come home. I know he had malaria and two bouts of pneumonia, as well as serious burns after being scalded in an accident with some boiling hot soup, so I suppose compared to what some of his pals endured, he probably thought he got off quite lightly. I found some notes he had written in 1943, when he was on a ship sailing to India before embarking on eight weeks jungle training, where he contracted sand fly fever, soon followed by yellow jaundice, which gives a small insight into his 'good war.'

*Wed Oct 27*th*: Very packed in, am looking forward to an unpleasant time. Thurs Oct 28*th*: Wakened up and we are well on our way. Sailing down the west coast of Ireland. Heavy seas. Fri Oct 29*th*: Out of sight of land, weather rough, most of lads sick. Feel sick myself. Sat Oct 30*th*: Bunch of red caps on board, everybody having trouble with them. Mon Nov 1*st*: Getting more fed up every day. No sight of land. Weather calmer. Tues November 2*nd*: Lovely day but don't feel in the mood to enjoy it. Packed like flies below decks, and altogether having a miserable time. Wed Nov 3*rd*: Lectures & PT started today, rather a farce but still, passes time on. Thurs Nov 4*th*: On fatigues in the officer's quarters, just like the Ritz Hotel. Not fair to the lads. Sighted Gibraltar, lovely Mediterranean weather. Fri Nov 5*th*: Grub hardly eatable, only the bread is any good, real white bread. Sat Nov 6*th*: Jerry attacked us with torpedo planes about 5oclock, everybody ordered below deck. Our gunners bring one down, whizzes past our mast and let's fly at the Marmax (sic). Sun Nov 7*th*: We turned back last night and picked up over 1000 survivors. Condition's terrible, worse than the Altmark (naval incident in 1940). Only allowed on deck half an hour in the morning and evening, so many at a time, danger of ship keeling over* *owing to having no ballast. We have been lying off Phillipville since last night. Monday Nov 8th: Entered Phillipville harbour this morning to disembark survivors. The Africans look poverty stricken. Tuesday Nov 9th: One of the ships hit was towed into harbour, but unfortunately sank before all our eyes, rather a majestic sight. Total loss of convoy was two troopships and one destroyer, not many lives lost. Wed Nov 10th: Left Phillipville last night under escort of two British Destroyers. Thurs Nov 11th: Armistice Day. Last Post sounded at 11 o'clock. Port Said reached at 4 o'clock. Lovely place but no chance of shore leave. Fri Nov 12th: Still lying off Port Said. Lovely weather, but wish I was home. Sat Nov 13th: Sailed down the Suez Canal today and took all day to do it. Dropped anchor again at Suez. Mon Nov 15th: Lot of speculation about how long we will be in India which is now definitely our destination. Tues Nov 16th: Sailed tonight, our next port is Aden at bottom of the Red Sea. Fri Nov 19th: Was on guard tonight. Lovely moonlight night and feel very homesick. Sat Nov 20th: Aden reached at 8pm. Mon Nov 22nd: Spuds are scarce now owing to survivors being on board. Getting bags of rice. Tues Nov 23rd: Set sail today, convoy of 3 troopships and 1 cargo boat escort, 1 cruiser and 3 destroyers. Wed Nov 24th: Well out in the Arabian Sea. Sat Nov 27th: Dropped anchor at Bombay about 4pm. Sun Nov 28th: Disembarked today. First thing the natives say is buckshee sahib. Caught train to Devailali, arrived about 3am. An hour's walk to camp. Very tired. Jan 23rd: Posted to Budin for 8 weeks jungle training. March: We lost two good lads on the river. Drowned whilst bridging. Another lad broke his leg and hip through falling down a nullah (sic) in the jungle. Mar 24th: Taken in hospital with sand fly fever. Not surprised either, just finished 5 days deep penets (sic) action in the jungle and it was pretty rough going. April 4th: Left hospital today. May 9th: Went in dock again today with yellow jaundice. My liver and tummy swelled up pretty high. Getting a lot of patter from the boys about being pregnant. June 27th: My stay in hospital nearly up. I think I am earmarked for a month's convalescence at Poona. June 28th: Saw the boys up at camp today. They are all on a draft for Special Force. To hell with Poona, I'm going with them. June 29th: Have managed to get off the Poona stunt but now they won't let me go with the boys. July 10th: Am browned off to hell with this monsoon. Just a sea of mud outside and only providence is holding this tent up. Aug 2nd: I leave here tomorrow for Special Force. Hope I catch up with the boys.* Diary ends.

Dad on parade, nearest camera 2rd left

Mum and Dad also spent time at the Empire Services Club on Hartington Road, where they made many new friends. He was an entertaining man was Joe, he always had a tale to tell, and people liked him. He always carried old photographs in the inside pocket of his jacket, in what he called, his archives. He was proud of his family and wanted to share his stories about them. But tragedy was lurking just around the corner. Mums' cancer returned and she had to have more major surgery in 1982 and I did lose my faith for a while during this period. If there really is a reason for everything, and it was extremely difficult to find any reasons for her pain and suffering to be honest, but I am staunchly of the opinion that the pioneering surgery my mum went through, undoubtedly helped the medical advancement of the treatment and procedures for those unfortunate enough to suffer a similar fate. I'm sure they learned a great deal from what they did to her, but she was a bit of a guinea pig if I'm honest, and I genuinely wonder if such invasive surgery was perhaps a bridge too far. Maybe the surgeons learned that too. And secondly, what I personally learned from the experience of seeing her suffer so much, I'm sure helped me have more empathy towards others and a deeper appreciation of just how precious, and yet so fragile, life really is.

The second operation was a marathon and much more severe than the first one. It took quite some time for her to get some confidence back and to find some kind of normality given her situation. She did really well, bless her, and after a lot of TLC, she did eventually start going out again. But some time down the line, she started getting a bit forgetful and repetitive and it wasn't easy for Dad looking after her while working full time as well. But he soldiered on as long as he could.

In 1987 I went to work at South Ribble Borough Council as a Rent Collector/ Cashier. We were living in Lostock Hall at this time, having sold our flat in 1985 and bought a 3-bed semi, so I did have a little knowledge of the area. It was a good move and I was now able to pay in to the local government pension scheme, a bit of security for the future. The council had the policy of collecting rents from the elderly and disabled and I really enjoyed being out and about meeting people and helping them whenever I could and would often go the extra mile for them. My job evolved into becoming a Visiting Officer in the Housing and Council Tax Benefits Department, helping people to complete the necessary forms to claim benefits. My philosophy was always to help the people I visited, and treat them with the same dignity and respect as I would expect from anyone coming into my Mum and Dad's home, and it always served me, and the residents, very well. But I did have a bit of an up and down time of it working for SRBC, some of which from 1995 is noted in another chapter, but for whatever reason, I don't think my face really fit with the man eventually in charge of the money.

Dad retired from BAC in 1987 but he didn't stay idle for long, his works pension wasn't enough to live on and got himself a job on the car park at the Fishergate Centre, opposite the train station. He had a party at Empire Services Club to celebrate his retirement and it was lovely seeing all the younger lads he worked with come to share in the night with him, showing what a popular man he was. All the family were there too and it was a wonderful night enjoyed by all. Pat and I wanted to do something special for him and had the idea of trying to get the name of his Uncle included on the huge marble Roll of Honour in the Harris Museum. Uncle Joe, who he had been named after, was killed in action during the First World War, and for some reason his name wasn't included among the over 2000 local soldiers who were commemorated. Dad was always proud of being named after Uncle Joe, but deeply sad about his name being omitted from the list of men from all the other local military regiments. He seemed to think the omission was due to the cost at the time and the family being unable to afford it. We contacted Preston Corporation and the War Office, and eventually got the go ahead to have Uncle Joe's name added to the commemorative list. There was just enough room to fit it in at the end of the last section, and Dad was absolutely delighted.

114

Dad's Retirement party – Mum, Dad, Kash 1987

Pat and Andy set up a Horse Racing Club, Laurel Leisure, in 1989. For many years, Andy was the Racing Editor at the *Lancashire Evening Post*, and also wrote for *United Newspapers Group*, the *News of the World,* and the *Scottish Sunday Mail*. What began as a hobby, with a small column on the racing section of the paper, *Andy's Choice*, where he selected three potential winners for the readers, grew to be a very successful career, and he also contributed to BBC and Independent radio stations. His consistent record of tipping winning horses proved he had an excellent knowledge of form for picking a winner. He won the *Sporting Chronicle* Gold Cup for his accurate selections in the early 1970s, and, the *Sunday Times* did a survey of racing tipsters and their nap selections, covering a ten-year period of flat racing, and our Andy easily came out as Britain's number one tipster. He also wrote two books about horses, *Silver Buck* and *Laurel Queen*. It was after taking early retirement from the LEP, he had the idea of setting up the club. Pat knew nothing about horse racing, but soon learned the ropes becoming club secretary. It was a very successful venture attracting over 2000 members, all run by just the two of them. Some of the horses were trained at Jack Berry's stables in Cockerham, and Mary Reveley was another notable trainer for them. It really was a wonderful achievement. *Laurel Queen* was their most successful horse, winning over twenty races, and *Surrey Dancer* was another star performer among many others. Just look him up on YouTube the 1994 Stanley Leisure, Children in Need Handicap Hurdle, to see him in action.

Andy receiving an award for Laurel Queen

Pat leading in Laurel Queen after her 20th win

Kash passed away suddenly in June 1989, after suffering a heart attack. I remember the day vividly. My Dad rang to tell me the news and I was devastated, I loved Kash very much; she was a lovely lady with a wonderful silly daft sense of humour. I hoped it had been quick and she didn't know anything about it and wasn't afraid. I remember driving down to see Dad and I cried in his arms. It was a beautiful summer's day, and I was thinking, how can she be gone on such a lovely day? For her funeral, Pat and I got her a wreath made into a lovely little piano, she would have liked that. Not long before she passed away, she was telling me about some money she had in a Building Society Account. She didn't say how much it was but she didn't want Luke to know about it and kept the account book hidden. I think it might have been from the sale of her house on Whittingham Street. When they got married she sold it and moved to his home on Bucklands Avenue, and after a while, they moved to a council flat on the corner of Plungington Road and Aqueduct Street. They had only lived there for a couple of years when she died. I often wondered if the book was ever found and who inherited the contents. One of my abiding memories of Kash was when Mum and I were walking with her down Plungington Road, I was linking one arm and Sadie was linking the other. Everyone we passed by was saying 'hello Kath', 'hello Kath', and smiling, they all knew her; It was lovely. Kash is very much missed but always remembered. I still take a wreath to her grave every Christmas Eve.

Dad, Mum, Kash, Luke

In June of 1992 I climbed Ben Nevis with a group of friends. We were lucky with the weather, it was a lovely sunny day, clear blue skies with the occasional fluffy cloud, but there was lots of snow when we eventually got towards the summit and it totally covered the hut at the top. The views over the mountain range were spectacular and well worth all the effort of getting up the tallest mountain in the UK, I was very proud of the achievement. A few years later, my friend Yvonne, was diagnosed with breast cancer and needed to have a mastectomy. She wanted to raise money for some iced head caps they used to help prevent hair loss when going through chemotherapy, so we did a fundraiser climb up Ben Nevis for her. We weren't as well blessed with the weather this time and couldn't see very much at all when we reached the top, but I did see the hut that was covered by snow on the previous climb, which gave a sense of just how deep the snow actually was. Another long day with an even greater sense of achievement, but this was my last adventure as a mountaineer.

Mum and Dads Golden Wedding was on the horizon, and our Pat and I saved up every month for a year to put on a special celebration for them. We had to tell them what we were doing to prevent Dad from arranging something else. He was a bit worried about having a disco, but we assured him it wouldn't be as bad as he thought. I booked Bernie Wareing (Clive's brother) to do it for us, he'd done a lot for me at football functions I'd organised, and I knew Bernie would do a good job. We booked St Anthony's Social Centre for 25 July 1992 and arranged a surprise of white Rolls Royce to pick them up and take them to the venue. The doorbell went, and we said, *'taxi's here Dad,'* so he would answer the door. His face was a picture when he saw it. *'Bloody hell Sadie, come and look at this.'*

Mum and Dad on their Golden Wedding Day

118

It was obvious Mum wasn't her old social self, her memory was failing and her confidence going, but she looked lovely and she did have a wonderful time with many of her Scottish family there to share the night with us all.

Sisters Ina & Patsy, Mum, Cousin Maureen

Mum and her brother Phil

My friend, Anne Swarbrick came along to take photographs for us and we also organised a video recording of their special night, which Dad enjoyed reliving for the rest of his days. We managed to get in touch with his best man from their wedding day, and also found one of his old pals from the Army. Dad had no idea we had invited 'Blondie', it was a special surprise, and it's lovely to see them hug one another, once Dad realised who he was. And to see just how much warmth and affection everyone had for Mum as they greeted her, really brings a lump to my throat. Dad often liked to get up and sing, and he didn't disappoint that night. It's wonderful to look back at the video and see him singing his heart out. He was quite an entertainer was our Joe, definitely had a touch of the Frank Sinatra's. He was in his element and thoroughly enjoying the whole occasion. During his thank you speech he said, *'thank heaven for little girls.'* Pat and I were really chuffed to have made them both so happy.

Me, Dad, Pat

Sadly, Martha and I parted company in late 1992 and I went to live in Blackpool. It was a deeply sad and difficult time, and the move to the coast would be relatively short lived. It wasn't the happiest of times.

Mum's condition continued to get worse over the next few years, and looking after her was taking its toll on Dad. He had been totally devoted to his little Sadie, he honestly couldn't have done more for her, but looking after her 24/7 had a price. I went down to see them both one day and the situation was pretty serious. Dad was ill in bed and obviously in a bad way, with Mum unable to take care of him because of her own failing health. The doctor had been to see Dad and was sending him to hospital. While we were waiting for the ambulance to arrive, I had to make a mad dash into town to get him some pyjamas and a dressing gown fit for a hospital stay, it was a bit of a frantic rush to say the least. Mum couldn't stay home on her own and I had to arrange for her to be taken to Ribbleton Hospital while Dad recovered. It was a dreadful situation having both Mum and Dad taken to hospital on the same day, not knowing what the hell to do for the best. It's all a bit of blur now but I went with Mum to Ribbleton hospital and tried to get her settled. It was heart breaking when I was trying to leave, she kept saying, *'you're leaving me on my own', I'll be on my own.'* I tried to explain I had to get to Royal Preston Hospital to find out what was wrong with Dad and I'd be back soon. I knew she was safe but it broke my heart to leave her and I cried my eyes out as soon as I closed the ward door behind me. I couldn't bear the thought of her being scared and alone but I had no other choice. I made my way to RPH and found out where Dad was, and they informed me he had been given seven pints of blood. Apparently, he had been passing dark stools and thought it was because he'd been drinking Guinness to build him up a bit, but the diagnosis revealed he had an ulcer and it had been bleeding for quite some time. Talk about getting him there before it was too late. He looked a bit better for having the transfusion when I saw him and he told me not to worry about visiting him, just make sure Mum was ok. When Dad got back on his feet, we arranged for someone to look after Mum while our Pat and I took him to the Edinburgh Military Tattoo to give him a bit of a break. He religiously watched it on the tele every year, and we thought it would be lovely for him to see it live at the actual event. It turned out to be a bit of a marathon of a weekend though, with long coach journeys from a hotel on the outskirts of Glasgow to Edinburgh Castle, and a trip to St Andrews thrown in, which we could have well done without to be honest. I think it was a bit too much for him and he was glad to get home, but he did appreciate the visit to the Castle and all the military displays.

In 1996, I bought my own home, a small two bed semi detached on Kiln Croft in Clayton le Woods. It was quite scary at first living alone but I did get used to it and was eventually quite proud of myself. Mum only came there once, and I don't think she understood, but I think my Dad was proud of me and I enjoyed taking my turn making Christmas dinner for Dad, Pat, Andy, Ian and Elaine. Although I say so myself, I made it quite homely. Over time, I had a new bathroom, thankfully replacing the burgundy one I inherited, a new kitchen, new windows, and had a conservatory built, mainly for use as a dining room. I had a lot of help from my Dad though, I could never have done it all without him.

Mum's condition continued to worsen and it became obvious things couldn't go on like they were. Dad was under enormous pressure and simply just couldn't carry on. Mum went into a nursing home for two weeks respite, but it was obvious it needed to be permanent. We chose Priory Park Nursing Home in Penwortham because it was easier for Dad to get to, and also because it seemed a really nice place where Mum would be taken care of. Leaving her was always the hard part, she often said she wanted to go home, but we think it was Scotland she was referring to, even when she was at home, she still said the same thing. She hadn't been in Priory Park very long when there was a change of management, and things were never the same. We weren't really happy with the new regime, but we were so scared of moving her somewhere else and unsettling her. It was so hard, so very hard.

Pat, me, Dad, Elaine, Ian, Andy

Our Ian invited Dad down to his home St Albans for a bit of a break and to take him to France to visit the Somme area. Ian was aware of Dad's Uncle Joe, and wanted to take his Grandad on a visit to the battlefields, and to see his name listed among the missing on the Thiepval Memorial. Uncle Joe was the youngest brother of Dads Dad, and up until then, Matthew had been the first name of the first born son in the Newsham family tree going back several generations. It illustrates just how much young Joe meant to his Dad to break from the time honoured tradition by naming his son after his brother. Ian got on really well with his Grandad, they had a special bond, and it was a wonderful thing he did taking him all that way. I know it made Dad very happy, not just the visit to Thiepval, but also spending time with his grandson, and the whole trip meant the absolute world to him. But, just as not eating Christmas dinner at mine or our Pats house, our Joe was the same wherever he went when it came to food. Ian told us how he wouldn't have anything to eat anytime they offered him something, he'd just say, *'no thanks son, you're alright, I've got a bit of a meat pie here.'*

Ian said it was just the same on their trip across the channel and he told us the tale of this mysterious meat pie that really made us laugh, he said, *'I don't know how big this meat pie was, we never actually saw it, but it travelled on the train from Preston to St Albans, on the Channel Tunnel to France, all the way to the Somme, and back again to St Albans.'* But that was our Joe, he always loved a meat pie.

It was good for Dad to get to do these things, he'd worked hard all his life and always did the best he could for his family, and he could never be faulted for the way he took care of Sadie. He deserved to be spoiled once in a while. I took him up to Glasgow for a weekend to see our Scottish family, they thought a lot of their Uncle Joe and he was chuffed to bits they all came to have a drink with him at the Black Bear, attached to the Premier Inn where we were staying. My cousin Margarets husband, Stephen, took him to Celtic Park to watch the football, and he had a wander around Shettleston, where Mum used to live, walking down memory lane, and went for a pint in the Drum for Auld Lang Syne.

In 1997 I was involved in a road traffic accident on the motorway when my car was written off. I was in the middle lane, slowing down as I approached a traffic jam just north of Forton Services, but the car behind me wasn't paying attention. They crashed into the back of me and shunted me into the car in front, it was a right mess and couldn't be driven. I was a bit sore with various bruises and whiplash from the collision, and pretty shaken up by the whole incident, but otherwise physically unscathed, but I went to A&E to record my injuries, just in case. Included in the terms of my employment at SRBC was having a car allowance for using my own vehicle while carrying out my duties for the council. Upon returning to work with a different car, my first port of call was to the payroll department to notify the details of my change of vehicle that would be necessary to calculate the car mileage allowance going forward. And then I just got on with my job.

Several months down the line, I was informed by payroll I had been overpaid to the tune of £180 due to the change of my car. I was naturally perplexed by this as I had given them all the correct details when I returned to work after recovering from the accident. I hadn't noticed any increase in my salary and obviously questioned how this could be my fault. I was living alone with a mortgage to pay and didn't have a great deal of salary left after paying all my bills, so offered to pay the money back at £5 a month for as long as it took. However, there was to be no room for manoeuvre and I was informed that the new director of finance was insisting on all the money being repaid by the end of the financial year, which wasn't too far away. Working in the revenues department, I had seen how easy it was for the council to simply write off thousands of pounds of debt at the stroke of a pen, yet the director of finance was adamant I pay everything back to his timescale. I couldn't understand why I was being treated in such a disgraceful way. The benefits manager called me into his office and told me the director was insisting I give access to my pay in order to deduct £20 a month. I refused and told him I couldn't afford it. To be fair to the benefits manager, he did think the director was being rather heavy handed and said as much to me, but it didn't make any difference. In the end, a friend loaned me the £180, and I metaphorically put two fingers up to the director of finance.

Mum passed away on 27 March 1998, it was just over twenty years since her first operation for oral cancer, and her battles were finally over. We were all with her at the end, she slipped away knowing that we loved her more than words could ever say and we let her go with all our blessings.

Not long after we had said goodbye to Mum, I booked a holiday to Corfu, and at the last minute, our Pat decided she wanted to come too. She booked everything separately and neither of us knew where her accommodation would be, whether we'd be close together or what. Her flight set off before ours and we watched her plane take off, but we ended up being delayed for twelve hours. I was frantic with worry about Pat being on her own in Corfu, not knowing what had happened. I tried to get the airline people to send some info out for her, but they weren't very cooperative. When we eventually arrived at our apartment, our Pat was in the block right next to us, she heard our transport arrive and came out to meet us. Neither of us could believe it, but thought that perhaps '*someone*' had been looking after us. And the holiday did us both the world of good.

Me and Pat in Corfu 1998

SADIE'S COURAGE

When I left the Army in 1977, like a lot of ex-service personnel, I wanted to have my own business and be my own boss. Mum loaned me and Martha some money to buy a small take-away sandwich shop called the Cabin, on Blackpool Road, near Lane Ends. We sold pastries, freshly made sandwiches, sweets and tobacco. I was really grateful to her for giving us this chance and she said not to worry about paying her back anytime soon as the money was, in her words, "*only to bury me*". A lady called Molly helped me in the shop, we got on well and she was a great help. We didn't make a fortune; in fact, we didn't make anything at all and it was a total disaster. Realistically, there was a lot of competition in the area, and we didn't have enough money to be able to stock the shop to its potential to be competitive and it looked a bit sparse, but it was an experience nonetheless. Mum would call in to see me from time to time when she did a bit of shopping around Lane Ends. She had begun complaining about her gums being sore on the left side of her mouth under her lower denture, but like most of us do, she thought it would clear up. She came to the shop one day and her cheek was swollen, she had been putting cotton wool under her denture because it was painful to wear and she didn't want to been seen without her teeth. As I watched her walk down Blackpool Road that day; she was wearing a beige mac, a brown headscarf, and carrying a tan coloured shopping bag, I had a strange feeling of foreboding that something was wrong, but she still went off to London a day or two later to attend a family funeral.

I eventually persuaded her to go to the dentist after antibiotics from the doctor were having no effect at all. I asked her if I could look inside her mouth, and was shocked to see some sores, they looked like blisters, on her cheek. I found it difficult to believe how a doctor couldn't see it looked a bit concerning and just continued prescribing antibiotics that clearly weren't working. Thankfully she took my advice, and went along to the dentist who immediately made her an appointment to see Mr Vero, an Orthodontic Surgeon at Preston Royal Infirmary. I asked our Pat if she could take her to the appointment because I was rather worried. A biopsy revealed she had oral cancer and it had gone into her jawbone. We were all absolutely devastated, scared of what lay ahead, and even more terrified of losing her. I'd never heard of anyone having cancer in the mouth before and found it difficult to comprehend. Why, how? They said there could have been several causes, some of which included, spicy food, ill-fitting dentures and smoking, to name just a few. Mum was a smoker. Our Pat and I took her to the next appointment to see a plastic surgeon, Mr Charles Beard. He was in his forties; a really kind man and one of the top surgeons in his field. He explained what procedures he would do during the operation, which would mean the removal of her lower left mandible (jawbone), and taking a large flap of skin from her forehead to build up the side of her face and replacing what needed to be removed from the inside of her cheek. (Presumably the blisters I saw) He said there wasn't a bed available straight away, but she would be informed as soon as possible when the arrangements had been made. We went back to Whittingham Street absolutely pole axed and tried to give Mum as much support as we could, while trying to explain to Dad what was going to happen. We hadn't been there very long, when there was a knock at the door. We were surprised to see Mr Beard standing there, he had taken the time to come personally to tell Mum a bed had been made available and he could get the operation done as soon as possible. Mum had a lot of faith in Mr Beard, and he really did his best for her.

It was a bit of whirlwind till the time came and Mum was really scared about what lay ahead, well not to put too fine a point on it, she was absolutely terrified. We tried to reassure her and keep her spirits up, trying not to let her see how scared we were for her. Mum had a half sovereign ring I had always admired, and used to joke with her about leaving it to me in her will. She gave it to me to wear while she went in hospital and I promised to take good care of it till she was home. She had given me her gold signet ring when I was still at school and I always treasured it. I visited her in hospital before her operation and she was rather upset about one of the nurses. Mum had asked for a cup of tea without any milk, so the nurse poured the milk out of the cup and then poured the tea into the same cup. But even though there was only a small amount of milk, Mum couldn't drink it, it was still too much for her. The nurse was a bit off with her and I went over to get a cup of tea I knew she could drink. How much trouble would it have been to just rinse out the cup? Mum was on the verge of her life changing forever with this surgery, she was petrified, and the nurse didn't have the good grace, or the compassion, to sort out a cup of tea she could enjoy, without tutting like a spoilt child. I was bloody furious. I collared this lass in the corridor later and told her exactly how I felt about the situation, and said, *'If ever your Mum is ill, I hope she gets a nurse just like you,'* then I walked away and left her to think about it.

Mum's operation took place on 3 March 1978, and although Mr Beard had explained everything he was going to do, it still couldn't prepare us for the shock of seeing her after the surgery. It looked like a scene from a horror movie. There were tubes and machines all over the place, and at first, her head was band-aged covering the wound of the flap taken from her forehead. She had been cut through from the middle of her bottom lip, under her chin and up the side of her face above her ear, there was also a large bandage on her arm where skin had been taken to graft on to her forehead where the donor flap was taken from, and she had a tracheostomy. I was completely heartbroken, we all were, my poor little Mum looked so tiny, fragile and battered, I could hardly bear it, I felt so desperate and collapsed on the floor in tears when we came out of her room. It was only a day or two later when they removed the bandage from around her head to reveal the size of the wound. It looked like she had been attacked by someone wielding an axe, it was from the middle of her forehead, just below her scalp to above her eye brow, right to the side of her head. Her hair was matted with all the dried blood and it was stood on end making it look even more shocking. Looking at the depth of the wound, it was hard to believe there could be so much flesh to take. While she was in hospital, she was being fed through a tube and was unable to speak to us for some time due to the tracheostomy. She had to write things down for us, but even through all that, she still retained her sense of humour. To illustrate, she wrote this for me on one of our visits: *'when my voice does come back, I have only to use it moderately. Your Dad will break his heart.'*

God only knows what must have been going through her mind, how she must have truly felt about everything. How her mouth felt, how she looked, would she get better. I didn't care what she looked like; I loved her with all of my heart and I just didn't want her to die. But she obviously cared, and sometimes when I look back, I feel I let her down because I perhaps didn't take into consideration how deeply she must have felt about her facial disfigurement. I know it was terribly upsetting for her when they first brought a mirror for her to see herself but she didn't say a great deal to us about it. I remember vividly a photo of her when she and Dad had gone to the Isle of Man on holiday. Someone had taken a photo of her at the dining table, and she told me how it broke her heart when she saw it. I still have the picture today, and it still breaks my heart knowing how upset she was. Of course, she had to learn to eat again. She needed a new top denture to be specially made, but could no longer wear a bottom denture. It must have been so hard and terrifying for her, but she did find the strength to fight back and I couldn't be more proud of her for her courage.

After Mum became ill, we sold the shop because I wanted to pay her back the money she had loaned us, the words she used about it just being to bury her, were praying heavily on my mind. But she wouldn't take it and insisted we keep it. So, we bought a stair carpet and a fridge for our new council flat. Mum was really pleased with our purchases, and she also paid for the installation of our first telephone. Selling the shop meant I was able to look after Mum when she came home, and Dad was able to go to work with a little peace of mind knowing I was there. She only wanted to see family when she first came home, and we would have a bit of a joke if someone came to the door, we'd shout, '*are you family*', before we'd let them in. I prayed so, so hard every day for God to take care of her, and I eventually had the feeling He would. Being faced with losing someone you love certainly makes you think about so many things. I wrote this poem during Mum's recovery.

WHY?

Why are we born if only to die?
What is the reason, Please tell me Why?
Should we be grateful just for the chance?
Of learning to walk and learning to dance
Learning to laugh, learning to cry
Why are we born if only to die?
What is the reason for all of this?
Learning to Love and learning to kiss,
Learning to hold, learning to share,
Learning to want and learning to care,
Learning to question, wondering why,
Why are we born, if only to die?
Could there really be a life after death?
Do we go to heaven when we've drawn our last breath?
Is something better waiting when our life is done?
Is it as the Lord's Prayer says, that 'Thy Kingdom Come'.
There must be an answer and one day we shall see,
The Ultimate secret of what God's Will is to be.
Yet here I am living, still wondering Why,
Why are we born if only to die?

Gail J Newsham

When she was feeling well enough to be left at home while Dad was out working, I managed to get a job at Peter Craig's, and when she felt ready to start going out again, I felt like we'd been given a second chance. I went playing bingo with her every week at Ashton Labour Club and I treasure the memories of those very special times, just me and my Mum. I offered to give her back the gold sovereign ring I'd been keeping safe while she was in hospital, but she let me keep it. It meant so much to me because I could have all the pleasure of wearing it while she was still here, rather than it being left to me and feeling sad wearing it when she had gone, and I have never taken it off. Mum went back to her job as an evening cleaner at Thorn Lighting on Fylde Road, and one of the stories she told still upsets me to think of. It was late, there weren't many people about and Mum went to clean the ladies toilets. As she opened the door, a woman was inside and she was a bit startled. Mum said, *'I'm sorry, did I make you jump',* and she said, *'oh it's alright love, I'm used to seeing people who've been in accidents.'* Mum made a joke about it at the time, but I know it hurt her very much.

Although Mums' sense of humour always shone through, she did go through a period of deep depression, and our Pat took her to see a doctor on Moor Park to try to help her cope with life as it now was. They prescribed some anti-depressants and she had some counselling, but she never really talked to us about it, she must have been completely heartbroken. All we could do was try to make her feel better and give her as much love and reassurance as we could. We had lived from check up to check up since her operation. Pat and I would take her, and it was such a relief when she was given the all clear till the next time. Mr Beard always seemed pleased to see her, he had a wonderful down to earth way of putting her at ease, and us too, truth be told. He was the kind of man who didn't let his position get in the way. He was always approachable and he did tell us that things had progressed since he did Mum's procedure, and relating to the flap they took off her forehead, he said they wouldn't do that kind of surgery on a woman again because of the disfigurement. It was good of him to be so open but unfortunately it was too late for her. But he did seem to care about Mum rather than her being 'just another patient', he was a blessing in disguise, and was exactly what Mum needed. But sadly, we were soon to learn he had his own battles to face after being diagnosed with terminal lung cancer. The news broke and it was all over the local press, but Mr Beard carried on working as long as he could. I remember the last time we saw him; Mum thought the world of him and asked him how he was. He didn't really give her an answer, he just said, *'have a good summer.'* He knew his time was short and he wouldn't see Mum again. Not too long after, we heard he had passed away, he was only forty-two years old. Mum was devastated, as were we. After his death, the Royal Preston Hospital named one of their operating theatres in tribute to him, The Charles Beard Theatre.

After Mr Beard died, Mum saw another plastic surgeon for her check-ups. Mr Jones didn't have the same bedside manner as Mr Beard, but had excellent credentials nonetheless, but Mum never took to him in the same way, I don't think any of us did if I'm honest, but you're at their mercy I suppose. Time passed, and check-up visits were now every six months or so and we were past four years since her op, hoping all the worries were behind us. For this particular check-up in 1982, neither our Pat nor I, were able to take her, so Mums sister Nan, and daughter Una, kindly stepped in for us. Neither of us had any cause for concern. Mum seemed well and there were no signs of anything untoward. However, life was to throw another enormous battle in our way. Mr Jones said he had discovered some 'ulcers' at the back of Mums' throat. Why the hell did it have to happen when we weren't with her, we had always been there? What did he mean by ulcers? Ulcers are ok, aren't they? I often got ulcers in my mouth but they cleared up after a few days. Please God, not again. Please let it be ok?

But it wasn't. The bloody cancer had returned and Mum had to undergo yet more life-saving surgery in July 1982. It was a ground breaking procedure, and Mum was probably the first person to undergo such complicated, invasive, and dare I say experimental, surgery for oral cancer. I don't recall being given any explanation of the procedure as was the case with Mr Beard, and we were shocked at how long the operation was taking. Every time we rang the hospital to ask for some information, they just kept saying she was still in theatre. In a mammoth ten-and-a-half-hour operation, little Sadie had a third of her tongue taken away, all the soft pallet at the back of her throat, and tissue from her left breast moved up to replace what they had taken away, which pretty much meant most of her breast. It was an absolute unimaginable nightmare.

I can't describe the terror in her eyes when I visited her in hospital, she must have been in so much pain. Another tracheostomy, the same cut from her bottom lip right up the side of her face in front of her ear, and loads of staples on her chest towards her shoulder, too numerous to count, where the breast tissue was used to put inside her mouth, and God knows how many stitches were inside her mouth. Her face was so swollen, it was almost twice the normal size, and when I arrived for one particular visit, she was sat leaning forward with a huge amount of green mucus dangling about six inches from her mouth. It was so distressing; how long she had been left in such a state, heaven only knows. I truly believed she was put back on a ward far too soon and should have been in intensive care where she could have, and should have had, specialist attention for much longer. I still have some of the notes she wrote and it breaks my heart to read them. You can see the pain in her words.

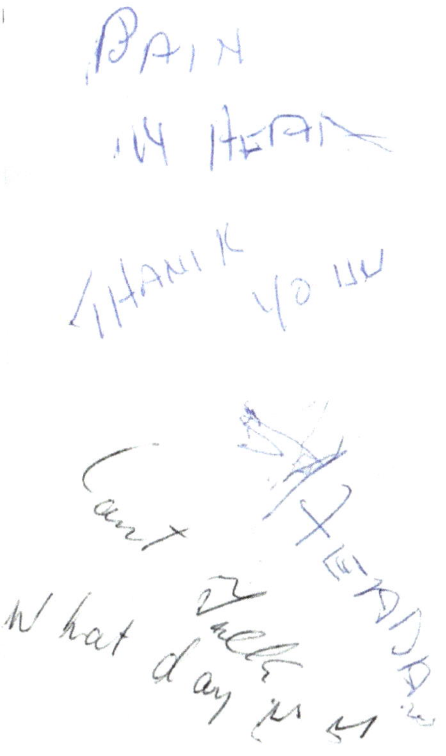

PAIN

IN HEAD

THANK YOU

Can't

What day is it

It became apparent she had gone all night without any pain relief, and because of the tracheostomy, she was unable to ask for any. The ward Sister was very apologetic and assured us it wouldn't happen again. We wrote a sign for her to hold up, '*more pain killers please*', but the next day when I visited, the sign was nowhere to be seen. It was clear the length of the operation, and its magnitude, had taken its toll on Mum, she was hallucinating and very, very distressed, so much so, Pat and I had to make some out of hour's visits to try to reassure and calm her. Whatever was going on in her mind, trying to come to terms with what had happened to her must have been utterly terrifying, far beyond anything I could ever comprehend. What the inside of her mouth must have felt like for her is completely unimaginable and doesn't even bear thinking about. It was all just too traumatic for words. It was a terrifying and devastating time for her and I suspect she was suffering from PTSD. I'm sure, had it been me, I would have been thinking, what the fuck have they done to me. Thankfully, she did start to settle, but this was going to be a long haul and as can be seen, she didn't care very much for the surgeon, and the more I re-live all this now, I can understand

131

why she felt that way. It does seem like it was more experimental than we ever realised.

Mum's own words

Mum was always a tea belly at home, she always had a teapot, or a pint cup and a cooling cup, in front of her, and when she started to feel a little better, that's exactly what she was looking forward to. It was wonderful to see some improvement, no matter how small, because it truly was a dreadful time. I did lose my faith a bit during this period, but looking back, I can see help may have been at hand.

While Mum was in hospital, I was working at Fairways Garage on Blackpool Road, a Vauxhall dealership then, owned by the Rawlinson family. I thought it was going to be a step up from my job at Peter Craig's, but it really wasn't a happy time in my working life. I would never have accepted the positon had I known how I would be treated. They promised so much at the interview, new bonus scheme and a pay rise to bring me in line with my previous salary, but none of it ever materialised. Who would leave one firm to be employed somewhere else for less money? I was given the job under false pretences, and there was always an 'edge' to working there. They knew Mum had undergone major surgery for cancer, and how devastated I was, because I was visiting her in hospital every day during my lunch break, and going straight back again after work. I booked a week off to look after her when she came home, and while I was actually at Mums caring for her, they telephoned to tell me I was being made redundant and not to bother coming back. I was absolutely staggered by the callous and cowardly way they informed me over the phone, rather than face to face, and by their total lack of human decency and compassion. What kind of an employer does that when you are taking care of your Mum with her life in the balance? How could they be so cruel at such an emotional and critical time? It was an added worry for me inasmuch as concerns about paying our mortgage, and I hadn't been employed there long enough to be able to take them to a tribunal for unfair dismissal. But my belief in everything happening for a reason, put the Fairways debacle into perspective; it meant I could be with Mum as long as she needed me and Dad could carry on working knowing Mum wasn't on her own. Perhaps the Fairways episode was some kind of divine intervention to get me in the right place again. In reality, it needed a lot longer than just a week to be with Mum; and the mortgage was always paid. Many years later, I met Margaret, the lady I had worked with at Fairways, and she told me they all wondered what had happened to me, why I just disappeared and never went back. No one had the balls to be honest with their staff and tell them what they had done. She was absolutely disgusted when I told her the truth.

It was very difficult for Mum to speak at first, she was unable to make all the guttural sounds we do from the back of our throat when forming words, particularly those beginning with G and C. She was very self-conscious about it and thought people would never be able to understand her. I kept trying to reassure her that she could be understood, I always knew what she was saying, but she had to get used to a whole new way of speaking. She was having speech therapy, but all her confidence had been taken away because her speech just wasn't the same, and on top of all that, she had more facial disfigurement. Added to those two massive concerns for her, was the fact that eating was now a much bigger problem, and it was heart-breaking. One of Mums' simple little pleasures in life was eating out, she used to love going to Blackpool and having fish and chips at the Lobster Pot, or going into town to the Jolly Farmer for a meal, and I have fond memories of her taking me to Booths Café when I was younger, she used to really enjoy going there, but all of these things were now to be a thing of the past. She would never eat in front of anyone outside the home.

Mr Jones was delighted with his handy work, but did confess to having used too much of her breast tissue to build up the side of her face, it drooped a bit under her chin, and he said, in an ideal world he would have taken some away to correct it. But she had been through enough already and none of us wanted her to be put through anymore butchery. I doubt she would have agreed to it anyway, if it had been seriously suggested. Mum was one of his star patients, being probably the first to undergo such incredibly invasive and pioneering surgery. When she went for check-ups, he would often show her off to his students as they all looked inside her mouth while he was preening himself explaining everything he had done. If there is any crumb of comfort at all to be had for what she had to endure, or any reason why it should have happened, there is no doubt in my mind that what my Mum went through, would without question, have helped others in the future who may have suffered the same fate and aided the understanding of similar surgery. In fact, there was another lady who had undergone a similar operation just after Mum, I think her name was Margaret, and coincidentally, she lived just a few streets away, on South Meadow Lane. They thought it would be a good idea for them to meet up and I took Mum along to see her. Trying to see the funny side of things, I was acting as interpreter because Mum couldn't understand what she was saying, so the visits didn't last very long. I think the lady sadly passed away soon after, and we didn't hear of any more similar operations after that. Who really knows, but perhaps they may have concluded such invasive surgery simply was just a step too far.

I tried to help build Mums' confidence and took her out shopping to get her out and about again. Going round the shops was something she had always enjoyed. I took her to some grocery stores, and while we were stood at the counter, she would tell me what she wanted, for me to then ask the shop assistant for whatever it was, and this went on for a while. Then we had a break through moment, and it still brings a lump to my throat when I think about it. I took Mum to Kwik Save in Penwortham, and we were stood at the fresh veg counter. Mum told me she wanted a pound of carrots, and without further ado, the shop assistant went and got her the carrots without me asking for them. It was absolutely wonderful, I don't think that lady will ever know just how important it was, I was so happy, I could have cried. I said to Mum, 'see, people can understand you'. She did begin to get a little more confident from then on, and when I took her out on more shopping trips, I would make her ask for things herself to try to build her confidence more. As Mum regained more strength and began to improve, I managed to get a part time job back at Peter Craigs, working on the same section as before. It meant I could bring in a bit of money but still be able to be there some days in the week so she wasn't on her own all the time while Dad was out at work. When a vacancy came around for full time, I was taken back on again so everything worked out for all of us.

Mum did really well to come back from this massive operation, and she and Dad made Christmas dinner for us all at Hassett Close only five months later.

But her recovery certainly wasn't easy and there were many dark moments for her. She never really shared how she truly felt about what had happened or how she looked, and again, looking back I do feel I let her down because I didn't pay enough attention to her feelings in that respect. I was desperately sorry for her, but selfishly, I simply just didn't want her to die; the thought of losing her absolutely terrified me. But she cared how she looked, she cared very deeply, and must have been more devastated than words could ever say. I wish with all my heart she would have talked to me about it, it will always be one of my regrets. I was having a party for my thirtieth birthday at the Highbank Hotel, where our Pat and Andy had their wedding reception, it was just over a year since her operation, and I was so happy she felt well enough to be there. I love this photo below. It was taken on the actual day of my birthday. We even sit the same way.

Sadie and me – 17 July 1983

Being the little trooper she was, she continued to fight her way back, and without telling anyone, she went and got herself a little job, helping with breakfasts and making beds at the Moose Hotel on Fishergate. Knowing how much she had lost all her confidence when we were going shopping, when she wouldn't speak to anyone, to finding the true grit and determination to want to get out there and earn some money of her own again, words could never express how proud I am of her for having the inner strength and being so brave. She was only 4'10" but she had the strength and courage of a Lion. My heart literally bursts with pride at the courage shown by my little Mum. I loved her so very much, I know we all love our Mums, but during all those years of worry, I felt that no one else in the world could ever love their Mum as much as I loved mine.

Things were going reasonably well for a few years until Mum had quite a bad fall at home. She tripped over a mat in the hall way and hit her head right on the corner of the sideboard. It was on the same side as the scar on her forehead, so there wasn't much protection for her at all, and she made a right mess of herself. We then began noticing she was becoming a bit forgetful and repetitive. Her sister Nan passed away in 1988 and she didn't really grasp what had happened. Perhaps just as well, she would have been devastated to lose her sister, they had always been quite close. Rose, the home help, stayed with Mum while we went to Nans funeral, and when we came back, she asked us if we'd had a nice time. I also remember a particular occasion when we asked her for a pencil, and she didn't know what a pencil was. Thankfully she was reasonably alright for their Golden Wedding. Pat took her to choose something nice to wear and helped her pick a special outfit, but she was struggling with the zip and didn't quite know what to do with it. She looked lovely at the party and did enjoy seeing her brother and sisters again, but it was obvious her confidence was going and she was very uncomfortable being in the limelight, which was in stark contrast to how she used to be. Over the next couple of years things began to deteriorate, Mum was getting more confused and didn't know how much money she was giving out when she went shopping. We were getting very concerned. And the eating situation was becoming much more of a problem for her. Because of all the reconstructive surgery at the back of her throat, where the soft pallet had been removed and replaced, her swallowing mechanism started to break down and she would often have terrible choking fits. It was very distressing for her, and for us watching on helplessly. Food was going the wrong way and ending up in her lungs causing repetitive chest infections. I suppose in essence, the surgery, and their experiment, had failed.

The last five years of her life were a total nightmare for her and we thought we were going to lose her a couple of years before we did. Due to the food situation and the recurring chest infections, she was really quite poorly and had another spell in hospital. She had lost a lot of weight and was down to less than five stone. They were feeding her through a tube up her nose, but she became agitated with it and kept pulling it out. During one visit, she needed the toilet and I carried her in my arms myself, she was so frail. We were told that the best option would be to have a tube inserted into her stomach to be fed that way for the remainder of her days. There was nothing else they could do. And I was ready to tell her. But once again, Sadie's fighting spirit shone through and she still tried to eat as normally as she could. Food had always been a pleasure for Mum, she had a wonderful appetite and lived to eat rather than ate to live. I used to make extra portions of meals I knew she enjoyed, and would puree and freeze them for her, and I always kept each part separate so that it looked like a proper meal rather than just slop on a plate. I know she appreciated that. I remember one stay in hospital when they gave her a meal where everything had been blended up together and it looked bloody awful. She just looked at it and said, *'it's not what I normally eat.'* I felt so desperately sorry for her. It wasn't too long after she was officially diagnosed with dementia and she continued to decline. We'll never know for sure, but I often thought it was because of the length of the last operation. It may well have been a bridge too far really, I have often wondered if it was too experimental, but life is precious and I suppose we have to try everything. We'll never know what the alternative would have been. Dad looked after her for as long as he could, he never really shared with us how hard it had been for him. He was a good man, and was totally devoted to Mum, he did his absolute best, above and beyond really, but it just became too much. Mum went into Priory Park Nursing Home for some respite care, but it was obvious it needed to be permanent. I know Dad felt a huge burden of guilt, we all did, we were heartbroken having to leave her in a place like that, it was a situation none of us wanted, or were happy about, but we couldn't change anything, or make her better. With all of my heart I truly wished we could have, that feeling of helplessness never goes away.

Mum forgot most things, she didn't remember her family in Scotland, and could never remember any of Dad's visits. She used to say to me, *'he never comes to see me,'* and I'd say *'who'?* Her reply was just, *'him.'* She didn't know my name either, but she always knew I was hers, and I will always be eternally grateful for that. Her face would light up when I visited her and she would touch my cheek with her hand and say, *'you're beautiful'.* I was with her one time, and one of the male carers was walking down the corridor and Mum said, *'he doesn't like me, him.'* I didn't really pay much attention thinking it was just her imagination. But when I went to see her soon after, as I was walking up the stairs to the floor she was on, I could hear some shouting going on in the corridor. When I opened the door, the same male carer Mum said didn't like her, was shouting and pointing his finger at her. I was absolutely bloody furious, I don't know how I kept my hands off him, and told him in no uncertain terms, pointing my finger right in his bloody face, *'don't you ever speak to my Mum like that again, or it will be the last thing you ever do,'* and then I reported him to the manager. Thankfully, he was never seen again.

In Priory Park Nursing Home, Mum, Dad and Ian

I went to visit Mum on Christmas Day 1997 to take her present and spend some time with her. I found her sat alone in the sitting room, nursing her hand, and I had to open the parcel for her. I brought it to the attention of the staff but no one seemed to know how it had happened, and I presumed they would do something about it now they had been made aware, and she was in their care. Our Pat went to see her the next day and the nursing home hadn't done anything for Mum, her hand had swollen up and the bruising was starting to come out; we were appalled. They reckoned they were short staffed and couldn't take her to the hospital. Pat and I took her to RPH to have it x-rayed, and it was no surprise to discover it was broken. The photos below show Mum in the nursing home with her battle scars on view. It would have been nice had the hair dresser been more considerate and covered the scar on her forehead with her hair, as she always had.

Sadie in Priory Park, 2nd pic with hand in plaster

138

Visiting Mum in Priory Park was always hard, especially at meal times when she had her choking fits. No one ever seemed to make proper allowances for it, I don't suppose they could understand the amount of reconstructive surgery she'd undergone, and it's only by writing this now, that I'm beginning to comprehend just how hard it must have been for her living like that. No wonder she felt like she did about the surgeon. I remember once visiting her in RPH and they had given her pie, chips and beans for her dinner. There was no way on earth she could have eaten it, she did try, but the look on her face said it all to me. It was so distressing, I couldn't handle it towards the end and it gets to a point where you really just want it to be over so that she could have some peace, she had suffered enough. The chest infections were still occurring and Mums' condition was deteriorating. The doctor suggested stopping the antibiotics, and we all agreed.   I visited Mum not long before she passed away, and she was still singing one of her favourite songs '*Magic Moments.*' She was too weak to walk down the corridor so I went to get a wheelchair to take her to her room, and as I helped her get ready for bed she was saying, '*I never knew, I never knew.*' I don't know what she never knew, but I like to think *someone* was there for her.

The phone call came early in the morning of 27 March 1998, our precious little Sadie was preparing to leave us. We all got there as quickly as we could and were with her as she was fighting for every breath. Dad was finding it difficult to deal with and went into the corridor to try to compose himself. I was sat holding Mums' hand and I just said to her, '*it's alright sweetheart, you can give in, we won't be mad at you*'. I didn't want to make it hard for her, I didn't want to be weeping and wailing at her bedside begging her not to go. I knew she wouldn't want to leave us; I didn't want her to leave us, but I didn't want her fighting any more, she had fought so very hard for so long, it was time to let her go, and after only a few minutes, her breathing changed. Our Pat and I looked at one another, then back at our Mum, and watched as her breaths became less and less. I said to Pat, '*I think she's gone,*' and Pat nodded; but Sadie had to have the last word. She took just one more breath, and then she was gone. It was so peaceful, and I am so happy we were able to be with her and let her go with our blessing and all our love. She had put up such a courageous fight for so long, she deserved to finally be free from all her pain and suffering. We loved her enough not to begrudge her that.

One of the nursing assistants, a nice lass named Polly, who was there when Mum was first admitted, came to offer her condolences and to mention Mums' belongings were in the safe. She had a gold gate bracelet and some other jewellery when she arrived at Priory Park. Pat and I went to the office to collect her things, but the gate bracelet had vanished into thin air and we never did get it back. We didn't make a fuss, what was the point, it wouldn't bring Sadie back. We felt utter contempt for whoever at Priory Park was responsible for the negligence and theft, and hoped it never brought them any joy.

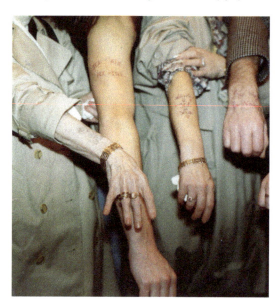

Mum first left, wearing her gate bracelet

Clifford Ward was the funeral undertaker, and what a lovely man he was, very compassionate and kind, and he took care of Sadie just as we wanted. Mum would never tell anyone how old she was, when asked she would always say twenty-four. When Clifford came to Mum and Dads flat to attend to everything, he asked her age for the official notices. Well, we couldn't tell him could we, and just told him what Mum used to say; twenty-four, she was forever twenty-four, and that's exactly what he put in the paper. Sadie Newsham, aged forever twenty-four. She was in the room of repose and she looked so lovely and peaceful. We had her dressed in her own clothes, and as it was so close to Mother's Day, we put all her cards and presents in with her. Mum always carried a handbag and when she was well, she never liked to be seen without any makeup. I put her handbag next to her with some of her makeup inside, and wrote her a note telling her how much I loved her and how I would miss her every day for the rest of my life.

We gave our precious little Sadie the best send-off we possibly could and I'm sure she would have loved it. Clifford had made sure Forever 24 was engraved on the nameplate on her casket, and it made us smile; he understood what kind of family we were. Pat and I got her a wreath made into a teddy bear, Mum loved soft toys, they always made her smile, and we knew she would be chuffed with that. We had a Piper outside St Walburges Church playing 'Flower of Scotland',

and the pall bearers were the McCabe boys, Michael, Andy, John and Patrick, her four Scottish nephews, who safely carried their Auntie Sadie, into the church.

Michael, Andy, John Patrick (at a family wedding)

During the service, I read out 'Ode to 42', as a homage of our lives together in Whittingham Street and we also played her favourite song, '*It's all in the Game.*' Ian and Elaine were unfortunately out of the country and unable to be there to say farewell to their Nana, but Elaine organised a beautiful floral tribute and Ian sent a heartfelt message to be read out for her:

No other Nana ever made a jam butty taste so good. Just the thing for a hungry lad after playing on the cobbles outside 42. Thanks for the memories.

No other Nana ever fought so bravely against the big C. It must have been so hard and so painful, but you never let on. You never let it beat you. Thanks for the strength you inspired.

No other Nana ever had a bigger fan than me. And now it's time for your well-earned rest. I want you to take with you all my love. Goodbye 'Sal'. Always remember your number one boyfriend. He'll always remember you.

As we were leaving the church, a recording of '*Scotland the Brave*' echoed loudly as her coffin was carried out to the hearse. The Piper was waiting at the crematorium and played *Amazing Grace* as she was taken on the final leg of her journey. She would have loved every minute, and now that very proud Scots lassie from Glasgow was finally at peace.

Life was never going to be the same again, as four became three. Joe, Pat and Gail now had to learn to live without the woman they all loved so very much. I felt I could cope as long as I knew she was ok, and only a short while after Mums' funeral, I had a dream about her; they say your loved ones come to you in dreams don't they. I was outside Marks & Spencer, and all of a sudden Mum was there, it was so wonderful to see her, she looked so lovely. No more facial disfigurement, she was whole again. She spoke to me and all she said was, '*I'm alright, and there is somewhere else,*' then she had to leave to walk up a big white staircase in front of us. I wondered if it might have been something to do with what she said she never knew, just before she left us. I went to see a spiritualist a few months later, I was struggling without her and just needed a bit of reassurance. I'd heard lots of good reports about her, she had a very good reputation and I wasn't disappointed. I always talked to Mum and I told her I was going to see this lady and asked if she could send me a message only she and I would know. The spiritualist told me lots of things which I knew were from my Mum and as the session was coming to a close, she looked to one side as if listening, and said, '*your Mum says I've to say, thanks for the makeup, do you know what that means*'? Of course I knew what it meant, there was only me who could have known, and it gave me a great deal of comfort.

I know my Mum was around spiritually for quite a long time. There were certainly lots of things happening in my home to let me know she was there, and not just when I was alone, friends also witnessed it. It started with pinging noises coming from the delph rack in the living room, but there was nothing up there to explain the noise and this went on for quite some time in all parts of the house. Photographs would fall to the floor. Flowers would move right in front of my eyes, a vase jumped off the television, and the computer printer would switch itself on in the middle of the night. Most of these things were witnessed by others, and there was no logical explanation for any of them. But I knew. I never felt I was truly on my own at Kiln Croft, there was always a really nice 'feel' about the house, and things happened regularly. I still get signs to this day and I feel truly blessed. The love never dies, the link is never broken, she's just in another room and I speak to her often. Love you Sadie, always will.

Mummy Sadie xx

Last photo I took of her before life changed forever

LIFE WITHOUT SADIE

I think Dad was content enough in his own way after Mum died, but he obviously missed her very much, and certainly never stopped loving her. He kept her ashes at home in a wooden casket, with 'Sadie', engraved on the gold name plate, it seemed to be a comfort for him. He always spoke to her when he came back from the Legion or Empire Services, *'It's only me little girl',* he would say as he came through the front door. It was a comfort to me too if I'm honest, I would talk to her as well. Dad seemed happy enough with his own company, he was a great reader of the history of both World Wars and had many books on the subject. He would watch any programme about it on the television and record them to watch again. I don't think there was anything he couldn't tell you about either war, and he read every page in the newspaper from front to back, he didn't want to miss anything. He kept himself occupied and never complained about being lonely, he never complained about anything really, and when he woke up each morning, he would draw back the curtains and say *'thank you Lord for another day.'*

Sadie's casket

It wasn't until after Mum passed away, he told me she had confided to him about being abused by one of her Uncles when she was younger. He said it was the main reason she wanted to get away and came to England during the war to work in munitions. She told him after she left, he turned his attention to another of her sisters. I can't describe the anger I felt to discover she had to go through something like that. It did sort of explain why she seemed to have been 'troubled' in some way during her life, and how these childhood experiences maybe shaped the person she sometimes was. It did put things in a different perspective, with a far greater understanding. He also told me about the possibility of having a half-sister on the other side of Preston. Things weren't always great in Mum and Dad's relationship, and I certainly wasn't angry with him for any infidelity, I know he had enough of his own feelings of guilt, and I did understand. And maybe he was processing his own grief and loss, and wanted to talk about these things. I was touched that he loved me enough, and trusted me enough, to share it with me. I don't know any more than that, and I've never felt the need to try to find out.

Dad was made President of the Middleforth Branch of the Royal British Legion later in the year after Mum passed away. Our Pat was his Lady President on Presidents Day, and he was proud as punch.

Joe and our Pat – RBL Presidents Day 1998

145

Having written a few poems over time, a friend once asked me if I had ever written one for my Dad. No, I hadn't, and said, I wouldn't know where to start. But it planted a seed and I thought about it for a while. I sat down and wrote this one for him and he loved it. He was chuffed to bits and showed it off to all his mates.

AN ODE TO JOE

If I was to sit down to thank you Dad, I wouldn't know where to start,
To thank you for your love for me, that's always in your heart.
To thank you for your devotion in caring for my Mum,
To thank you, Dad in every way for all the things you've done.
For being a loving father, no matter what I do,
And I'm so very proud to have a Dad, as wonderful as you.
I have so many childhood memories of you I'll treasure evermore,
Combing your hair; Daddies Red Badge; and wrestling on the floor.
The Cadley; the milk round; and you, 'crackin' on yer grateful',
Abel Heywood's papers and fresh cockles by the plateful.
Without you Dad I know, I wouldn't be who I am.
Your qualities are an example; you're a very special Man.
You believe in Trust and Honour, you believe in being True,
And Dad, I want to be like you in everything I do.
You seldom have a grumble; you always have a smile,
And you have a special gift of spreading happiness all the while.
You're more than just a father; you're my very special friend,
And it means so much that I can be myself and not pretend.
I'll always be so grateful for the Special Love we share,
And whenever I need my Daddy, I know you're always there.
But when the time does come Dad and we really have to part,
My love for you will never die; you'll be Forever in my heart.

Gail J Newsham – July 2000

Over the next few years, our family was expanded when Ian got married to Sarah, his long-time love, in August 2000, and they later had a beautiful daughter Sophi.

Ian and Sarah

Elaine was married to Nick in 2001 and they went on to have four wonderful children, Finlay, Jamie, Oliver, and Fern.

Nick and Elaine

Pat and Andy loved spending time with their grandchildren and were very proud of them all. They would often visit Elaine and Nick in Peterborough, and the kids loved their Nana Pat. I love this pic of them below, it's a lovely moment captured in time. Ian, Sarah and Sophi live in Bristol, but Sarah's family were Preston based and they often came to visit her Mum and Dad. They always came to Pat and Andy's on Christmas Eve and we would all meet up there for a night of festive cheer.

Nana Pat in her element

Andy with all his grandchildren on his birthday

Fern, Sophi, Finlay, Jamie, Ollie

In March of 2001, we heard that Doreen Dawson had passed away. Doreen was Mum to my first best friend Mal, who I hadn't seen for many years. Doreen lost her husband Frank very suddenly from a heart attack on New Year's Day 1980 and I would visit her from time to time. She was lovely was Doreen, I was very fond of her and really sad she was gone. My Dad, our Pat and me, went to her funeral to pay our respects to a friend and neighbour from our Whittingham Street years. I didn't get a proper chance to speak to Mal, or swap addresses, but she said when she saw me in the church, her heart nearly burst. I didn't know how to get in touch with her, but fate played a hand when her Uncle Bert came in to the council office in Bamber Bridge, where I was working. I was able to get her contact details from him just in time; tragically, he had a heart attack only days later and passed away suddenly, just like his brother Frank. If he hadn't come in to the office that day, Mal and I may never have got back in touch.

Dad was doing ok on his own. He had always been a good cook and was looking after himself really well and keeping the flat clean and tidy, he was rather domesticated was our Joe. He never wanted to be a burden and would go to Morrisons on the docks most days to get the bulk of his shopping. I would ask him to let me do it to save him going every day, but he insisted he wanted to do it while he still could. But he did let me bring him his weekly supply of Long-Life cans of beer. Going to Morrisons gave him a bit of a purpose and got him out of the house, and he had got quite attached to one of the cashiers, little Christine, as he called her. He was a very likeable man was Joe, and she used to look after him when he went in so he always went to her till. She would send him postcards when she went on holiday and she always made time to have a chat with him. It was really kind of her. All was going well until he had a really bad fall at the Legion. He tripped over a loose carpet rod coming out of the toilet, and landed very heavily on his hip and was unable to get up. They had to send for an ambulance and he ended up being in hospital for about six weeks. Thankfully his hip wasn't broken but had been injured quite badly. It took a long time to heal and he was in a lot of pain. Our Pat and Andy were away for a month on a Caribbean cruise, and I was visiting him every day to make sure all was well. I was really worried about him, he just seemed to be fading away. He was hardly eating anything at all so I asked if I could bring in some fish and chips for him in an effort to kick start his appetite again. He was funny about food at the best of times but he did enjoy a chippy tea, so I was hoping this might do the trick especially as we would be having it together. But he didn't eat much of it at all.

They seemed to be concerned about him going home with living alone, and we were waiting for social services to come and see him to assess the situation, but as always with these things, it was taking far too long. I kept trying to hurry things along, I knew my Dad was very unhappy and I was worried about his general wellbeing, but it made no difference. In the end I just told them I was taking him home because he was just fading away in front of my eyes. I took some time off work to look after him and slept on the settee and stayed with him till he got some strength back. He was better being home. Social Services did get things organised and they arranged for some aids at home for him; a raised toilet seat, a tilted chair to help him have a shave, a seat in the bath and a trolley to bring cups and things from the kitchen, and they also removed any trip hazards. And we sorted a home help to keep an eye on him, a lady called Rose who I had worked with at Tweedales. She had also helped out when Mum was there.

I was blessed to have a very close relationship with my Dad, we could say anything to each other. He was a bit delicate when he first came home and needed time to get everything working properly again. I jokingly said to him, *'if you don't shit your pants today, I'll let you have a pint tonight'.* He killed himself laughing and took great pleasure telling all his mates, *'You'll never guess what she said to me'.* He made a good recovery and did get back on his feet again, but he did start to let me do more shopping for him. My job enabled me to see him most days. I was working as a Visiting Officer for South Ribble Borough Council, and I would make sure I arranged my visits to be in the right area so I could call in and have lunch with him. He was a good cook and he'd always done his share when Mum was with us, and I've never tasted a broth better than the one he used to make. As he got older, he'd make hot-pot on Monday which lasted most of the week, and this was usually my daily lunch date with him. Because I saw my Dad most weekdays, and every Sunday to take his shopping, I hadn't really noticed he was becoming a bit frail, or that he wasn't going out as much. He had started walking with a stick, but I thought it was down to the fall he'd had, to give him a bit more confidence. Pat and I organised a surprise party for his 80th birthday on 19 August 2002, and little did he realise that a quiet pint at the Legion was actually full of family and friends who had all come to share in his big day, and the Scottish contingent were there in force once again to celebrate with their Uncle Joe. We had a special cake made for him with all the little things on it that mattered to him the most. On the top was his military service, and his jobs as a bus driver, milkman, newspaper delivery driver, and on each of the four sides were, 'ARYB', an abbreviation for Always Remember You're British, from when he used to write letters to me, 'LITTLE SADIE', for the love of his life, and the other two sides had 'HRH', his title for our Pat, and 'WACKER', his term of endearment for me. It perfectly illustrated the difference between us both. He was made up with all the fuss and chuffed to have made it to eighty.

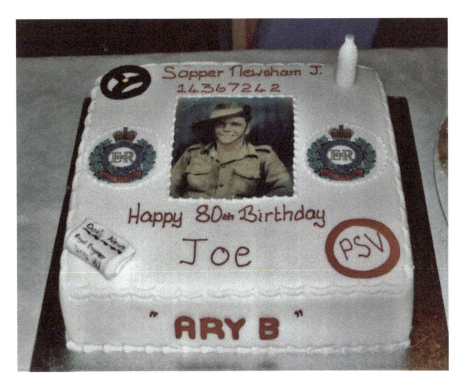

Dads' cake

Over the next few months, I was still going for my lunch most days, and started noticing little things he wasn't doing like he used to. He had a home help, but had always done most things for himself. He never complained about anything, he was no bother, and just quietly got on with things, but he told me there was something wrong with his back. He couldn't put his finger on it, but just said that he '*didn't feel right*'. He had a fall in his flat, and couldn't get up but managed to get to the phone and our Andy came to help lift him up, but it really knocked his confidence. It was around the 24th of April he asked me to get him some laxatives. It was an unusual request coming from him because he never had any problems at all with going to the toilet, he would often joke he could '*shit through the eye of a needle*,' and so, asking for laxatives was a bit of concern. They didn't really help him and his appetite was also starting to fade. His mobility was getting to be more of an issue and even walking with the trolley from room to room, he was still terrified of falling. We got the doctor out to see him and he actually suggested getting some physio. I couldn't believe how he could conclude something so utterly ridiculous. I have no medical qualifications whatsoever, but even I knew something was seriously wrong. I was going down to see him and he was telling me he had been eating, when it was clear he hadn't. I knew things were getting worse and I had a good idea what it meant, and what

151

the consequences were, and I just said to him, *'it's ok Dad, if you don't want to eat, I won't shout at you'.*

I sent for the doctor again and he finally arranged for him to be admitted to hospital round about the 14/15th of May. Even right up to going into hospital, he still didn't moan. A friend rang to ask how he was, and he just said, *'I can't complain'.* I knew my Dad was coming to the end and I stayed with him for a few nights before he went into hospital, he wasn't fit to be left alone. I would walk behind him as he was pushing his trolley into the bedroom, he was so scared of falling. I told him not to worry, *'I promise Dad, I won't let you fall.'* He was embarrassed that I had to look after him, he said I shouldn't have to do those things for him. I told him not to be so daft. Our Pat came down as well and stayed with him for his last night at home. His two little girls were close by. The ambulance came in the morning and I went with him. His next-door neighbour come out to wave him off in the ambulance, but Dad couldn't wave back because he was strapped in for safety reasons. He was worried in case he thought he was being rude and asked me to be sure to tell him why he couldn't wave. Pat followed in her car and we stayed with him until he was settled. Pat drove me back Dads to get my car and I told the neighbour why Dad couldn't wave, just as he asked me to. They did lots of blood tests that revealed he was riddled with cancer, it was in his bones and all his major organs, it was just a matter of time and wasn't long before he slipped into unconsciousness. Two days before he passed away, I was sat by his hospital bedside holding his hand, I'm not certain, but I think he knew I was there. I was singing songs to him that he used to sing to us, songs that made him happy. *'I've got sixpence'* and *'Two Preston Mashers'* were just two contained in his repertoire, and I think he enjoyed it. I visited again the next day, but he seemed a bit agitated, I think I was getting on his nerves making too much of a fuss, or he was getting ready to go and he was upset. He passed away not long after midnight on 19 May 2003, but neither Pat nor I managed to get there in time to be with him before he left. Something happened to both of us to cause a delay and prevent us getting there. I think that's how he wanted it really; it would have been too hard for him to leave his two little girls.

We had Clifford Ward to look after Dad on his final journey, and he gave him the same loving care and consideration as he did for our Mum. Throughout his life, Dad was never money oriented, he never craved it nor sought it, and he would always say, *'as long as I've got the price of my next pint'.* All he needed was the love of his family, and he was the richest man in the world. When I went to see him in the room of repose, I put £3.00 in his suit pocket, so he could buy a pint when he got there. He was a good man my Dad, he was my mate. We had a very special bond and there was nothing left unsaid between us when he passed away, and I am eternally grateful for that. The love we shared was almost tangible. I'm so grateful we were able to talk and had our times together. I knew I couldn't go through a similar journey with my Dad like we had with Sadie. I was devastated and heartbroken to lose him, but I wasn't angry, I was glad that God had been good to him. And as he always used to say, '*old soldiers never die.*'

Sapper Joe Newsham

Dad, smiling at me

We asked Clifford if they would drive us down Strand Road so we could pass by where BAC used to be, where Dad had worked, then up Fylde Road passing by Ashton Street, and then down Deepdale Road to see Preston North End for the last time. As we were following the hearse and came to the end of Strand Road, turning right to go up Water Lane, just where Umberto's chippy is, the rear car door opened on the left side where I was sat. We all had a laugh about it, imagining the headlines in the paper, '*Daughter falls from car on way to father's funeral.*' The driver was very apologetic, but all was well. There was a wonderful turnout at the crematorium, it was standing room only, which shows how well thought of our Joe was. He would have been so chuffed that so many people wanted to come and pay their respects, including our Scottish family who came to say goodbye to their Uncle Joe. It was lovely to know they all thought so highly of him.

153

From the McCabe's

His funeral was exactly what he wanted. During our many conversations I asked him what he would like when his time came, he told me he wanted, '*Jerusalem*', and a piece of military music called '*Old Comrades*,' and that's exactly what he had. I read out the poem I'd written for him, and our Pat arranged with the Royal British Legion for a military send off. He had the Union Flag on his coffin and a bugler played '*The Last Post*' before the committal. We left the crematorium to one of his favourite songs, '*Gentle on my Mind*'. A funeral is the last chance you have to do something for your loved ones. We did the best we possibly could for both Mum and Dad, and daft as it may sound, I enjoyed both of theirs because I knew they would have enjoyed it too. But it did take some time to process the grief. It's hard losing one parent, but it was exceptionally hard when Dad passed away; Your Mum and Dad's love is unconditional, and whatever ups and downs we may have had during our lifetime, I never felt un-loved, and I found it hard without either of them here to love me. But on a spiritual level, I knew they were both watching over me and that was a great comfort.

When I was sorting out Dad's flat, I came across a verse he'd written on a piece of old card. Whether he had composed it himself, or just copied it from somewhere, I don't know, but it fair summed him up.

Do not let yourself be bothered by the inconsequential.
One has only so much time in this world
So devote it to the work and people most important to you.
To those you love, and things that matter.
One can waste half a lifetime with people one doesn't really like,
Or doing things when one would be better off somewhere else.

It was incredibly difficult going through all of his things and emptying the flat. I only had two weeks to get it all done before the keys had to go back to the council. I felt as if I had thrown half his life on the tip, and it was breaking my heart. Looking back I know I gave away far too many things that I later wish I would have kept. If I can offer any advice to anyone, it would be to not make any decisions while you are grieving. I also made the mistake of clearing out my own loft and getting rid of many old photographs and other things I had put up there out of the way, things I thought I would never want again. I was so wrong, and now they're gone and I can never get them back. But one thing I did keep; my Dad gave me baby June's grave number not long before he passed away, which I kept safe, with the thought that one day, I must do something about that. I asked Dad what he would want me to do with Mum's ashes after he had gone, and he just said, *'whatever you think Wacker',* and this is what I decided. I had Dads' ashes put in the casket with Mum, but there was quite a lot left over. Clifford assured me he had mixed them all up so there was half in each, so I sprinkled what was in the urn in several places. As close to where 42 was as I could possibly get; at the entrance to Lidl car park on Strand Road where Dad worked when it was BAC, and at Church Deeps in Walton le Dale, where we would all go swimming when I was very young. The casket was given a new plate engraved with Joe and Sadie. Dad said, *'whatever you think Wacker',* and so I pondered a while. Where would my Mum and Dad rather be? And I reckoned they would want to be with me, and that's exactly where they are. The weeks and months after Dad passed away were incredibly hard, but speaking to people during the course of my work, helped me a great deal. Everyone has 'stuff' to deal with and listening to other people's stuff, helped me with mine. I can't count the times I had to pull over in the car when the song, *Dance with my Father*, by Luther Vandross, came on the radio, and I cried my eyes out every time. I still can't listen to that song. It tells it just like it is, and I'd love, love, love, to dance with my father again.

I had kept Dad's tele when I was emptying his flat. He'd not had it long and was really pleased with it when he bought it. I told him I'd have it when he was gone and we laughed about it. It took a while for me to feel able to watch it and

I was quite emotional when I eventually got it tuned in. I swear, you wouldn't believe the creaking noises that tele made, even when it wasn't switched on, it was uncanny. It had never made any noises at his flat and I was there often enough to know. When I went upstairs to bed at night, it would make really loud noises that I could hear from my bedroom, and I'd just shout, *'Night God Bless Dad.'* When I used to visit him for lunch, now and again I'd shut my eyes for a few minutes and ask him to wake me in ten minutes. Since he'd been gone, I went home for lunch, and if I needed a kip, I'd say, *'wake me at quarter to Dad,'* and sure enough, the tele would creak at quarter to and wake me up. I can't explain it, but it really did happen, just like all the things that occurred when Mum passed away.

It still fills me with immense pride when I meet people who knew my Dad and they say what a lovely man he was. Same with Mum, she was a very popular lady and had a great sense of humour. They were a well loved and respected couple and I am very proud of them both. They weren't perfect but they were mine and I loved them more than words can say. I would never have wanted any other Mum and Dad than Sadie and Joe. And despite the sometimes-difficult times in their relationship, I think deep down she really did love him. During her recovery from one of her cancer operations, she wrote in a wedding anniversary card, *'might I add a special thank you for your devotion and loving care shown to me all through my recent ordeal, God Bless you my love, Sadie xxx.*' I know it meant the absolute world to him and he kept it for the rest of his life.

I have a lot to thank my Mum and Dad for. Their constant unconditional love and support has always sustained my spirit. A life without them was unthinkable, a dreadful feeling of emptiness, and a broken heart, but something we all have to face, and learn to come to terms with, at some time or another. I will always treasure the memories of our days at 42 and be grateful for everything they did to shape my life. I have been truly blessed. They will always be in my heart.

LIFE WITHOUT SADIE AND JOE

When I lost my Mum, I still had my Dad and our Pat. When I lost my Dad, I still had our Pat, and although she had a family of her own, we still had each other and the shared memories of our lives together with Sadie and Joe, and I never ever contemplated losing her. She was just our Pat, who I had always looked up to, HRH, LFP, and she had always been a huge part of my life. I nicknamed her LFP in the early 90s because she often complained about being fat; she was anything but fat, so I started calling her Little Fat Pat for fun, which was eventually abbreviated to LFP, and it stuck.

It was my fiftieth birthday just two months after Dad passed away, my first birthday without a Mum and Dad. Dad and I had joked earlier in the year about me turning fifty, '*who'd 'ave thowt*,' as he always used to say, and I never thowt for one minute he wouldn't be here to share it with me. It was sad reaching this milestone without him, but a friend was kind enough to put on a party for me at her house. I'd joined a women's group in Preston, several of them came along, and so did our Pat. It turned out to be a really good night.

Our Pat at my 50th

157

Pat and I both struggled enormously after Joe had gone and had many phone calls where we just sobbed our hearts out together. She said she never realised how much she loved him until he had gone. We would often reminisce and support each other in our grief. I wrote a poem for her.

An Ode to L.F.P.
If I was to sit down to thank you Pat, I wouldn't know where to begin,
To thank you for your constant love through all the scrapes I've been in.
To thank you for your loyal support, and always being there,
To thank you for your Trust in me, and the secrets we both share.
My memories they are many, and what I remember most,
Our Saturday's at Holme Slack, and jam bubbling on my toast.
The picnic's on our days out and our holidays together
I'll treasure every moment, tucked inside my heart forever.
You're more than just my Sister, you're my confidant and friend,
I know you'll always be beside me – on you I can depend.
You have been an Inspiration, my candle in the dark,
You helped to guide my life for me: you have truly left your mark.
To say You are My Sister just fills my heart with pride,
The love and respect I have for you, I never want to hide,
Without your love and your devotion, just where would I be?
There is no doubt I would be lost without my L.F.P.
Of all the Sisters in the world, I know I have the best,
And I thank my lucky stars for I have been truly blessed.
Through our trials and tribulations with our precious Sadie and Joe,
Because we bore it all together, means more than you will ever know.
I am who I am today, coz of Sadie, Joe and You,
And the times we shared together in our days at 42.
But now there's just the two of us, it brings us closer still
I Love you Pat with all my heart, and I always will.

Gail J Newsham – 2004

I was nominated for an Employee of the Year Award, in the North & Western Lancashire Chamber of Commerce Outstanding Business Achievement Awards, by the Leader of South Ribble Council in 2004. I didn't really understand why I had been nominated and was a bit gobsmacked by all the fuss, and I don't think it went down very well with some of the 'higher ups,' who no doubt thought they were far better than a lowly visiting officer. But when the Leader said jump, they had to say how high, and I'm sure that's the only reason why some in management went along with it; to my face at least. It was a pleasant evening at Park Hall, in Charnock Richard, for the awards ceremony. Several colleagues were delegated to attend and we had a very nice dinner consisting of Chilled Melon, Noisettes of English Lamb, and Chocolate & Orange Roulade, all paid for by the council. I didn't win, I never expected to, but it was quite an honour being one of the finalists, and to piss off one or two people in the process and spend some of the council's money. Working in local government certainly opened my eyes to the 'jobs for the boys' establishment. Making sure they all got themselves very big pay offs and golden handshakes with early retirement at fifty-five, and seeing who really does control things, even at a local level. The stories I could tell. The shenanigans aren't just peculiar to Westminster. But this is not that kind of book.

I also met Lenore in 2004. We worked together at South Ribble and started seeing one another towards the end of the year. I wasn't looking for another relationship, I'd been on my own for several years and was quite settled. I didn't really want to get involved, I didn't want any more hurt or conflict in my life, but Lenore was different, in fact probably the kindest and most genuine person I have ever met, and I think it was simply one of those things that was just meant to be. We both had our own home, with no complications, and it worked out very well for the time being.

It was in 2005 when Andy was diagnosed with cancer in his bladder. I remember the day vividly. I'd nipped into town to get some new glasses adjusted at Specsavers, and just parked up on Avenham car park when my phone rang. It was our Pat calling to tell me the news. She said he had a good chance because the tumour was contained within his bladder and it could all be taken away without the need for chemo or radiotherapy, but it obviously meant he would have to have a stoma and a bag. I prayed for him to be ok and asked God to give him a few more good years before it was his time to go. The operation was a success and, with a lot of support from our Pat, he learned to deal with his new situation. He'd had a couple of mini strokes a few years earlier, which he made a good recovery from, but apart from those, and having a disc removed from his back, he wasn't in bad nick. They continued going on their annual Caribbean cruise and things were reasonably ok for a while.

Things had been going well with Lenore and I, she sold her house in 2007 and moved in with me. In 2008 I sold my house at Kiln Croft and we moved to Bamber Bridge in November of that year. We bought a bungalow in a quiet cul-de-sac and it needed a great deal of work doing to it. We moved in on the Friday, and the builders moved in with us on the Monday. Looking back, I don't know how we managed to live with those conditions, we had just two rooms we were able to make liveable while all the work went on around us, and we didn't have a proper kitchen for ages, we used our camping stoves and washed up in the bath, but we got through it and loved our new home once we had put our own stamp on it. On the Monday before Christmas, I started to feel unwell with pains in my abdomen and I thought it was just a sickness bug that was doing the rounds. The day before, we were on our hands and knees scrubbing the plaster off the floor boards in the living room, so it all seemed to appear from nowhere. I did see a doctor on the 23rd who examined me, but he didn't think there was any cause for concern. The next day was Christmas Eve, I was still in pain, and realised I needed some help before everything closed for the festivities. Lenore took me to the doctors and I struggled to get up on to the examination table. The doctor examined me and said I was to go to hospital straight away. I asked could I go home to get some things, but she advised to go straight there. When we arrived and got parked up, I tried to walk all the way to the assessment ward, but couldn't manage it and Lenore had to get a wheelchair for me. When we got to the ward, I was asked to give a urine sample, and as soon as I saw it, I knew I was in trouble. It was a dreadful colour with lots of nasties floating around in it. The doctor thought I had cancer and said they might have to take away part of my bowel. I had a CT scan and thankfully, it just turned out to be a gangrenous appendix and I had an emergency operation on Christmas Day. The whole procedure took around four and a half hours; they said it was a mess when they opened me up and had to clean it all out. I was very lucky by the sound of things and very grateful to the doctors and nurses for their care. I was put on intravenous antibiotics for a week and also had a drain. During my recovery, I had a bit of 'an episode' with my heart rate. I was just lying there in bed and it went up to over 180. I felt quite calm about it really, I wasn't in pain as such, and I remember thinking well, if this is it, so be it. I wasn't scared, I just brought it to the attention of a nursing assistant. She took my pulse and immediately sent for a doctor. They put those pads on my chest to monitor my heart, but it settled after a while and all was well. I couldn't eat the food though, a bit like my Dad I suppose when he was in hospital. Lenore would bring me something every day and I honestly couldn't have got by without her. She was absolutely wonderful.

I have to say though, being in hospital certainly opened my eyes to the NHS. I can only speak for my own experience and I was rather surprised by some of the things I saw. There was a young lass in the bed diagonally opposite me who had undergone some major operations to do with cancer. She was being fed through a tube due to having had most of her stomach taken away. During one night, she was feeling very sick and needed assistance from a nurse, she pressed her buzzer several times, but no one came. She was quite distressed so I got out of bed and went to try and find someone for her. I was wandering up and down the corridor, pushing the stand holding the drip I was attached to, but there were absolutely no nurses to be found on the ward, not a single soul. Where everyone was, I have no idea. Another thing that took me by surprise was when the cleaning staff were doing their rounds. They used the same cloth for everything, even wiping around each bed space, and from the get go, the stand I had for the intravenous drip, had dried blood stains on the base. Then there was the toilet, oh my goodness me. There was no way you would have used that toilet if you weren't a captive audience, it was disgusting. Thankfully, I was allowed home on New Year's Eve but Lenore was worried about me coming back to the house with it still being a building site, there was muck, dust, and builders' tools everywhere. We didn't have much in the lounge by way of comfortable furniture either and only a camping carpet on the floor. Lenore set up a camp bed and cushions for me to relax on, and we watched the film *Chocolat* on the tele. Happy New Year. It was good to be home.

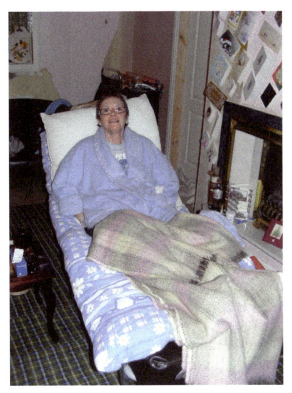

Home sweet home

In 2010, Lenore and I had our Civil Ceremony. It truly was the happiest of days shared with our family and friends. Lenore's Mum and our Pat were our witnesses, and my cousin Theresa and Lenore's sister Kate, each did a reading for us. We had our reception at Leyland Golf Club with our friends and families from Scotland and Ireland. The whole day was absolutely perfect.

30 April 2010

Pat and Andy celebrated their Golden Wedding Anniversary in 2011. They both just wanted a quiet time with family, and a small gathering at home with close friends and neighbours. This was when I first noticed a difference in Andy. Where he had always been great at speeches with his quick wit and dry sense of humour, words didn't seem to come as easy to him when we were making a toast to them both. It wasn't like him at all. He then began having some 'funny do's', and after a lot of going backwards and forwards with various doctors, they discovered there was something wrong with his heart and he needed to have a pacemaker fitted. The procedure didn't go totally as planned as they managed to puncture his lung during the process and it took quite some time to heal, meaning a much longer stay in hospital, and for him to get back to some kind of normality. The whole experience took a huge toll on Andy, and our Pat was greatly affected by it too, she was extremely angry with the outcome and what it did to him.

In August of 2012, I reached the milestone of having worked at South Ribble Borough Council for twenty five years. When I came into the office on the day, no one said a word, not a Scooby doo, and it passed without even a mention. I did eventually get some vouchers via Personnel, but I had to chase them about it.

I had a long, protracted issue with skin cancer on the third finger of my left hand. It went on for several years, first to get it diagnosed, and then trying to get it cleared up. At first, they were treating it as eczema, it was initially slightly bigger than a 5p coin and the skin would split and bleed. I think I must have been prescribed every conceivable cream on the market to try and shift it, but it had spread further down my finger during that time. I eventually had numerous biopsies to diagnose the condition, squamous cell carcinoma, followed by several doses of chemotherapy cream, photo dynamic light treatment, and laser treatment to burn off the affected area, none of which were successful in curing the problem and it was all a bit traumatic, not least very painful. Consequently, I had to have several periods off work at SRBC. I'm sure there were those who thought it was 'only a finger', what's all the fuss about, but I suspect had the finger been on the other hand, they might have been a little more sympathetic. The final operation to remove the cancer in June 2013, was to surgically cut away the affected skin from most of the inside and side of my finger, down to the tip of my palm, and replace it with a full thickness skin graft taken from my upper left arm. Throughout all this, I was put through the 'sickness policy' by my department, having to be interviewed by Personnel about my absence, and warned against any future time off. When I came back to work after the last operation, none of those involved in the sickness policy malarkey, asked me how I was. We did remain friends as I liked to give them the benefit of the doubt that they were acting under instructions from above, 'towing the party line' so to speak; the manager did have a bit of a god complex, but it still hurt. And I wasn't sorry one iota when I left on retirement the following month. The CEO, formerly director of finance, had said in a briefing to all the staff after his promotion, if we didn't like the way things were, we knew where the door was. In my leaving speech, I made it perfectly clear just how happy I was to be leaving, and with my final parting shot, said I knew where the door was and delighted that Gail Newsham was finally leaving the building. I have never looked back. It was only thanks to being with Lenore I was able to retire at sixty, as I had to wait four and a half years before I got my state pension, but it was worth it.

Over the next few years, Andy's health was deteriorating, and so was our Pat's. Andy rang me on a couple of occasions because Pat had some 'passing out' episodes, resulting in several trips in an ambulance to A&E. I also took her for a couple of colonoscopies which thankfully came back all clear. But there were other issues, all of which were adding to her problems. It was a very difficult time all round. Andy was getting urinary tract infections quite often, he was hospitalised several times, and was also diagnosed with vascular dementia. Pat's health was also in decline both physically and mentally. She had numerous problems over a long period of time and the whole situation was a bit of a nightmare. And because she was ill, she found it increasingly more difficult to cope with Andy's growing needs. She needed help, but didn't want anyone coming to the house to make things a bit easier, and try as we might, no one could get through to her. There hadn't been any joy for a number of years to be perfectly honest, it was all such a very, very, sad situation and it took its toll on all of us.

Then we had the covid situation to contend with, and the isolation made it even more difficult for Pat having to deal with everything on her own. Lenore would do some shopping for her and I would take it over, but that was pretty much all we could do in the early stages. Pat was telling us about Andy wandering in the night, getting confused and sometimes falling out of bed. She had no option but to ring for an ambulance on a few occasions, and with things the way they were, Andy went into a nursing home for a couple of week's respite. However, it was obvious by this time that Pat was unable to cope, and the two weeks respite became permanent. As Christmas was approaching, the nursing home said Andy was unwell and he was taken to hospital. They said he had covid, and on 22 December 2020, Andy passed away, just a few months before what would have been their Diamond Wedding Anniversary. The last time I saw him was when I dropped off some shopping and he was stood at the top of the stairs with Pat. He had been such a big part of my life since I was five years old, and I never got to say goodbye. I hope he understood all the reasons why. I had always visited him when he was in hospital and we could always have a conversation, no matter what he was like. We always talked about football and North End, and I wanted him to know how much I cared about him. During one visit to see him in Chorley Hospital, I said, *'you know I love you don't you Andy,'* he said, *'yes, and I love you too, you've always been good to me, you've always come to see me.'* I am so happy we had the chance to share that special moment.

His funeral during the covid restrictions was a nightmare. While Downing Street were having parties because they knew there was nothing to fear, we couldn't give Andy the final farewell he truly deserved, and it will haunt me for the rest of my days. There was just our Pat, Ian and Elaine and their respective families, me and Lenore. I can't begin to imagine how Ian and Elaine must have felt under such circumstances, losing their Dad and not being able to give the kind of send-off they would have wished for him. They must have been heart broken. Despite the social distance rule, I was by Pat's side, and we did play some appropriate music for Andy. We chose the Grandstand theme for when he was brought into the crematorium, and during the short service, Ian gave a Eulogy and I also said a few words. We played Match of the Day for him when we were leaving, so we all did the best we possibly could under extremely difficult circumstances.

It was a steady decline for our Pat from then on really. She was on the phone to the doctor on a regular basis, but never seemed to get anywhere. With all her health issues, she was beginning to fail, she wasn't eating much at all and her weight went down to just over five stone. Again, she needed help but didn't want people coming to the house, and no matter what any of us said, she did things in her own way, as she always had. Lenore and I did go over to spend some time with her despite the so called 'rules.' I think she appreciated it. Pat had a fall in the back garden in early May 2022. She'd gone out to put some rubbish in the bin, and noticed a weed in the patio on her way back. She bent down to pull it up, but she lost her balance and fell over on her side. She sent for the doctor because she had injured her wrist and was also having trouble walking. He said she needed to go to A&E so Lenore drove us there on 3 May. As we were leaving her house, she said, *'I've left the computer on,'* and I told her not to worry, I'd sort it. *'The heating is on as well.' 'Don't worry, I'll sort that too'.* We arrived at 7pm and she didn't get an X-ray on her hip until twelve hours later, at 7am the next morning. We had both been sat in a very cold corridor the whole night, Pat in a wheel chair and me on a chair beside her. They did bring us a blanket each, but that was it. The doctor who finally arranged the x-ray implied some concern about her heart and then we were sent to another waiting area in a treatment room.

The x-ray revealed she had broken her hip and would need an operation to pin it. She said she wanted time to think about it, and choose who did the operation, but there was no alternative or choices, it had to be done. She was still 'playing it to the gallery' with the very nice doctor who showed us the x-ray results, showing him pictures on her phone of her Mercedes car, while I dashed back to her house to get some night clothes, toothbrush et cetera, and left her in their capable hands. When I returned, she had been given some pain relief and was in reasonably good spirits. They were going to operate later that day. I asked the doctor about the heart concerns, but he said the number levels were within the ok spectrum. I got home after mid-day, feeling more reassured and crawled into bed to try to get some kip. I messaged her in the afternoon to let her know I was thinking of her and hoping she was ok. I knew she wouldn't see it till she came round, but at least she would know she was in my thoughts.

I rang the hospital the next morning (5th) to see how she was and got the usual, *'she's comfortable'* report. I messaged her again about 10am to let her know

165

I was thinking of her and to tell her I loved her. She messaged back just before 4pm and said, *'Thanks darling – feeling very woozy and tired – still a lot of pain in the thigh. Let you know if it changes xxx.'* I replied telling her I would come up and see her that night, but she said, *'Can we leave it till I feel a bit better darling – not that I don't want to see you I just don't feel up to it. I hope you understand love – and I have a urine bag and stand xx.'* I replied, *'of course I understand. You rest up and know I'm thinking of you. I'm so sorry you're in pain, I hope you get some relief soon, and a good night's sleep.'* At 17.17pm she messaged me back with a smiley emoji with red hearts, and two xx.

The hospital rang early the next morning to say Pat was struggling to breathe and to get there as soon as possible. I was quite shocked, I thought she was doing ok. Lenore drove me there and we got to the ward just as she was to be taken down to intensive care. The sister in charge told me Pat had sepsis, pneumonia, and something wrong with her heart, and she said, ICU wouldn't take her if they didn't think there was a chance. This was serious; if there was a chance? How the bloody hell did all that happen from her message less than 24 hours earlier? I wish I would have asked more questions, how had it all happened so fast, but I was in a state of sheer panic.

I'd let Ian and Elaine know, and Ian was coming up from Bristol that day. Elaine had tested positive for covid and couldn't travel from her home near Peterborough. There was still the 'only one person' visiting restrictions malarkey at the time, so Ian obviously took priority and I didn't see Pat that day. I arranged to pick Ian up from Pat's to take him to the hospital the next day and he said I could go in with him to see her. She was still communicating, but only very slightly and in and out of sleep. We did manage a bit of a laugh, but she was obviously gravely ill. Ian went back to Bristol on the Sunday evening and the hospital rang me in the very early hours of Monday morning. Lenore drove me there again and we were both allowed into ICU to be with our Pat as she came towards the end of her life. She was attached to so many machines monitoring her heart, blood pressure, oxygen, et cetera, and we were watching as it was beeping and calculating her heart rate. It was fluctuating from the mid-100s to the lower 70s. We had been there since well before 5am and just after 6am the monitor started beeping as her heart rate fell to below 40, and then it stopped; we held our breath and waited. Two nurses were in attendance doing all the observations, and a good two minutes passed by, possibly more, as we watched Pat's lips turning blue, and I said to the nurse, *'has she gone'?* The nurse nodded, and they were just about to record Pat's time of death as 6.07am, when the monitor suddenly started beeping again and Pat's heart rate started to increase. No one could believe what had just happened, they said they'd never seen anything like it before. I think she was having the last word, and waiting for Ian to arrive. I can just imagine her saying, *'sorry, I can't come yet, our Ian's on his way, I'll have to nip back for a bit.'*

Lenore and I sat with her well into the afternoon, I was just holding her hand most of the time. The more I think about how long we held hands for the last time, makes it all the more precious, like making the most of every last second we could hold on to together. At one point I whispered to her and said, *'I'm sorry if I let you down Pat'.* It hadn't been easy over the last few years, and I wanted her to know I was sorry if I hadn't come up to scratch, but it had been so hard. Ian arrived late in the afternoon, and as soon as he whispered in her ear, there was a definite change, she knew he was there. The nurses were saying she was quite stable and appeared to be in for the long haul and advised Lenore and I to go home for a break, so we reluctantly left about 7pm to try to get some sleep. The phone rang just before 10pm; it was Ian telling us Pat's breathing had changed. We raced back to the hospital as quick as we could, but she had gone only a few minutes before we arrived. I was so sorry not to have been with her at the end, like we both were for Sadie, but I think happen she wanted it that way, with just her and her baby boy. And maybe the other incident at 6.07am was just for me.

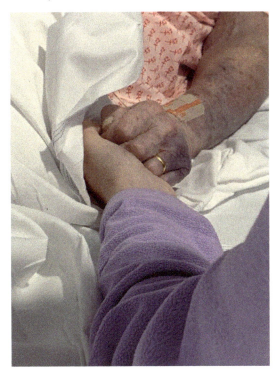

My last photo with our Pat

167

You never know when you'll do something for the last time. We left our Pat's to go to A&E, never thinking for one minute she would never come home. Computer and heating still on, everything in the house just the same, we never even took an overnight bag because we thought we would be bringing her back again after a few hours, just as on her other recent A&E visits. But this time, our Pat never came home. This has been extremely hard to come to terms with.

I think her funeral was just what she would have wanted. Ian and Elaine played a blinder. We asked if we could be driven up Ashton Street for her final journey, and the hearse stopped for a few moments where the fruit shop used to be, where her life began with Sadie during the war. It was a very poignant few moments. We then drove past where Whittingham Street was, and where she went to school on Wellfield Road, before heading through town to the crematorium. We asked everyone to wear some bling, and everyone obliged. Our Pat was the Queen of bling, she loved her sequins, stilettoes, hair pristine, nails done, diamond rings on, and being glamorous, she even had her own personalised LFP number plate on her beloved Mercedes. We chose 'Bolero' to be played as she was being brought into the crematorium. Our Pat loved Torvill and Dean, she made us sit through countless re-runs of their Olympic Gold medal winning routine, it seemed the perfect choice. Both Ian and I gave a eulogy during the service, and we played 'Don't Rain on My Parade' as we were leaving. She loved Barbra Streisand in *Funny Girl,* and we pretty much knew all the songs word for word having listened to the LP together hundreds of times, and that song was her favourite show stopper. She would have loved it. Afterwards we went to Bartle Hall for some hot pot and champagne. It was something we often said we would have for such an occasion, corned beef hash and something fizzy. Elaine organised a photo memory board, housed in an arch made up of black and yellow balloons, the colours of Laurel Racing Club. It was an ideal opportunity to remember their Dad as well. Andy was very much in all our thoughts. I think we did them both proud. I'm going to miss our Pat so much, there will always be a huge void. So I'll try and think of her as being on a never ending cruise on her favourite ship Arcadia, swanning around in her posh frocks, flashing her diamond rings, dining at the Captain's table, and winning the quiz with Andy every night. And we'll meet again when the ship comes back into port and it's my turn to get on board.

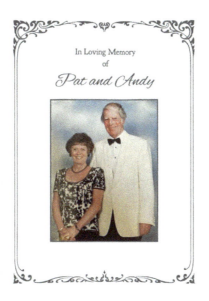

In Loving Memory

Elaine, Ian, Me

169

LFP

It took a long time to get the house sold and sorted with probate et cetera. I was going over quite often to get it how I knew she would have wanted it to be, ready to show to the world, and in some ways, it was good to have those months before finally letting go. It was comforting being able to go there and feel close to her, but hard at the same time. I cried buckets in her office, that's where I would talk to her because she spent most of her time in there. After one particularly bad day of getting upset, when I came down stairs, there was a white feather on the mat in the hallway. It definitely wasn't there when I came in, I always wipe my feet looking down at the mat, so I know for sure it wasn't there before. It was a great comfort and has been kept safe. While sorting through things at her house, I came across a 'Sisters Note Book', I had given her some years earlier. There were quotes on the bottom of each page about sisters, and this particular one, by Dale V Atkins, summed it all up for me: *'No one knows better than a Sister how we grew up, and who our friends, teachers and favourite toys were. No one knows better than she.'* No one knows better than our Pat.

The house was still furnished at Christmas, and Ian, his wife Sarah and their daughter Sophi, came up to spend their last Christmas at Dukes Meadow. For many years we had all spent Christmas Eve there with Pat and Andy; Lenore and I would make pizza for everyone and later we would have the present opening ceremony. It was obviously strange with Pat not being there, but it was comforting, in a sad kind of way, to have the chance to do it together one last time.

Last Christmas

Probate was eventually sorted and the house was finally sold in February 2023, just after what would have been Pat's eightieth birthday. I never thought of her as an old lady, she was just 'our Pat', and she had always been there, glamorous till the end. It was the end of an era, and life as we knew it was gone forever. It felt like losing her all over again. All the Christmases, barbeques, dinner parties, trivial pursuit nights, the happiness and good times, all gone. Pat and Andy bought the house from new, no one else had lived there but them. Now only memories remain and a new family is living there making their own. Before the house was emptied, I took pictures of every room, while they were still furnished, just as our Pat had left them. I can now look at the photos and wander around the house whenever I want and remember life just as it once was. I have something of hers now in every room in my home, just little ornaments and her little touches, so that I can feel close to her every day. Sometime after her funeral, I went to visit Barbara, one of our Pats long-time friends. Barbara told me that this photo over the page, is how she wanted to be remembered.

Pat and Andy

It's been incredibly hard since losing her. I'd honestly never contemplated her not being here. You sort of expect to lose your Mum and Dad, but losing a sibling really is a whole different set of emotions, I feel a deep sadness and emptiness. There's no one left to share memories with, or ask questions of and I will miss her for the rest of my life. But I don't begrudge her being at peace, the last few years were too much of a struggle. I don't feel the same without her and I never will, something will always be missing, but I treasure the memories of all the good times we shared, and even the not so good, because life is never perfect, we all have our differences along the way. And the thing is about losing someone, when they're gone, all the things that got to you, all the things that hurt you, or drove you up the wall, somehow don't seem to matter anymore, things take on a whole new perspective and you see things in a totally different light. I most certainly do, and hindsight is a wonderful thing. Death is so final, it's such a helpless feeling and there is absolutely nothing you can do to change it.

I know that without our Pat, I wouldn't be who I am, and I am so grateful for our time together, and all her love and support throughout my life, at 42 and beyond.

PAT

I never thought of ever losing you Pat
Couldn't think of owt as scary as that.
You'd always been the strongest link
I could never contemplate or even think
Of living my life without you in it
Never thought of it even for a single minute.
You were always the one who set the high bar
My Sister and my shining Star.
You taught me so many valuable things
And helped make me who I am,
And we shared so many happy times
Since our lives together began.
But I'm lost now that you're no longer here
You've left a place no one else can fill
And I'm struggling now without you Pat, but try my best I will,
To always smile whenever I think of you,
And I think of you every day,
And to keep alive your memory in the best and possible way.
I'll give thanks for you and our Mum and Dad
And keep you tucked inside my heart
I'll treasure our lives together before we all had to part.
I'll walk the path God planned for me and try to keep upbeat
Until we all meet up again
In heavens Whittingham Street.

Gail J Newsham – 14 September 2022

ME AND BILLIE JEAN

As a starry-eyed teenager, I fell in love with Tennis. I knew nothing about the sport but was once made to watch it on television at school during a PE lesson and I was immediately hooked. It was the 1968 Ladies Singles semi-final at Wimbledon, between British player Ann Jones and Billie Jean King from USA. Ann was serving for the match when the bell went for the end of our lesson and the end of the school day. I didn't have much idea about how they scored the points, or any of the rules of tennis, but I was really taken with watching the match and couldn't wait to get home to find out who had won. I was surprised to discover it was Billie Jean King who was the winner, even though it looked like Ann Jones was going to wrap it up when I left school. It had caught my interest enough to want to watch the final on the tele a day or so later. I think Mum and Dad must have wondered what on earth was going on having their football mad daughter now watching tennis. The final was played against a popular Australian, Judy Tegart, and Billie Jean didn't appear to be a great favourite of the Wimbledon crowd, but she certainly inspired me. She won the match in straight sets, 9-7 7-5. It was her third consecutive championship victory.

My love for Tennis grew, I learned the rules as I went along and BJK became my instant hero. I would buy all the daily papers during Wimbledon fortnight and meticulously cut out pictures and articles of the matches and put them in a scrap-book. I remember seeing an action shot of Billie Jean in one of the Sunday papers and said to myself, '*One day, I'm going to go to Wimbledon to see her play, and get her to autograph that picture;*' I was fifteen years old. From then on it was tennis, tennis, tennis. I loved watching Billie Jean at Wimbledon and I drove everyone mad going on about her all the time, no one was in any doubt of my admiration for Billie Jean King. Even if she was playing a British player, I still wanted her to win. I would send fan mail to her every year and I used to sneak a radio into work so I could listen to the match if she was playing. There were no video recorders in those days. When I came home from work, I would hit a tennis ball against the co-op wall at the corner of our street, trying to get to grips with the game. I went along to St Margaret's Tennis Club in Ingol, to try to learn to play properly, but my efforts were in vain, I was never very good, it takes years to learn to play properly and you need to take up a game like tennis when you're much younger, but I still loved watching it on the television, and still hit the ball at the corner of the street. It was thanks to St Margaret's Tennis Club I was fortunate to get two tickets for the Wimbledon Ladies Final in 1971. I could hardly believe my luck; my dream was about to come true, and I was so excited. Billie Jean was number one seed and expected to win the title and I had great seats on centre court. My friend Jeannie, who I worked with at Tweedales, agreed to come with me, and we arranged to travel down by coach. The day was fast approaching, I could hardly contain my excitement, but then disaster struck.

Billie Jean was beaten in the semi-finals by Australian protégé, Evonne Goolagong. I was heartbroken; completely inconsolable, and couldn't stop crying, it was the end of the world. My dream of actually watching my idol lifting the trophy at Wimbledon was shattered. It was with a very heavy heart I went to watch Evonne Goolagong beat Margaret Court to win her first Wimbledon title. Of course, it was a wonderful experience to actually have tickets for a Wimbledon final, and I know how lucky I was, but there will always be a kind of sadness for what might have been. After the final we wandered around outside Centre Court and saw a crowd gathering around court five. We went over to see what all the fuss was about, and beyond anything I could have ever wished for, it was Billie Jean King who was attracting all the attention having a practice session. After all the disappointment of her not being in the final, and thinking I wouldn't get the chance to see her, I will never be able to put into words exactly what that moment felt like. She was preparing to play in two doubles finals the next day, and she was only a few feet away from where I was stood. I couldn't believe it. When the practice session ended, she came over to the crowd and I was standing right next to her. I asked her to autograph the action photo I had saved, and as she signed it in my scrapbook she asked if I was the one who had written to her. I could hardly believe it; she actually spoke to me. I could never put a price on how I felt that day.

The photo from 1968 I dreamed of her signing

Because she was due to play in the ladies doubles and mixed doubles finals the next day, we decided to queue up all night in the hope of seeing both matches. We obviously weren't prepared for a night on the pavement, with no food and only a newspaper to put down on the floor. We had no waterproof protection either, but fortunately the weather was in our favour and we survived the long night. We discovered that after a final at Wimbledon, it was customary for spectators who didn't wish to stay for the doubles matches, to hand in their tickets for re-sale, and we were hoping we could buy some to see Billie Jean play on Centre Court. I think the ticket man was amused by my excitement and enthusiasm for the opportunity of seeing Billie Jean and he very kindly gave us the tickets free of charge. After all the disappointment came a very happy ending. Billie Jean King won the ladies doubles and the mixed doubles on centre court at Wimbledon, and I was there to see her do it. Absolutely Incredible. Dreams can come true. I still wrote to her at Wimbledon every year. I can't remember the exact year she sent me the autographed photo below, but it's obviously early 1970s. What a priceless gift.

Billie Jean King

Billie Jean announced her retirement in 1975, so I wrote to her at Wimbledon once more. I was in the Army by this time, posted at Camberley in Surrey, but I just wanted to thank her for all the joy watching her play had given me over the years, and to say a goodbye I suppose, because I thought I would never see her again. Sometime later, I had been unwell and was in sick bay when my room-mate, Karen Latham, brought in some mail for me. Her exact words were, 'here,

176

this might cheer you up'. I couldn't believe what I was seeing, it was a postcard from Billie Jean King, thanking me for my support. How kind of her to do that for a young fan, and how special it was for me. It is still in my box of treasures to this day.

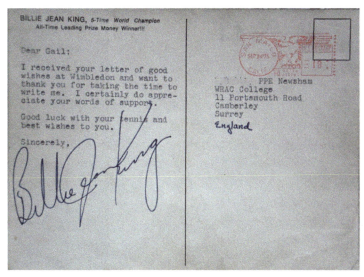

My postcard from BJK

I wrote to her at Wimbledon again in 1977, to ask if she would autograph the sleeve of her new book and enclosed a stamped addressed envelope for its return. The months went by and I didn't hear anything, until October when it finally arrived, duly signed and with a note which said, *'Dear Gail, this is just a note to let you know that I received your letter at Wimbledon some time ago and to thank you for writing again. I very much appreciate your kind words of support. Thanks again and best wishes to you, BJK'.* I was completely blown away, it meant the absolute world to me, she meant the world to me, she was a big part of my life. I enjoyed the BJK tennis years immensely and look back on them with great fondness.

I am lucky to have had the opportunity to visit Wimbledon several times over the years and share some of her moments of triumph. In 1978, Billie Jean was playing in the mixed doubles with Australian, Ray Ruffles, and made it to the final where she was attempting to win a record-breaking 20th Wimbledon title. I decided at the very last minute to go down to see if we could get in to see the match. Our Pat said, *'you'll never get in,'* but I thought it was worth a try. We travelled down on the midnight coach to London and found our way to Wimbledon, joining the queue very early in the morning. After waiting several hours, we finally got into the grounds and wandered around the outside courts taking in the atmosphere, and eventually managed to get used tickets after the men's final. They were great seats, almost looking down on the Royal Box from the stand on the right as you watch it on the tele. Frew McMillan and Betty Stove were their opponents and they were winning the game quite convincingly. Now in those days, people didn't really call out in the crowd, it was all just very polite hand clapping with lots of oohs and aahs, nothing like it is today. Things hadn't been going too well for Billie Jean and her partner, they lost the first set and were looking down and out as she came on court to serve to save the match from the Royal Box end, at 2-5 down. She was bouncing the ball getting ready to serve, and I just couldn't help myself, it wasn't planned, it just came out before I knew it, and I shouted, *come on Billie Jean,'* Well, it just echoed all around centre court didn't it, and our Pat was watching it on the tele at home and said, *'that's our Gail.'* The incident was reported in the press the next day: *'as Billie Jean served to save the match at 2-5 in the second set, a young fan shouted: "Come on Billie Jean." The 'old lady' stood for a moment and laughed. She has not always been popular at Wimbledon, but nowadays, as she has matured and become older, the young have taken her to their heart'.* The reporter obviously knew nothing of my ten-year devotion to Billie Jean, but that was a moment I shared with her, on centre court at Wimbledon. How special is that? Billie Jean and her partner lost the match 6-2 6-2 and the record-breaking attempt was dashed. But I'd love to see that moment we shared on video one day, if it still exists.

In 1979, at 35 years of age, Billie Jean was playing in the ladies doubles final with Martina Navratilova, once again attempting to win a record-breaking 20th Wimbledon title. She stood a very good chance this year with Martina as her doubles partner and I couldn't resist another trip to cheer her on. I was playing football with Ingol Belles, and we planned a trip to go to Wimbledon and support her. We made a banner and hung it on the wall as we queued all night. We were well prepared with sleeping bags and food and it was a great carnival atmosphere. There was a jazz band playing music on an open top bus to keep the queue entertained, it really was a fantastic night. Our Pat had let me take Ian with me and he absolutely loved it. She was worried about him getting cold, but her fears were unfounded as it was a really warm night, and our sleeping bags were army surplus, so we were toasty warm. We didn't get much sleep though. Ian rang Pat from the phone box close to where we were queueing, he was so excited he said to her, *'don't talk Mum, just listen'!* I was always going on about Billie Jean in those days, and when Ian was younger, he once won a goldfish on the local fair, and called it Billie Jean. A few months later, the goldfish died, and Ian said to Pat, *'Mummy, shall I tell Auntie Gail Billie Jean has died,'* to which our Pat replied, *'oh for heaven's sake no, don't tell her that'!*

Ingol Belles Supports Billie Jean King – Ian front right

We all got into the ground when they opened the gates and made the familiar dash to get standing room on Centre Court. We were quite close to the front of the standing area, and had a good view when Bjorn Borg and Roscoe Tanner came on court to warm up, but I was a bit concerned about the possibility of a crush with being responsible for Ian, so we decided to come off and see if we could get tickets again after the final to watch Billie Jean. There was still lots to see on the outside courts and lots of famous faces spot. We wandered round and did manage to bump into Billie Jean very briefly in the crowd and I was desperate to get a photo of her with me in the shot, but it was not to be, a young girl walked in front of me just as the shutter was pressed. I was wearing a white beany hat and had put an American flag on it, along with Billie Jean's name on the rim. Tracy Austin spotted it and came right up to me to see what it said. I can't recall our conversation, but she got the gist that I was a big BJK fan. We did manage to get tickets again after the men's final and I was absolutely made up to be sharing the experience with our Ian. After all my rambling about her since he was a toddler, here we were to see if she could beat the record of Wimbledon title wins. Immediately after Bjorn Borg won a record 4th singles title, Billie Jean King and Martina Navratilova played Wendy Turnbull and Bette Stove in the Ladies Doubles Final. It was a tough match going to three sets, but Billie Jean and Martina ran out the winners, 5-7 6-3 6-2. History was made that day as Billie Jean King won her 20th Wimbledon title, and although she didn't know, I was there in the crowd to share the joy.

Billie Jean and my white beany hat

In 1987 I did get to meet her again and managed to have my photo taken with the Legend herself after waiting for hours for a chance to see her. She sort of appeared out of nowhere and I was desperate to get a photo with her, I told her I'd only come to see her, but I'm not sure she believed me. She was in a hurry going to do some post-match analysis or something, and then she was gone. We waited ages for her to come back out, and time was getting on for our drive back to Preston. We were just about to leave when she suddenly appeared again and made my day. I said to her, *'I'm still here, I told you I was only here to see you,'* and she very kindly posed with me for a picture. What a wonderful moment captured in time. Another dream come true. This was the last time I ever saw her in person.

Me and Billie Jean

My book about the Dick, Kerr Ladies was published in late 1994, and I wanted to send a copy to Billie Jean at Wimbledon in 1995. I had her books on my book shelf, and it would mean the world to me if she had my book on hers, and I hoped she would enjoy their story. I parcelled up the book and also sent her a copy of the photo I'd had taken with her, along with some other things to show her the times I'd been at Wimbledon to support her. As you can see above, she signed it and sent it back for me, and she thought my book was terrific. I couldn't have been more delighted. Now that tennis has become a multi-million dollar sport, people realise just how important Billie Jean King is to the history of the game. Without her dedication, drive and sacrifice, fighting for equality for women's tennis in the 1970s, the game would be a mere shadow of what it is today, and she has become an icon. Rightly so in my humble opinion, but I remember the days when the Wimbledon crowd didn't really care for BJK, but this young lass from Whittingham Street certainly did.

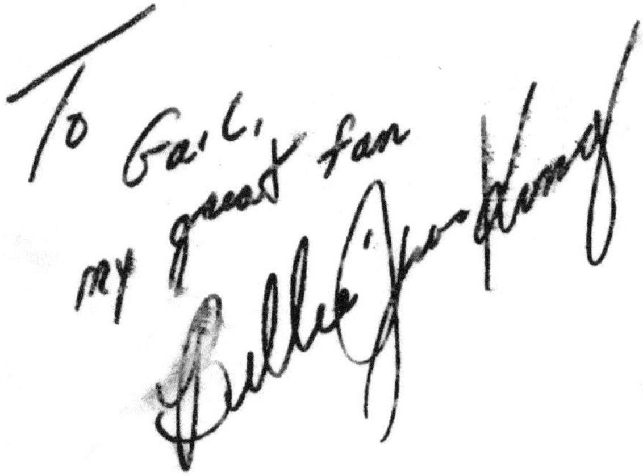

To Gail,
my great fan
Billie Jean King

ME AND SHEILA

The Philadelphia sound became prominent in the early 1970s, and a new group called The Three Degrees, hit the airways. It was my kind of music and I remember playing *Year of Decision,* on the juke box in 1974, and later in the year, *When Will I See You Again,* reached number one in the charts. After I left the WRAC in 1977, The Three Degrees were on tour and appearing at the Guild Hall in Preston. We got tickets to see the show and I was blown away by their harmonies, dance routines, and of course their talent. I soon joined their fan club and went to see them whenever and wherever I could. The lead singer, Sheila Ferguson, was my immediate favourite, and the Degrees were billed as, *The World's Number One Female Vocal Group,* which I wholeheartedly agreed with. The fan club was great. The lass who ran it was really good at giving out information on upcoming tours, and sharing info about Sheila, Valerie and Helen. It seemed a really friendly group, and Sheila said in one newsletter *'they're not our fans, they are our friends,'* and that's how it appeared to be. I liked that, I thought it was a lovely sentiment.

When I was going through a bad time with my Mum being very ill, their music was sometimes a welcome escape from all the heartbreak, and I wanted them to know how much listening to them had helped me getting through a very difficult time in my life. I wrote a letter telling them as much and sent a couple of poems I'd written, to see if they could use them for songs. I didn't want anything in return, it was just a genuine thank you. I didn't hear anything back and soon forgot all about it, until out of the blue, a letter came from Sheila saying how much she liked the poems and would try to use them if she could. It never happened, but it was good to know they hadn't been lost, and they were liked.

I used to get so wound up with excitement when we were going to one of their shows, it really was such a special time in my life. We would take our seats full of anticipation, and the atmosphere would build as the audience could sense their imminent arrival. You could hear them back stage joining in with some harmonies to the overture music, and to add to it all, you could actually smell their perfume before they came on stage to be greeted by their adoring fans. By the time they finally made their appearance, I was just about ready to burst. They were truly wonderful times and I wouldn't have missed it for the world. As part of their show, they always sang the song *'We are Family,'* dedicating it to their fans in the audience, and it became something of an anthem. It was an eagerly awaited part of the whole night, when the love from Sheila,

Valerie, and Helen for their fans, seemed to be emanating out from the stage touching each and every one of us, as we lapped it all up and gave all of our love right back to them. It was absolutely magical.

Being part of the fan club was like being part of a family, I loved it and always looked forward to the newsletters. One article told the story of an elderly lady who often went to see them perform at a club in Wakefield. This particular time, the lady wasn't at their show and Sheila said, *'We got a bit worried, so after making some enquiries we found out where she lived. Poor thing was ill.'* So what did they do? They went round to see her, cleaned the house and did some shopping. I really liked that, it genuinely touched me, what a special quality and how thoughtful. I bet the lady was completely blown away. The fan club were looking for area reps to organise coaches to shows and possible meet ups, and I volunteered to help. It was all going great until the lass who ran the club, sent out a letter to everyone saying how the Degrees weren't letting her have information on time, all was not well, and she wasn't portraying them in a very good light, it was quite upsetting and bitterly disappointing. I didn't know what was really going on, but thought something must have happened to make her react so strongly. I had believed in them, I thought they were different and genuinely cared about us, but she was painting a different story. I felt let down, so, I wrote and told them exactly how I felt. They were appearing at The Opera House in Blackpool and I had tickets for the show. I posted my letter to the theatre, addressed to The Three Degrees, to tell them of the letter from the fan club, and how disappointed I was in them. I also mentioned the song *'We are Family,'* and how it now seemed insincere, they didn't really care, it was just part of the act, and when it came time to sing it in Blackpool, at least there would be four of us who knew the truth. I didn't know if they would receive the letter, or if they would even read it, but at least I had got things off my chest. So, when it got to the part of the show where they were introducing the song, *We Are Family*, Sheila actually said on stage, *'and this is for the four of us.'* They had obviously read my letter and it seemed to have struck a chord. After their shows, they always signed autographs for the fans, so I went along to see them and made myself known. Sheila asked if she could see the letter from the fan club, but I didn't have it with me. She suggested I came to their gig at the Alhambra Theatre in Bradford and bring it along then. So that's what happened and this photo above right, was my first proper meeting with The Three Degrees, just me and them. Look at that smile.

The Three Degrees and me: Sheila Ferguson, Helen Scott, Valerie Holiday

I don't know what the outcome of it all was with the fan club, I gave the letter to Sheila and there were obviously some issues for the Degrees to deal with. The club sort of ceased to be after that and the lass who ran it was never heard of again. Looking back, I should have realised there are always two sides to a story, there is often more to something than meets the eye. I continued going to their shows as often as I could and became a bit of a familiar face and the end of show autograph sessions, which was always a bit special.

Showing off the bottles of Blue Nun I brought for them

They were once doing a gig on New Year's Eve at the Night Out club in Birmingham, in the mid-1980s. We'd driven down to stay at Martha's Mum's and were unpacking our luggage, when I noticed we hadn't brought a blue bag containing our shoes. I was stood there in a pair of tatty grey trainers, covered in paint from decorating, and panic set in. It was too late to rush into the Bull Ring to get new ones, so the only option was for me to drive back to Preston, pick up the blue bag and drive all the way back down the M6 to Birmingham. It was about a hundred and five miles each way but thankfully the roads weren't as busy in those days. I managed the journey and got back in time for the show without missing out on the food, and we saw in the New Year with the Three Degrees after all. But a few speed limits were broken, and lots of swear words uttered, during the course of the emergency.

Sheila had married Jersey Property Developer, Chris Robinson, in 1980 and given birth to twin girls, Alicia and Alexandria, in September 1981, so the Degrees hadn't been touring until Sheila was up and running again. She did return to the group and they were just as popular as ever, but in 1986 Sheila made the difficult decision to leave. Being on the road so much meant she didn't see the twins as often as she would have liked, and she wanted to spend more time at home being a Mum taking care of her girls herself, rather than the nanny looking after them. And although I understood her reasons, I reckon I was among the many fans who were devastated she was leaving. Sheila was the lead singer, the voice of the Degrees, and the songs just wouldn't be the same without her. It was a sad time not having another Three Degrees gig to look forward to. Not to mention the thought of never seeing her again.

The Three Degrees, complete with new member Rhea Harris, came to the Guild Hall in Preston in 1987. I went along to see them, and while it was lovely to see Helen and Valerie again, for me, the magic had gone. *When Will I see You Again, Take Good Care of Yourself,* and all my other favourites, just weren't the same. But all was not lost. Sheila began embarking on her solo career and news filtered through that she was appearing at the Flamingo night club in Blackpool. I could hardly contain myself. We arrived early and I stood at the front near the stage all night so I didn't lose my place. It seemed ages until she made her appearance, but then she was there, the wait had been worth it, and it was wonderful to see her again. She was strutting her stuff and the magic had returned. The crowd were giving her a great reception, and then mid song, she noticed me and said, *'Gail, what are you doing here?'* I said, *'I've come to see you.'* I couldn't believe she remembered me, let alone my name. It was amazing. I had such a good spot at the front of the stage, I was able to take some great photos of her, which I developed and printed myself.

Sheila sings! 1987 ©

After her performance, I went up to the dressing room. It was so good to see her, I can't begin tell you. I told her I'd been taking photos all night and would send some for her if she wanted, and post them to the office address, but she gave me her home address instead and said to send them there. Wow! And she signed an autograph for me which said, '*Forever Friends.*' I was on cloud nine. And then she was gone, into the night.

I got to thinking after seeing her in Blackpool, if she could go to a small night club like that, I wonder if I could persuade her to come to the women's football tournament I organised, to present the trophies to the winning teams. We'd previously had female jockey Geraldine Rees, and Olympic Athlete Shirley Strong, and now that Sheila was making a solo career, there might be a very small outside chance she'd consider our theme of successful females. I wrote to her to ask the question, and waited. I didn't get a reply, so I wrote again and waited. The tournament was due to take place at Edge Hill College in Ormskirk in July 1988 and plans for the event were well underway. Time was marching on so I had the crazy idea of driving down to her house in Berkshire to see if I could get an answer that she might consider coming. I thought she would see me if she was there, and if she wasn't home on the Saturday we'd travelled, we'd stay over and try again on the Sunday before heading home. Well, that was the plan. We arrived in the beautiful village of Bray in Berkshire, looking for the mansion house built by Edward VII for Lily Langtree, where Sheila was living with her husband Chris and two beautiful daughters, Alicia and Alex, and I was about to ask her to come to a women's football tournament in Ormskirk. We pulled up outside the house, I got out of the car, opened the gates and nervously rang the doorbell expecting a maid to answer, but it was Sheila who came to the door. She'd been doing some ironing in her den and was obviously surprised to see me stood there and said, *'what are you doing here?'* I said, *'well, you didn't reply to my letters, please will you come to our tournament?'* She laughed and invited us in and made us very welcome. She made us a brew, gave us one of her delicious home-made blueberry muffins, and then showed us all around her beautiful home. It was absolutely beyond words incredible.

Sheila Ferguson, former lead singer with the chart topping, world number one female vocal group, the Three Degrees, who performed at Buckingham Palace for Prince Charles 30th birthday, agreed to come to Ormskirk to present trophies at a women's football tournament. Never give up on your dreams. She got on a train in Reading, to meet me in Preston, not having a clue where she was going, but somehow, and for some reason, she trusted me. Everyone at the tournament was completely gobsmacked, they couldn't really believe it, but it was happening and there she was. Sheila presented the awards to the winners and people were shouting for her to sing something for us, and she duly obliged with, *Stand by me*, sang A cappella. It was perfect. Everyone joined in, and she promised she would come back and perform for us next year. We had managed to get Dutton Forshaw to sponsor a car for us to take Sheila back down to Bray, so when all the photos were taken, and autographs signed, I drove Sheila home. Our Pat came with me to help keep me awake on the way back. And to have a cheeky peek at her stunning home of course.

Sheila at Edge Hill College 1988

Me and Sheila

I think in the early part of her solo career, Sheila found it strange being on her own when everything she had achieved before, was part of a group. All the decision making, the travelling, the performing, it was all shared with the other girls. But to then have to do all that on your own, it must have taken time to come to terms with. It's like a divorce I suppose, getting used to a whole new way of life, we all need time to heal. I think maybe she lost a bit of confidence being home, not being out there performing. She wrote me a thank you note for taking her home and looking after her, and she said, '*if ever I doubt my worth, I can always come to you for reassurance.*' I kept telling her how much everyone wanted her to come back and did everything I could to show her how much love there was for her. And Sheila kept her word, she did return to the Lancashire Trophy in 1989. I drove down to pick her up this time and it was nice to spend that time with her, just the two of us, even sharing a couple of secrets. I couldn't believe it really; it was more than a dream come true. I often thought our souls must have met in a past life, and we were just somehow reconnecting, which might have explained how a superstar, and a lass from Whittingham Street, could possibly be friends.

Sheila, our Pat, me, Elaine, Ian, Andy

189

Sheila performed a rock and roll medley, and of course, a string of Three Degrees hits, finishing up with *When Will I See You Again*, and it brought the house down. She looked fantastic, sounded fantastic and I'm sure she felt all the love in the room. And then it was time to go. I only had to drive her to Manchester this time as she was taking part in a television programme with Hudson and Halls the next day. I was doing my best to treat her like the star she is, trying to ensure every last detail was attended to, as Sheila waved her good-byes. We got in the car, and a few miles down the road, I happened to glance at the petrol gauge, it was nearly empty and I realised I didn't have any money with me. I had to borrow a fiver from Sheila to top up the tank. So much for attending to every detail, eh? We had a good laugh about it though and I posted the fiver back to her the very next day.

Sheila at the Lancashire Trophy 1989

Sheila returned to the Lancashire Trophy in 1991 and again I went to collect her from her home in Bray. The tournament was now at Myerscough College, and we arranged for Sheila to stay at Guys Court, by the side of the canal. On the way up she suggested calling in to see my Mum and Dad. As we were approaching junction 29 on the M6, I said, '*If you're serious about going to see my Mum and Dad, we'll need to come off the motorway at the next junction.*' She was, and so we did. We arrived at Mum and Dad's small council flat on Hassett Close. Sheila hid out of view while I rang the doorbell. My Dad opened the door and I said, '*you'd better go and put your teeth in Dad, I've got a very special visitor for you.*' They could hardly believe their eyes when Sheila Ferguson walked in and sat down in the living room with them. She stayed a good while chatting with them, she knew about Mum's illness and talked to her trying to give her some encouragement, and she even had a can of lager with my Dad, it was just like she was part

190

of the family, so comfortable. Mum and Dad were thrilled to have a superstar in their 'little palace,' and couldn't wait to tell everyone about it.

Sheila was putting on a bigger performance for us than the previous time at Edge Hill. We had to clean out the gym to make it more presentable and had a stage erected for the show. But to be totally honest, it was a far cry from anything she would have ever been used to. The college provided a caravan for her to get changed in at the side of the building, but it turned out there was no electricity connected to it and Sheila had to put her make up on, pretty much in the dark, but she never complained, not once. She put on a fantastic show for us and everyone loved it. We all ended up congregating in the courtyard at Guys later in the evening and Sheila joined in with us. It was a lovely warm summer's night, we were all singing songs in party spirit, and simply having a great time in each other's company. It was a bit special.

Over the years, Sheila has invited me to some private functions where she was performing. The Watford Hilton hosted a charity event, with performances from Sheila and Bobby Davro. Before the show, Sheila invited us to dinner with her and the band. We were also invited to the Oasis night club at Porth in South Wales. It was another fantastic performance from Sheila, strutting her stuff as only she can and I took the opportunity to take some more photos to add to my collection. I am proud to say that this one below, is on display in her home.

Sheila in action ©

In 1989 Sheila published a cookery book about Soul Food. It was a brilliant idea bringing this unique cuisine to a whole new audience. It's more than just a cookery book, it has lots of family history and is extremely well written. Sheila set up most of the location shots herself, with family members and loads of family recipes. The Jambalaya and Sweet Potato Pie are a revelation. We were invited to her star-studded book launch at Stringfellows night club in London for an incredible night. Next came Land of Hope and Gloria, a sit-com especially written for Sheila in 1991, and she invited us to a pre-recording of one of the episodes. In the bar afterwards, Sheila introduced me to some of the cast, including Joan Sanderson.

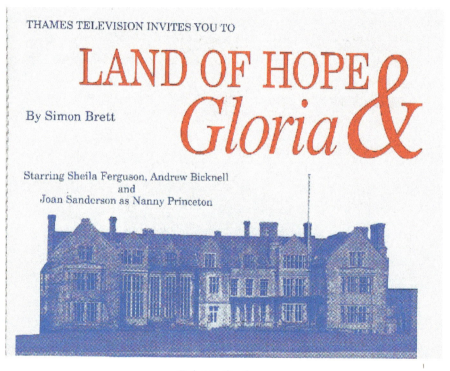

Ticket to the show

Sheila, me, & Andrew Bicknell

In 1996 Sheila was appearing at the Grand Theatre in Blackpool with Cannon and Ball, in the Rock with Laughter show for the summer season. I went to see her many times during that summer and took my Dad along and to meet her back stage. He was really chuffed to see her again, he loved the show and meeting her again made his night. I asked Sheila if she would like to come out with me to the Stocks restaurant in Poulton le Fylde. It was a German restaurant, very popular during that period, and one of my favourite places back in the day and I was delighted when she accepted my invitation. I had to arrange with the management for our late arrival at the restaurant, and they were very accommodating. I met her at the Grand after the show in my car, a Peugeot 106. When I picked her up at the stage door, I said, '*welcome to my small limo.*' She laughed, but it got us to the restaurant and back and we had a really lovely evening. I introduced her to Bratkartoffeln (German fried potatoes with bacon and onions) and she loved them, and even took some in a doggy bag back to her pad for later. It was a wonderful summer having her so close by.

The Lancashire Trophy came around again in 1997 and everyone was thrilled when Sheila made another visit to perform for us once more. The tournament had moved to the Nautical College in Fleetwood and the converted gymnasium was in a much better condition than her last visit at Myerscough, and this time, the makeshift dressing room had an electricity supply. We hired a proper sound system and the whole night was magical. Sheila's performance brought the house down, as it always does, and many more new fans were made. Four visits from an international superstar to a women's football tournament, when the game had nowhere near the profile it has today, isn't half a bad record now is it? Just shows what an incredible person she is.

Since then, I have followed Sheila's solo career travelling all over the country. From stage shows like, *Soul Train, Oh What a Night, Hot Flush, Fame the Musical* in Belfast, *Respect la Diva*, to numerous Christmas panto's, *Cinderella*, where Sheila played the Fairy Godmother, *Aladdin, Dick Whittington*, and have always been made welcome. Another time we went to see her at a Warner Hotel, Alveston Hall in Cheshire. We met up with her when she was doing her sound check and she didn't mind us hanging around to listen in, so we got to see the show twice in one night! David Gests, The Legends of Soul tour, took place in 2013, and we had tickets to see the performance in St Helens. Sheila invited me and Lenore to meet her in the dressing room before the show, and afterwards at the post show party at the Radison Blu Hotel in Liverpool. What an unbelievable experience it was to be in the dressing room with so many soul legends. Sheila Ferguson, Kim Weston, Candi Staton, Martha Wash, Martha Reeves, Dorothy Moore, and Deniece Williams. The banter between them all was so funny and a joy to hear, and a privilege I will never forget. We were a bit apprehensive about meeting David Gest back at the hotel, but he really was a lovely man and made us feel very welcome. Rowetta, from the Happy Mondays, was there too, she is friends with Sheila and we gave her a lift in our car to the hotel. What a truly unforgettable night that was. Truly, truly unforgettable.

Sheila, Rowetta, me, David Gest

David Gest brought his, (I've Had) The Time of My Life, tour to the Guild Hall in Preston in 2015. Nearly forty years since I first saw Sheila perform there with The Three Degrees, she was back doing her thang. We had a meet and greet with some of the cast before the show. So many legends: Sheila Ferguson, Bill Medley, Deniece Williams, Dorothy Moore, Billy Paul, The Tymes, Freda Payne and David Gest. Another fantastic and memorable night that will live long in the memory.

Sheila in Preston 2015 ©

In 2017, Sheila invited me and Lenore to her 70th birthday party at Tramp night club in London. We didn't realise until we got there, but it was just a small intimate gathering of people, chosen by Sheila, who had been part of her life. There were only around fifty people present made up of close family and friends. It was such a special night, and very comfortable. We all sat down to a delicious three-course dinner, to celebrate the life of this incredible woman who had touched us all with her stellar talent and her love. It was absolutely wonderful. The whole night was just amazingly comfortable and warm. Words cannot express how much it all meant to this lass from Whittingham Street.

Me and Sheila – the warmth of friendship

I have been truly blessed to have been a small part of Sheila's incredible life, and for her to be part of mine. I will treasure each and every moment we ever shared; always. Forever Friends.

MY LIFE IN FOOTBALL

I grew up in the late 1950s early 60s, and was often out in the street or on the park playing football with the lads. During one of our many games on the park, I remember hearing a passer by say, *'she's good, she should be playing for the Dick, Kerr Ladies.'* I didn't know who they were, but I was chuffed he thought I could play. Football wasn't regarded as a girls sport back then, it was often frowned upon and we were certainly never allowed to play at school. My Dad first took me on Preston North End when I was about nine years old. We went on the Town End to watch them play Northampton Town and we won 2-0. I remember watching England winning the World Cup in 1966, and playing in the street with the lads after the game. We all wanted to be Bobby Charlton or Geoff Hurst. My first memory of seeing an all ladies team was on Moor Park in Preston in the late 1960s. Preston North End Supporters Club Ladies were having a training session and I could hardly believe my eyes, I was amazed something like this could actually happen. They were skilful and well organinsed, I was very impressed. Seeing them made me quite envious and I would have loved to have been part of something like that but didn't know how to go about getting involved and looking back, probably didn't have the confidence to approach them. I didn't know any of them then, but later learned they were being coached by Keith Aspinall and Brenda Busby, two very well respected people in the women's game in those early days.

The Women's Football Association was formed in 1969, followed by the North West Women's Football League in 1970. At that time I was working at Tweedales Shoe Factory and it transpired that a couple of my colleagues were playing football for Peter Craig Ladies, who were in fact one of the founder members of the League. I asked if I could come along and join in and began playing for the team circa 1971. As a left footer I hoped to play on the left wing but when I finally got my chance in the team, it was at left back. I was a bit disappointed not to be playing up front but grateful for the opportunity to play and soon realised this was where I belonged, I was a natural defender. It was an exciting time for me and I loved being able to play in a proper team in a proper league and I was revelling in it. The most vivid memory I have from those early days with Peter Craigs was when we went up to Kendal to play against Paper Dolls. We travelled up sat on the floor in the back of a transit van, it was wet, but warm, drizzley day, and I made what was probably the last kick of the match with a desperate goal line clearance to keep the score level at 4-4. A good away point for us. Most of the teams back then were pub teams, with names like,

Wheatsheaf Bandits, Ribbleton Diamonds, Duke of York, and Prince Arthur, who all played in the league during the early 70s.

The facilities in those days often left a lot to be desired, and quite a few pitches only had a wooden hut to change in, with no showers. Woodplumpton had a very uneven playing surface, literally with up and down dips. But Catforth was the one that really took the biscuit. I think it must have just been a farmers field that was marked out as a football pitch. It was surrounded by hedgerows not far from the touch line, with just enough room for the playing area and not much else. The changing rooms, and I use the term very loosley, were what can only be described as old chicken huts. The home team had the luxury of getting changed in the biggest hut, which was open to the elements down one side, and there was a rusty old oil drum if you needed the toilet. The pitch itself wasn't up to much either, it had a very uneven surface, the grass wasn't mown very often, it had certainly never seen a roller, and was frequently very muddy and water-logged. But we were playing football and that was all that mattered. The things I remember most from those early days, were coming home covered in mud, smelling of wintergreen, and sitting down to eat my Sunday dinner in front of the fire, watching *Black Beauty* on the tele. The theme tune to that programme always reminds me of those times.

I was spotted by Preston Dolphins, (formerly Duke of York, later Preston Rangers) and asked if I would come to play for them. They had seen me playing with Peter Craigs and said I was running the game. I was sorry to leave because I had known most of the girls for some time, but Dolphins were a better side and I wanted to play in a better team. Our trainer was a guy called Frank Shaw and I think I probably played some of my best football under his coaching. He had the ability to make you believe in yourself and knew how to get the best out of you. I remember vividly playing one of the best games of my life against Sandra Graham, who played for Blackpool Seabirds. Sandra had just returned from playing in the first official England game in 1972. She was a very strong player and well known in our league. We had never won a match against Blackpool before and were playing them on our home ground in Bamber Bridge, near where the Milk Marketing Board used to be. Sandra was playing on the right wing and I was a bit nervous because I had the task of marking her. The first half went really well for us, I was making a good job of keeping Sandra at bay, and she had little or no impact on the game. In the second half they moved her to a different position and Frank told me to stick with her. It was the same story for the rest of the match, I was like her shadow. We were leading by 2-1 when they equalised in the dying minutes of the game and the final whistle went for 2-2 draw. It was a great result for us and a superb game for me, I've never forgotten it. I didn't put a foot wrong.

Preston Dolphins 1973

Back row: Sheree Jameson, Pauline Burke, Janet Jones, Susan McCann, Janet Tracey, me, Drina Hope
Front row: Ann Brindle, Janette Sherliker, Maureen Hayes, Sally Pilkington, Brenda Metcalfe, Kath Montgomery

It wasn't long before I was asked to take on the role of treasurer for the club. I had no previous experience of doing the job but took to it like a duck to water. There were no sponsorship deals to be had in those days, or grants from the FA, we had to raise all the funds ourselves. Every week I would collect subs from the girls to enable us to pay for pitches, new kit, referee's, footballs and first aid equipment. For away matches we would travel in a convoy of cars and all contribute towards the petrol. Managing the team during this period was Tom Pilkington, and Frank was still putting us through our paces as our trainer. We were up near the top of the league and doing really well. I was one of seven Dolphins players who were selected for the first stage of England trials in 1973, with Frank being selected to act as coach during the trials.

For a short spell in 1974, I went to play for Preston North End Ladies, who were the team I had first seen training that day on Moor Park. They were one of the top teams in the country at that time. One of the players, Lesley Stirling, had been selected to play on the right wing for England several times. She was a very skilful player with great pace and we had played against each other on numerous occasions in many a hard fought battle. We had been friendly rivals, left back versus right winger, and I always knew I'd been in a game after playing against Lesley. When I signed for PNE, Keith Aspinall said he was really pleased I had joined the club and said I played Lesley better than anybody in the country. Hearing that from someone like him, was a great compliment and confidence boost, a bit of recogniton never goes amiss and I was delighted he believed in my ability. I scored a couple of memorable goals during my time at PNE, one in particular sticks in my mind against Manchester Corinthians, a great left foot volley from a few yards outside the box, straight in the top right hand corner of the net. Sweet as a nut, the keeper had no chance.

There were no career pathway opportunities in women's football in those days and in 1974 I joined the WRAC (Womens Royal Army Corps). I served until 1977 before returning to Preston and eventually moved to a brand new council flat in Ingol, on the outskirts of the town. I had lost touch with friends from my earlier football days, and in 1978 I saw an advert in the paper for players to join Ingol Belles, a local ladies team who played in the second division of the North West Women's League. I went along to meet the manager, Mick Bell, to see about joining and instantly became a regular in the side and Mick soon made me team captain. I mainly played at left back but sometimes played in midfield and scored quite a few goals. A memorable match for me was when we played against Cumberland Rangers on Kingsfold Drive in Penwortham. We weren't playing particularly well and went in all square 1-1 at half time. In the second half, Mick moved me up front and I scored a hat-trick. One of goals was another of those unforgettable ones, a cracker of a shot from well outside the box that hit the back of the net like a bullet. We won the game 5-1.

I was really chuffed when our Pat, Ian and Elaine came to watch me when we were playing away against Barrow White Arrows. It was quite a long run on the coach with sandwiches and a flask required for the journey home. Ian would sometimes come training with me on the fields at the end of Cadley Causeway, and occasionally at Penwortham Holme, I loved that he wanted to play footy with his Auntie Gail. We would also go on the North End with Pat and my Dad. Special memories.

Pat, Elaine, Ian

At the end of the 1978/79 season, Mick arranged for our presentation evening to be held at Maudland Labour Club on Maudland Bank, and he invited Preston North End star player, Michael Robinson, to come and present the awards. It was great to have a player of his calibre come to an awards night for a small club like Ingol Belles, and he was very apologetic about not being able to stay too long as he was on his way to sign for Manchester City. Imagine that, about to sign the biggest deal of his life, but still made time to come to present the awards for us, for no fee, just because; and I won an award for Goal of the Season, presented to me by Michael Robinson. What a lovely man. I'm pretty sure that kind of thing wouldn't happen today, certainly in men's football, and sadly now in women's football too.

Ingol Belles end of Season Presentation Night with Michael Robinson

Back row: Lynne Singleton, Alison Reid, Caroline Wilkinson, Brendan Hobin, Alison Gahan, Diane Lawrenson, Helen Coulthard, Lynn Cureden, Mick Bell, Janet Wilkinson, Kath Bell, Debbie Blackshaw, Bob Cavies.
Front row: Dawn Clayton, Julie Fallon, Loretta Bell, Andrea Trigg, Michael Robinson, Janet Wallbank, Me, Louise Cavies, Karen Titley

It wasn't long before I was asked to take on the role of treasurer and got into organising mode straight away. In 1979 we had a trip to Wimbledon which was a great weekend for us all. Not long after, I saw an advert for teams to enter a women's football tournament in Holland and thought it might be a good experience for us to take part. We all worked hard raising funds for the trip and went to play in The Hague in 1980. We were based in Sheveningan, and played against teams from Belgium, Germany, France and two English teams, Friends of Fulham and Tiverton Town. It was a big thing in those days for a small club like Ingol Belles to be travelling abroad to play football, and Mick and I were interviewd on BBC Radio Lancashire before we left. The oppositon was pretty tough but we had a great weekend and came home with a trophy for the Most Sporting Team. Our Pat, Ian and Elaine came with us and it was great to have them along to watch us play. We had an embarassing moment one evening when out for something to eat, mistaking some savoury pancakes for sweet ones. We often went to the Pancake House at home for sweet pancakes, they were all the rave in the early 80s, and that's what we assumed these were on the menu. The restaurant thought we were a bit strange asking for fresh whipped cream to accompany ours and were giving us very funny looks, but our Pat assured them we had them all the time in England. We realised our error as soon as we cut into them and felt really stupid. Trying to explain our reasoning when you don't speak the language was hilarious.

Ingol Belles in Holland 1980

Back row: Brendan Hobin, Diane Lawrenson, Alison Gahan, Lynne Singleton, Diane, Alison Reid, Sharon Livesey, Mick Bell
Front row: Me, Debbie Blackshaw, Michelle Parkinson, Louise Cavies, Julie Fallon, Andrea Trigg, Caroline Crewdson

I was asked to return to Preston Rangers later in 1980. I was sorry to leave Ingol Belles, I had a great time playing with them, but I wanted to rekindle old friendships with Rangers and play for a team in a higher division. I soon resumed the role of treasurer and many fund raising events were to follow, from fancy dress treasure hunts, jumble sales, selling football cards, pontoon tickets and any other conceivable means of raising money, and we soon had a very healthy bank balance. I also organised for the team to play in the same tournament in Holland in 1981. We faired better than the previous year with Ingol Belles losing only two of the nine games we played. I was injured with a really bad 'dead leg', and missed some of the games on the second day. Bucks Fizz won the Eurovision that year, and '*Making your Mind Up*,' was being played everywhere. In 1981 I was elected on to the Management Committe of the North West Women's Football League as Disciplinary Chairman, a post which I occupied until 1987. The League was self funded and self administered and we all worked hard to keep things running. As Disciplinary Chairman I was responsible for dealing with all on and off the field offences, non fulfilment of fixture and administering fines to individuals and all member clubs. I was also responsible for convening and chairing disciplinary hearings when required. I look back on those days knowing that I was always firm, but fair, no preferential treatment, or a blind eye afforded to anyone. I remember once playing away in the WFA Cup and the manager was considering playing an unregistered player. I couldn't allow us to break the rules and have an unfair advantage, but the manager said, '*no one will know*'. I replied, '*but I will*.' The player didn't take any part in the game.

We had a new team manager at Preston Rangers for the 1981-82 season in local footballer Jim Clitheroe. He transformed the team from being a good side, into a very good side, with a strong emphasis on fitness. At the end of the season I was absolutely delighted to be awarded Managers Player of the Year, especially as we had two former England Internationals, Sheree Jameson, and Sandra Graham, in the team, I was very proud.

Recovering from a training session on Lytham Sand Dunes

Lytham Sand Dunes whatever the weather

Under Jim's management we reached the semi finals of the Women's FA Cup in 1983. In the last sixteen, we beat local rivals Preston North End with a convining 5-1 scoreline. It was a great result for us and showed how much we had improved. We had never beaten them before and this set us up well for our home tie with Howbury Grange in the quarter final. They were a team made up of England Internationals with Debbie Bampton and Terri Wiseman among those in their ranks. Before the game, they were all strutting around in their England tracksuit tops and we thought they didn't give us a hope in hell. But never underestimate the underdog. We scored first with a great goal from Oonagh Matthews, but just before half time, Debbie Bampton headed home a good goal from a right wing corner. They took the lead in the second half when Debbie Fox found the top left hand corner of the net with a good shot from outside the penalty area. We were pressing for an equaliser and in injury time, we managed to keep ourselves in the game by the skin of our teeth when Michelle Smith hammered the ball past England goalkeeper Terri Wiseman. We were absolutely ecstatic, and we all ran and mobbed Michelle, who could be found at the bottom of a huge pile of very happy sweaty boddies. The winner was scored in the first period of extra time when Louise Coleman, drew out Terri Wiseman in goal, and coolly kicked the ball into an empty net. We played out of our skin to beat them by 3-2 in a thrilling quarter final match. It was a superb victory for

205

us and lives long in the memory that's for sure. After such a great performance, we were bitterly disappointed to lose to St Helens in the semi final by 5-1. We were beaten by the better team on the day, the conditions were awful and we never really got going, but had some compensation in our next match when we held them to a 2-2 draw and then went on to beat them 4-1 the following season.

That winning feeling during our cup run

We played in the Emgals Women's Football Tournament in 1983. It was a well established annual competition played in Leicester, and it attracted many of the top teams in England, as well as clubs from abroad. It was great to finally have the opportunity to take part in such a strong event and we were drawn against Rowntrees, Howbury Grange, Emgals A, and Maarssen A, from the Netherlands. Travelling with us was our previous manager, and former assistant manger of Preston North End Women, Tom Pilkington. His daugher Sally, who began her career at PNE, was our goalkeeper, and he came to watch us on a regualr basis. Tom had been watching all our matches that day and during a break in the afternoon, we were chatting about how we were fairing. He said he thought I was the best left back in the country. I was really chuffed he thought so highly of my ability. It was a wonderful compliment, and one I have never forgotten. At the end of the season, I was presented with the Club Award.

We were drawn away against Brighton in the last sixteen of the Women's FA Cup in 1984. It was a great weekend by the seaside and we won the game 3-1. I almost made it 4-1 hitting the crossbar with a thumping volley in the

206

closing minutes of the match. In the next round we were drawn away again for the quarter finals, and travelled down to the south coast once more, to play Southampton. They had previously won the cup eight times and we knew we were in for a hell of a game. I was marking Eileen Foreman, the then England centre forward, and I played the game of my life. Wherever she went, I followed and I ran myself ragged. So much so, in the second half I went down with severe cramp in both my calves, and needed help from the touchline. We lost 2-0 but I won an award for the Best Individual Performance of the Season for my efforts that day, another game I will never forget.

Preston Rangers at Brighton 1984

Back row: Louise Coleman, Sally Pilkington, Janis Bremers, Chris Shepherd, Sandra Graham, Jayne Mottram, Oonagh Matthews.
Front row: Me, Sheree Jameson, Alison Farnworth, Wendy Skerritt, Julie Hindle, Michelle Haylett

We won League and Cup double in the 1983-84 season, pipping St Helens to both titles. Interviewed in the press before the cup final, Sheree Jameson said, *'our back four have not conceded a goal in the previous eight or nine games, and we are looking to this department to lay the foundation for victory.'* We took the lead in the first half with a well taken goal from Lynn Arstall. In the 13th minute of the second half, St Helens were awarded a penalty. Liz Deighan took the spot kick and hit the ball to the left of our goalkeeper, Sally Pilkington. Sally made a brilliant save, getting her hand to the ball and turning it past the post. St Helens kept up the pressure and were pushing for an equaliser and I made a last ditch goal line clearance to keep us in the lead. We ran out the winners by 1-0.

Preston Rangers League and Cup Double winners 1983-84

Back Row: Shona ?, Bev Hills, Chris Shepherd, Sally Pilkington, Louise Coleman, Oonagh Matthews, Sheree Jameson, Lynn Hatton, Carol Carr, Carol Cadwallader, Janis Bremers, Tina Clitheroe
Front row: Jim Clitheroe, Julie Hindle, Sandra Graham, Me, Lynn Arstall, Wendy Skerritt, Alison Farnworth, Jayne Mottram

In September of 1984 we played in the Reckitts Arco Cup 7-a-side tournament in Hull. We played really well, coming runners up in our group, just one point behind Rowntrees, to reach the semi final. We lost 2-1 to Doncaster Belles who went on to beat Rowntrees in the final 6-5 on penalties after a 1-1 draw. It was a great day, but the pitches were very hard. I took the skin off my left thigh several times on the same spot, when sliding in to make a tackle. It was a bit of a mess and I had to sleep with my leg out of the bed due to the wound literally dripping with puss. I had a desk job at work, which involved sitting down all day processing customer orders on a VDU screen. My leg was too sore to sit at my desk and I had to ask to do a walking around job for a few days until it scabbed over. I don't think they were too happy, but at least I hadn't gone off sick.

Arco Cup 1984- Sandra Graham, Sheree Jameson, Louise Coleman, me

We were League Champions again in 1984-85 and runners up in the League Cup, although I wasn't there at the end of the season to receive my trophies. With enormous sadness, I had to leave Preston Rangers in 1985 after a dispute with the team manager about the clubs finances. I was in the process of organising a trip to Germany for us to play in a football tournament. I had been looking into the travel arrangements and knew we needed to do a lot of fund raising to cover the cost of the trip. However, the manager decided the club should pay for the coach travel, which was not far short of everything we had in the bank. There was no discussion, he just decided this is what would happen. There would have been practically nothing left for the day to day running of the team. In my opinion as treasurer, it was a huge mistake and certainly not in the best interests of the club. The trip was for an out of season summer tournament, a holiday, and it wasn't what the funds were intended for. I simply couldn't agree to spending almost all our hard earned money on a whim. I felt he was undermining my position as treasurer, and chief fundraiser, and I was left with no alternative but to resign. I hoped for some support from the girls, but they stood with the manager and went to play in the tournament in Germany. It was the hardest decision I have ever made. Football was my life, Preston Rangers were my life. I was absolutely devasted and totally broken, it felt as though someone had died. Perhaps part of me had. I couldn't go to work for the next few days because I couldn't stop crying. I'd heard about some of the things that were said at their meeting, and I was shattered. It was hard to accept how no one spoke up for me after all the work I had done fundraising for the team. I put my heart and soul into Preston Rangers and now it was over, just like that. Not long after, there was an England Women's match being played at Deepdale and I went along to watch the game. When we were leaving the ground, we saw some of Preston Rangers walking in our direction and they blanked us without a word. We trained twice a week together, played football on a Sunday together, socialised together. What on earth was I going to do without football? I joined Vernon Carus, for a short while, to try to fill the void but my heart simply wasn't in it. In truth my heart was broken, so I hung up my boots and I had no desire to play anymore.

But, life has taught me everything happens for a reason, and only a year later, in 1986 I was responsible for setting up The Lancashire Trophy, a two day residential International Women's Soccer Tournament. It was a huge task to get it off the ground, but all our hard work paid off. As well as putting together the format for the football weekend, accommodation for the travelling teams had to be arranged, coach transfer for those arriving at airports, all the entertainment for the players, First Aid cover for their welfare, any sponsorship we could beg, and also send out press releases. And all this before the internet and mobile phones. We sent out hundreds and hundreds of invitations by post all over the country, and to as many continental teams we could reach. There was just a small team of us and we created something really special. The first event was held at Edge Hill College in Ormskirk and along with the North West entries, we had teams travelling from Sweden, Republic of Ireland, and Scotland. It was a great success and it gave local clubs the opportunity to play against teams from other countries for the very first time. Geraldine Rees, the first lady jockey to complete the Grand National Racecourse, came to present the awards to the winning teams. The event was a huge success and we were already making plans for it to continue.

I was elected as Chairman of the North West League during 1987, and also spent a short time coaching Penwortham Girls High School, who took part in the Lancashire Schoolgirls Cup competition during its early years. I didn't have an official coaching badge, I was just helping out with the team for a short while sharing some of my experience. It was very rewarding watching the girls do on the pitch something you had tried to teach them in training.

Penwortham Girls High School football team 1987

In 1988 I was contacted by a couple of the girls from Preston Rangers who wanted to apologise for how I was treated when I left the team, and asked if I would consider returning to the club. The manager had moved on and there wasn't much left in the bank. They said I was the best treasurer they ever had and were very sorry for what happened. I didn't really know what to do because it didn't feel the same anymore. It was good of them to apologise, and I was genuinely thankful for everything they said, things like that are never easy, but after all the hurt, I wasn't sure what to do. People often say you should never go back, and I was in a quandary. I thought about it for a while, I didn't want to have any regrets and be left wondering 'what if', so I agreed to return. They desperatley needed a new ground to play on so I spoke to some contacts and got them a pitch at BTR Sports Ground in Leyland. It was quite a good move as the ground had a club house with a bar, so the opportunity was there to make a real go of it. I hadn't played football for over three years, so it was going to be hard to get fit again and see what I could do. I was older now, I was thirty five and I didn't want to play until I felt ready, but I was more that happy to resume the treasurer role and help get some money back in the funds.

Preston Rangers at BTR Sports Ground 1988 – me far right

I worked hard in training to get fit again, but I have to be honest and say I could never quite recapture my best form. I think I was pretty much at my peak in the early 1980s and was confident in my own ability, I was pretty quick over short distances and I always felt the right winger would have to be good to get past me. Maybe I was expecting too much of myself after not playing for several years, not to mention getting a bit older too, but I felt like I had lost something. I don't know if it was just being older, or a loss of confidence, or a hangover from what had happened, but it took a while to get back in the swing. But I did manage to play again, and I was chuffed. Even if I wasn't as good as before, I was enjoying being back, and at the end of the season, I was presented with the Club Award by team manager, Mick Livesey.

Keeping watch at the back post v Rainworth Miners (Nottingham) WFA Cup 1988

On the ball v Leasowe at BTR 1989

In 1988-1989 I returned to the Disciplinary Chair and also acted as League Rep, which involved attending WFA meetings in London and Birmingham during those years. I was present at the inaugural meeting when the WFA became a Limited Company. For the 1989-1990 season I took on the role as Development Officer on the League Management Committee and finally returned to the Disciplinary Chair again in 1990 and 1991. During this time I was still involved with organising the Lancashire Trophy which was growing in stature and at the height of its success was regarded among the best organised in Europe. There had been nothing like it before and perhaps there won't be anything like it again. I think what made it so special was it wasn't run for profit, everything went back in to making it better every year. It was all about promoting women's football and having a great weekend in the process.

We had more success in the WFA Cup in 1990, beating Ipswich Town 2-1 in the quarter finals at Springfield Park, Wigan, with Channel 4 in attendance to record the proceedings. I was on the bench for this game but it was exciting to sit and watch. Ipswich were a strong team with Linda Curl and Jackie Slack among their ranks. We took the lead five minutes before the end of the first half when Debbie Anyon hit a blistering 25-yard shot past the Ipswich keeper. Karen Masheter had received a kick in her back during one tackle and was taken to hospital at half time. X-rays later revealed she had two cracked ribs. We extended our lead to 2-0 in the 80th minute when Debbie got her second goal with a well taken free kick from just outside the box. Ipswich pulled one back when Jackie Slack scored from 20-yards out and they were pressing hard for an equaliser.

With only a few minutes remaining, Linda Curl found herself unmarked in the box, and it looked like she was going to score, but Sally Pilkington bravely dived at her feet keeping the score at 2-1. It was a great result and the champagne corks were popping loudly in the dressing room afterwards.

The semi finals were staged at Millwall FC, at the Old Den, and once again, Channel 4 were on hand to record the game. Our manager, Mick Livesey was unable to travel with us due to his wife, and our star striker, Sheree (nee Jameson) being about to give birth to their first child. We were playing against Friends of Fulham and I was selected to play in the second WFA Cup semi final of my football career. We were definitely the underdogs against a much more expereinced team with several England internationals in their line up. We lost 3-0 to the better side, but gave a good account of ourselves with Louise Cafferkey testing goalkeeper Terri Wiseman with a long range shot early in the game, and Sally Pilkington making a brilliant finger tip save at the other end. England international Brenda Sempare for Fulham, scored a peach of a goal to add to her sides scoreline and Marieanne Spacey played a good powerful game contributing to their well earned victory.

Womens FA Cup semi final v Friends of Fulham 1990

214

Me and Brenda Sempare after the game

It was during this second spell with the team I was given a special award at the end of season presentation night. It was a lovely pewter plate engraved with the words, '*Gail Newsham – For your loyalty to Preston Rangers.*' It was a lovely gesture and meant a great deal to me, perhaps a bit of closure, and definitely something to treasure.

In 1992, I organised the first ever reunion of the Dick, Kerr Ladies football team which took place at the Preston Guild Lancashire Trophy held at Myerscough College. It was through meeting these amazing women, I realised that something needed to be done to preserve their history and had the idea of writing a book about them. There was very little known about them at the time, and if something hadn't been done then, their story could have been lost forever. As a result of organising their reunion, and for my efforts of promoting women's football, I was nominated for the Lancashire Woman of the Year Award, held at the Gibbon Bridge in Chipping in October 1992. I was one of only 100 women selected to attend. I didn't win, but it was a huge honour to be nominated and a wonderful experience being part of such a special occasion and mixing with so many inspirational women.

Due to a change in my personal circumstances, I reluctantly left Preston Rangers in 1993 after going to live in Blackpool, and the less said about that the better but I am happy to say I left the club with a healthier bank balance than when I returned. My last position on the Management Committee was as Treasurer in 1992/93. During my time as an officer for the North West Women's Regional Football League I introduced individual awards for players and unsung hero's to recognise their contribution to their team and to the game. I was given a special award by the League for my services to women's football in 1992-93.

Circa 1993/4, the Lancashire FA were advertising a vacancy at their head-quarters in Blackburn, for someone to deal with disciplinary offences relating to affiliated teams under their jurisdiction. In contrast to local league men's foot-ball, whose disciplinary offences were sent direct to the Lancs FA, any and all women's football offences were dealt with in house by our own leagues, and we administered all these matters ourselves. We followed the same rule book so all the procedures were exactly the same. I thought I might be a suitable candidate for the job given the number of years' experience I had as Disciplinary Chairman of the North West Women's Regional Football League, and I duly sent in an application to be considered for the post. I was given an interview, but wasn't successful. Unsurprisingly, the job was given to a male applicant.

I was unable to get the Lancashire Trophy up and running again in 1993, but 1994 saw a welcome return. In that year, local women's football historian Rod Prescott conducted a survey and produced a programme of summer tournaments staged throughout the North West. The Lancashire Trophy, Leyland Festival, North Wales Soccer Sixes, Brinscall & Withnell 5-a-side Tournament, Greater Manchester Youth Games, Padgate Premier UK 7-a-side Competition, Moss Farm Tournament and Vernons 7's. The Lancashire Trophy came out on top with a score of ten out of ten. Rod said, *"The organisation was superb. This tournament has everything. As tournaments go, this is the highlight of the Summer for women's football followers in the North West!*

Lancashire Trophy central control 1994. Seated: me, Brenda Eastwood, Nancy Thomson

After two years of extensive research, my book, *In a League of Their Own*, charting the history of the Dick, Kerr Ladies, was published in November of 1994. I was very proud of the achievement of revealing their incredible success story for the very first time, and it gave women's football a real sense of it's own history when it didn't really know it had one. I was also extremely proud that Preston's favourite son, Tom Finney, agreed to write the foreword for me. Since the books publication, I have been asked to take part in many radio interviews, and numerous television appearances in documentaries and general interest programmes, with many well known presenters and broadcasters including: Gabby Logan, Clare Balding, Gloria Hunniford, Michael Portillo, Amanda Vickery and Christina Trevanion from Antiques Road Trip.

Book Launch 1994

After the loss of my precious little Mum in early 1998, I found it a struggle dealing with things for a while, and the Lancashire Trophy didn't take place for a couple of years. But for the new century in 2000, we all got together for one last time to celebrate this wonderful event. The theme for the whole weekend since its inception in 1986 was Football, Friendship and Fun. Teams would arrive on a Friday, and after their long journey, we welcomed them with a barbeque, followed by a karaoke disco, which always proved to be very popular. Football was played all day Saturday and Sunday and the winners received their trophies at a gala presentation evening when they were entertained with a star cabaret and disco.

During the lifetime of The Lancashire Trophy teams from Austria, Switzerland, Germany, Sweden, Eire, Scotland, and all parts England, competed to be winners of this very special tournament. The competition was also staged at Myerscough College and laterly, Fleetwood Nautical College. Wyre Borough Council were very good to us over the years, and funded all the hospitality for dignitaries and guests, helped with the programme costs and generally supported us very well. Many well known players also took part in the tournament and here are just a few familiar names from over the years: Sue Buckett, Pat Chapman, Sue Law, Hope Powell, Karen Burke, Laura Montgomery, Kerry Davis, Angela Gallimore, Liz Deighan, Maria Harper, Alison Leatherbarrow, and Sheila Parker both as a player and a referee.

Lancashire Trophy referees – Vanessa Mcleod and Sheila Parker front right

I always tried to get a female sports personality, or female celebrity, to come and present the awards, and over the years we were fortunate and honoured to have guest appearances from Geraldine Rees, the first female jockey to complete the Grand National racecourse on her horse 'Cheers'; Shirley Strong, the toast of British women's athletics when she won a silver medal in the 100 metre hurdles at the 1984 Olympic Games in Los Angeles. Sheila Ferguson, former lead singer with The Three Degrees, who entertained us with her superb talent on four occasions. Top class comedienne Mia Carla who was always a big favourite with the audience and Rita Tushingham, the BAFTA and Golden Globe award winning British actress who presented the awards to the winning teams at the very last event in 2000.

Rita Tushingham and me

It was a fabulous weekend with a wonderful atmosphere which captured the true spirit of what this very special tournament had come to represent. Winning it was a bonus, being part of it was what really mattered. To this day I am incredibly proud of what was achieved at The Lancashire Trophy and the warmth in which it is still remembered. We received so many wonderful thank you letters and cards over the years, many of which have been preserved for posterity in my scrapbooks. One letter I have always been particulary proud of was from Martin Reagan. He had been manager of England Women's football team and he came to the tournament when we were at Myerscough College. This is what he said:

Dear Gail,

A brief note to thank you for your courtesy, kindness, and hospitality during my visit to your tournament. I know you had so much to do and many matters to attend to, and your attention was greatly appreciated.

The surroundings and the atmosphere of your tournament were excellent and you deserved to succeed. Football played in those conditions, and in that way, is a great credit to the game, and is an example for others to follow. You brought a lot of pleasure to a great number of people over the weekend and I hope that you think that all your efforts were worth while. It was a great pleasure to meet up with you again and to renew friendships with others.

Kind regards,
Yours sincerely,
Martin Reagan

Martin had soldiered with my Dad for a time in WW2 and he was heavily involved in raising funds for a memorial for twenty seven members of 284 Armoured Assault Squadron, Royal Engineers, and ten Canadian soldiers, all of whom died in Holland in 1944. He was keen to speak to my Dad about this and I put them in touch again. Martin was impressed with my Dads memory about these matters and they kept in touch for some time. My Dad served in the Royal Engineers, and he was always very interested and well versed in the history of both World Wars.

In 2002, the National Football Museum was hosting its inaugural Hall of Fame event and I was asked to nominate a female player. The museum was based in Preston in those days and I worked closely with them when they were initially setting up some of the artifacts on display, and I was a regular visitor when they needed help identifying objects relating to the Dick, Kerr Ladies. Given what I knew at the time, I suggested Lily Parr as a worthy candidate and they accepted my nomination. She was the only female inductee. I was invited to the first two presentation dinners at the Hall of Fame awards ceremonies and again in 2007 when they accepted my nominaton of Joan Whalley as an inductee. I was thrilled to meet so many of my football heros at these events, too many to name all of them, but a few notable legends were: Bobby Charlton, Nobby Stiles, Gordon Banks, Alan Ball, Peter Shilton, Pat Jennings, Kenny Dalglish, Dennis Law, Glenn Hoddle, Graeme Souness, Nat Lofthouse, John Charles, Tommy Docherty and Alex Ferguson.

It would be seventeen years since the final Lancashire Trophy in 2000, before

I would be involved in organsing another women's football tournament. During the the years that followed, I had been asked to take part in many television and radio programmes to share my knowledge of the Dick, Kerr Ladies. Film crews came to my home, or I travelled to meet them at various locations. In 2015, I was asked to take part in 'Antiques Road Trip' and the programme was seen by some members of staff at the University of Central Lancashire. They were captivated by the story and wondered why they had never heard of the team before.

Me and Christina Trevanion – Antiques Road Trip

To cut a long story short, we ended up having a wonderful year of celebration in 2017 for the Centenary of the formation of the Dick, Kerr Ladies. The university put on an academic conference, which I opened with my talk about the Dick, Kerr Ladies, and Alison Hitchen and myself, organised a Centenary Dinner and a National Women's Walking Football Tournament, the Dick, Kerr Ladies Cup. Ali came along at exactly the right time and her support over the years has been invaluable. The walking football tournament was the first ever national event of it's kind and has proved incredibly popular since its inception. Aimed at women in the over 40s and over 50s age groups, it has given the opportunity for those who have never played football before to finally get the chance to play, and for those who thought their playing days were over, a new lease of life, as they took up the game again. After not having kicked a ball in well over twenty five years, I even played in it myself. The winners of the over 50s were my old team Preston

Rangers. I would have loved to have played with them again but I was already commited to playing with a team of WRAC Veterans. It was a wonderful day of walking football enjoyed by all who took part. I am very proud to say, it is due to our initiative, that many other organisations have now set up more women's walking football events, and the sport continues to grow at a rapid pace.

Also in this centenary year, the first Blue Plaque in the world for women's football, was unveiled at the factory on Strand Road in Preston, to mark where the team was formed during the First World War. The original building was then occupied by Alstom, and I wrote to the Managing Director of the company to seek permission to have the plaque put on the wall. I had some funding available for the project and worked closely with Preston Historical Society to get the plaque made and installed. Later in the year, after a lot of hard work and support from a small team of volunteers and generous sponsors, my dream came true when a wonderful memorial tribute was unveiled at Preston North End, to commemorate their first ever match played there on Christmas Day 1917. It is all documented in much greater detail in my book, *In a League of Their Own!*

Alison Hitchen and me

Me, Ali and Seb Salisbury

Later in the year, Ali and I were invited to the FA Women's Football Awards at the Grosvenor House Hotel in London. We thought it was a reciprocal invitation after the FA had a table at our centenary dinner. It was a wonderful opportunity to meet some of the Lionesses after their semi final apparance at the UEFA Women's European Cup in the summer. We sat watching the night unfold as all the recipients received their awards, when suddenly a picture of the Dick, Kerr Ladies came up on the screen and we were presented with an award for the Dick, Kerr Ladies contribution to football. What a wonderful surprise.

Me, Ali, Rachel Brown Finnis

The walking football tournament was initially meant to be a one off as part of the centenary year, but as it proved to be so successful, Alison Hitchen, myself, and Lenore McNulty, set up the Dick, Kerr Ladies Foundation, and continued to orgainise the event, with the help and support of UCLan Sports Arena. Now regarded as the FA Cup of Women's Walking Football, we are all very proud of what we have achieved. Another legacy created. Also in 2017, Lambent Productions produced a documentary, *When Football Banned Women*, presented by Clare Balding. I spent a few days filming with Clare, at my home, at the original factory where the team was formed, and at Preston North End. It was very well received.

Me, Lenore, Clare Balding

In 2018, the Dick, Kerr Ladies were recognised by the Royal British Legion for their efforts during WW1, as part of their Ribbon Campaign to commemorate the centenary anniversary of the end of the War. And they were also given a special recognition award at the North West Football Awards, where they were described as probably the most important team in the history of women's football. I couldn't have been more proud.

NWFA Awards

During the lockdown period of 2020 and beyond, with a lot of spare time on my hands I decided to use some of it going through all the information I had accumulated about the Dick, Kerr Ladies over the last three decades. I knew there were some gaps in the story and felt it was important to try to uncover more details relating to the years after the ban. Having lived with these women for such a long time, and now with a much better understanding of their lives and personal history timeline, I wanted to leave as complete a record as I possibly could. I listened to all the recordings of the interviews I had with the ladies to see if there was anything I may have missed, and in revisiting their stories, some of the things they told me, now made more sense. There were new revelations needing to be shared and this led me to publish a revised edition of my book in 2021, and a hardback version in 2022. I think this now clears up some misunderstandings, and leaves a more accurate account. It really is a great story, and if you're interested in finding out all about them, at this time of writing, the book is still available with online outlets.

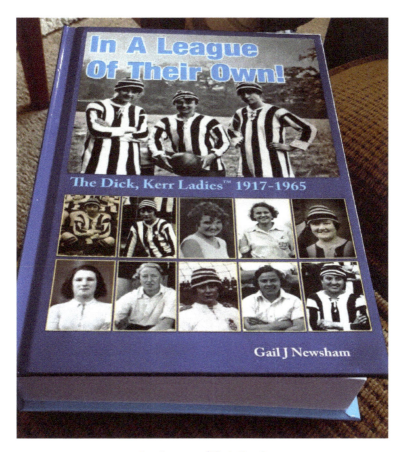

In a League of Their Own!

I was approached by Jenny Reeves from *About Time Dance Company*, exploring the possibility of putting on a dance routine based on the Dick, Kerr Ladies, and she asked for my support in helping the dancers with the story line and the real characters in the team. I was happy to work with them, but having no idea at all about interpreting dance as an art form, I wasn't convinced a dance routine could depict a women's football team. I had watched *Strictly Come Dancing* on the tele, but that was about it for my knowledge of dance. This was a completely new concept for the DKL story. The rehearsals were taking place at the Media Factory within the UCLan campus, and I went along several times to share my knowledge of the women they were portraying and the historical content of the timeline involved. It was good to have the opportunity to share the true facts about the team especially with all the misinformation on platforms like Wikipedia et cetera. They were putting on a preview of the routine on Ashton Park, on the very spot where the Dick, Kerr Ladies used to play, and Jenny invited me along to the performance. I have to say, I was totally blown away by their portrayal of these women who I had come to know and love so well over the years. It was incredibly moving and the superb choice of music added to all the drama and emotion. They were absolutely incredible and I was so proud for the Dick, Kerr Ladies to be remembered in this way on the very pitch they used to play on.

About Time Dance Company

Me with the girls, Jenny Reeves far right 2021

We had planned a Greatest Game Centenary Dinner in 2020 to commemorate the famous match played at Goodison Park, on Boxing Day 1920, when 53,000 spectators came to watch the Dick, Kerr Ladies play St Helens Ladies. Sadly, it had to be postponed due to the government policy of lockdown, and the opportunity was lost. However, we did manage to celebrate another centenary milestone in December 2021, to mark one hundred years since the FA ban on women's football, and also staged a first of its kind, Women's Football Grand Reunion. We brought together players from the first recognised England match in 1972, and from every generation of the game. People travelled from Scotland, Cornwall, and everywhere in between, to meet up with friends they hadn't seen in over forty years. It was an incredible night, topped off with a special performance from *About Time Dance Company* with their Dick, Kerr Ladies routine. It went down a treat.

I had approached Preston City Council, through Steve Daley MBE, about the possibility of having a plaque placed on Ashton Park in Preston, to commemorate the centenary of where the Dick, Kerr Ladies had played their first match after the ban, on an area known then as Lively Polly Corner. Everyone involved was very supportive and I was extremely proud to unveil the plaque with the Mayor of Preston in December 2021.

Ashton Park Plaque

During the Euro Women's Championships in 2022, I was invited by Copa90, to present the Player of the Match award at the France v Italy game at the New York Stadium in Rotherham. France were convincing winners by 5-1 with Grace Geyoro scoring a hat-trick and being voted player of the match. It was a great thrill to go on the pitch to present her with the award, although I'm sure she didn't have a clue who I was.

Grace Geyoro and me

The Women's Euro's broke all previous records for attendances at stadiums and viewing figures for television audiences. Right from the start, I had a gut feeling the Lionesses were going to lift the trophy, and nothing could persuade me otherwise. I truly believed the script for this moment had been written as far back as 1921, the day after the FA ban on women playing football. And sure enough, like any good script, and echoes of 1966, the Lionesses walked out at Wembley, against their old rivals, Germany. Gabby Logan was pitch side to give her pre match build up to the game, saying Germany had never lost in a final, and I thought, *well, they are going to today Gabby*. The stadium was packed to the rafters and the dream came true. The Lionesses became European Champions and women's football was back where the Dick, Kerr Ladies had left it in the 1920s. I couldn't have been more chuffed if I'd scored the winner myself.

We staged another successful Dick, Kerr Ladies Cup in 2023 but decided this would be our last event as organisers. We passed on the baton to Shiva

Omidvar-Christian at UCLan Sports Arena, where the competition has been staged since its inception. I hope new blood in the engine room will see the competition reach new heights, and with a fresh approach and new ideas, the legacy we created will continue from 2024 and beyond.

The Dick, Kerr Ladies Cup 2023 © John Shirras

Having celebrated all the centenaries attributed to the Dick, Kerr Ladies, I also decided it was now time to hang up my organising boots all together. This year marks the 30th anniversary of the publication of my book, '*In a League of Their Own*', and up until that point in 1994, many people were previously unaware of the team, or of their success. I am very proud to say they are now recognised as probably the most important team in the history of women's football. To mark the books 30th anniversary milestone, Alison, Lenore and I, organised a Legends Dinner at Preston North End on 15 June 2024, and invited Legends of the women's game to come along and celebrate with us for one last time. We have accomplished great things since the centenary year, and Alison came along just at the right time to help me achieve some of my DKL dreams. We managed a few quiet moments before everyone arrived, to take a deep breath and soak up the atmosphere. Something magical happens whenever the Dick, Kerr Ladies are in town, the room is always full of love as they sprinkle their magic dust from up there in DK heaven, and tonight was no exception. Everything came together perfectly, like it was all just meant to be.

Me and Ali

The FA came on board as our Gold Sponsor, just as they did for our first Centenary Dinner. They have always been very supportive of me personally, especially Rachel Pavlou, and Baroness Sue Campbell, when she was Head of Women's Football, and I will be forever grateful to them for all of their help over the years. I tentatively asked if it would be possible to have the Women's Euro Trophy on display during the evening and I was completely blown away when they arranged for it to happen. It was a definite crowd pleaser and everyone loved the excitement of having their photo taken with that magnificent piece of silverware that gave us all so much joy during that wonderful summer of football in 2022, when the Lionesses became Champions of Europe. I felt just like the little girl caught on camera at Wembley in the after match celebrations, who could be seen among the jubilant crowd singing her heart out to *Sweet Caroline*. So good, so good, so good!

It was also a great honour to share the evening with some of women's football's finest: Former players of the Dick, Kerr Ladies, June Gregson, who at ninety years of age, is probably the oldest surviving DK player, and the only one present who was with me at the first reunion back in 1992; plus Freda Garth, Lorraine McKenna and Anne Lymath, who all played in the late 1950s early

1960s. Pat Gregory MBE and June Jaycocks, who were paramount in the growth of the game during their time at the Women's Football Association; Wendy Owen, Pat Firth, Carol Thomas BEM, Kerry Davis, Rachel Brown Finnis, Jody Handley, and Lindsay Johnson who all played in the National team over the years; my former team Preston Rangers, along with Leasowe Pacific, PNE, FC Phoenix, Crawley COGS, and Garstang Lionesses Walking Football Club were also among the guests. Travelling all the way from New York USA, was Marios Christos Sfantos, who was representing Athens Women's Football Summit, and sponsor of our drinks reception, along with well-known podcaster, Ed Bowers. Karen Dobres, co-owner of Lewes FC, also made the long journey up north to be part of this very special night. Appropriately for me, some of the lads I played in the streets with, where my football journey began over sixty years ago, also came along; Clive Wareing, Steve Shaw and John McCann.

Marios Christos Sfantos, me, Karen Dobres

The perfect way to bring the curtain down on this magical and emotional evening, was a stellar performance from the incredibly talented Music Legend, Sheila Ferguson, who has supported us so well over the years. Her daughter, Alexandria Robinson-Lowles, flew in from Dubai especially to be with us to support her Mom.

Lenore, Sheila, me, Alex ©

When Sheila first came to the Lancashire Trophy in 1988, she autographed a programme for me and wrote, '*I won't ever let you down,*' and God Bless her, she never has. My gratitude is immeasurable and I can hardly believe how lucky I am. They say you should never meet your hero's; that you'll be disappointed; well there is always the exception to the rule. It was a huge honour and a great privilege for me to introduce Sheila Ferguson to the audience for one last time, and my heart was full.

Sheila Ferguson and me © Alex Robinson-Lowles

Sheila delivered an absolutely stunning performance, as only she can, and exactly as I knew she would. Her voice is just as amazing, if not better than it ever was. Rich and powerful, mellow and soft, she covered every note in the musical spectrum with effortless ease. All the superlatives have already been used to describe the calibre of Sheila Ferguson, and there is nothing I could add to what has already been said. The proof of the pudding, as they say, could be seen in the true quality of her unrivalled talent. She lifted the roof off the Greats Room at Preston North End, making many more new fans as she touched each and every one of us with her unique presence. Everything about it was simply sensational, but her version of the song *Love Train,* will certainly live long in the memory as everyone joined in and made a love train all around the room. It was absolutely sublime. What a star.

Sheila Ferguson performing the song, Love Train © John Shirras

Kate Ambler, me, Lenore with family and friends, lost in music © John Shirras

My Simple Heart will always love you

We had certainly saved the very best till last. Everyone in the room was touched by the magical spell of the Dick, Kerr Ladies, and the completely incomparable presence of Sheila Ferguson. As my Dad would have said, '*who'd 'ave thowt.*' An international superstar, and a lass from Whittingham Street. What a finale; the perfect way, and the only way for me, to bid farewell to a lifetime love affair with women's football.

That Champion Feeling

I feel so blessed to be in such a privileged position. Being so close to the history of women's football, I feel a special kind of spiritual connection to the Dick, Kerr Ladies having spent more than thirty years getting to know everything about them. There have been so many 'coincidences' along the way with things seamlessly falling into place, it's been uncanny, and they genuinely have become my extended family. Then of course, there is my own football history, beginning in the early 1970s when women's football was just making a comeback and pretty much starting from scratch, and culminating in my love of the game today. It's wonderful to have been around to see the pendulum swing right back the other way.

People sometimes ask me why I played football and where my love for the game came from. The best way I can explain it is to quote Jean Lane who played for the Dick, Kerr Ladies from 1950-1965. Jean was a Lay Preacher, and the three most important things in her life were her family, her faith, and her football. When I organised the reunion of the team in 1992 she was seen on television by some of her friends from the church. They had no idea she had played football and asked her if she would come and give a talk at the church to tell them all about it. Someone asked her a question; *'of all the sports you could have chosen to play, why did you choose football.'* Jean's answer was indeed very profound, but really quite simple, she said, *'I didn't choose football, football chose me,'* and that just about sums it up for me too.

I look back on my life in football with great affection and gratitude, and I like to think I have put in a good shift. During my career, I am proud and privileged to have played on the same pitch as many of our greatest players, too many too numerous to name, but I do want to mention Sylvia Gore MBE. Sylvia was playing for Fodens when I first met her, and we played against each other in some really tough games, and a gang of us would socialise together some weekends. She was the first player to score a goal for England in the first official international match against Scotland in 1972, but more important than that, as I often said to make her smile, she was my friend. I knew her family and met her Mum, and also her cousin Dolly from Ireland, who was involved in an IRA terror attack in the early 1970s, when she lost an eye, and one of her legs in an explosion. Before I joined the Army, Sylvia came over for a farewell meal with some friends at the Bell and Bottle. We lost touch for many years after I joined the Army, but we managed to catch up again at a Liverpool v Everton women's match in the early 2010s. Sylvia was always very supportive of the work I was doing to preserve the history of our game and she invited me and Lenore to some showcase matches where we were sometimes able to meet some of the players afterwards. We also went out for meals together and visited each other's homes. Sylvia had dedicated a great deal of her life to football and won more individual honours than most people I know. I wanted to write her life story and was ready to make a start by recording interviews with her, we talked about it but she said that someone else was supposed to be doing it. I don't know who it was but nothing has materialised thus far. I was devastated when she called to tell me she had been diagnosed with cancer in 2016, I thought she was calling to tell me about some other award she was about to receive. It was so unexpected and her battle was relatively short.

I visited her many times in the hospice to show her my love, support and respect. I know she appreciated it. When I visited her there for the first time she said, '*I knew you would come*.' She passed away on 9 September 2016. She is still loved and very much missed.

Me and Sylvia at MK Dons 2015 – inset 1974

After a lifetime love affair with women's football, I couldn't be more pleased with where the game is today. After all we have been through, it is nothing more than we deserve. All those who came before, and laid the foundations, who fought the battles and have the scars to prove it, can now be proud of the part we have all played in the history of the game. Not just those who played for their country, it's far deeper than that, all those people who ran the clubs and the leagues and worked their socks off simply for the love and belief in the women's game. Now finally getting the media coverage the sport deserves, it has convincingly shown that women's football is a spectator sport. Some attitudes do still need to change, but we will persevere and continue to grow the game. I am very excited about its future development, it is more than I could ever have dreamed of during my playing days, and I am thoroughly enjoying watching the game go from strength to strength. But I have to confess to having some reservations regarding NewCo taking over the Women's Super League and Championship for the 2024 season. They are an independent body established with the sole purpose of overseeing the top two divisions of women's football in England, and to commercialise both competitions, not dis-similar to how the Premier League is managed. Things change when the money men take over and I hope the game doesn't get priced out for the legion of loyal fans who have supported the game and helped grow the fan base for many years. Time will tell. But no matter what, it still fills me with great joy when we celebrate the history of women's football. No other town, or city, or country in the world has the history we have. We should preserve and cherish it always.

NB: Grateful thanks to Mick and Sheree Livesey for some of the Preston Rangers images in this chapter.

THE COST OF SAVING
A LOST HISTORY

I think most people are aware there is a copyright symbol © at the front of every book, and the usual blurb stating all rights reserved; no part of this publication may be reproduced, stored in a retrieval system et cetera, without prior concent. I certainly never gave it a thought that these basic rights wouldn't be observed and respected. To explain a little more, here is some info to digest according to the British Copyright Council: *How original literary works are protected by copyright in the UK. There is no copyright protection for ideas or concepts as such. It is only when those ideas are expressed in a form from which they can be reproduced or copied, i.e., as a literary work, that they are afforded copyright protection. UK copyright protection applies to all original literary works provided that the author is a British Citizen, subject, or resident within another country of the Berne Convention (i.e. most of the world)*

The term literary work means any work, other than a dramatic or musical work, which is written, spoken or sung, and includes tables or compilations, computer programs and databases. "Original" means that the work originates with the author. It is their own creation, not copied, but the result of exercising independent skill, labour and judgement. Copyright may be infringed by using the whole or a substantial part of the work without permission of the copyright owner. Infringing uses include, copying, republication, dramatization, performance in public.

In the spring of 1991, I went to watch a women's football tournament at Bamber Bridge Football Club. Brenda Eastwood was the guest of honour presenting awards to the winning teams. Formerly Brenda Keen, she played football for the Dick, Kerr Ladies, and made her debut in goal in their first game after the Second World War. I think fate definitely played a hand in taking me there that day and I will always be convinced it was more than just a coincidence. As a result of meeting Brenda, I had the idea of organising a reunion of the Dick, Kerr Ladies to meet up at the Lancashire Trophy during Preston Guild year of 1992. What better time to try to stage a reunion of Preston's once world-famous team. An appeal in the local press proved very successful and on Sunday, 2 August 1992, the Dick, Kerr Ladies were reunited at the Preston Guild Lancashire Trophy, for the first time in almost forty years. As a result of the reunion, and speaking with the ladies, it became obvious to me that their story was far bigger than anyone had ever realised and something needed to be done to preserve this incredible piece of women's football history from being lost forever, before it was too late. At that time, a complete record of the Dick, Kerr Ladies history simply did not exist. There was some knowledge of them in their home town of Preston, but no one knew anything about the origins of the team, the extent of their incredible success, who the women were, how long they played, or what they had achieved. Yes, there were the occasional team photographs here and there, and some may have been aware of a big match at Everton, and a trip to America, but there was no official documentation regarding any of these details. I took on this enormous task with much enthusiasm, and over the next two years put my heart and soul into researching their glittering past.

There was no internet in those days, or satellite navigation systems to get you from A to B, I had to rely on the old-fashioned telephone book, searching through hundreds of names and numbers before I found who I was looking for, and my trusty map to guide me all around the North West. I spent countless weekends and hours in the reference library in Preston, searching through the microfiche of all the old newspapers, and I interviewed players, family members and friends of deceased players, and recorded our conversations, getting first-hand accounts directly from them. Being the first female football player to come along and show any interest in these ladies, and their playing days, they were delighted to share their stories with me, and they gave me scrapbooks, photographs, diary records and other historical objects, all of which helped to piece the whole thing together. The team had played all over the UK and beyond, and without all of these documents and information in one place, I very much doubt it would have been possible to compile such a comprehensive record. It was a very proud day when my book, 'In a League of Their Own', an original work documenting the history of the Dick, Kerr Ladies, with a Foreword from Preston's favourite son and football legend, Tom Finney, was published in 1994. It was reported in the press as *'a story that until now, had never been told.'* And being probably the first British female footballer to write a book about the sport I loved, I was absolutely thrilled with how well it was received. I knew it was a great story, and I always believed it would make a great film, if it ever fell on the right desk. But never in a million years did I ever expect what would happen, right from the get go.

My book was published by Pride of Place Publishing, based at Euxton near Chorley. They seemed quite reputable and had some well-known authors on their books, mainly about horse racing, but sport nonetheless. I had no previous experience of writing books and I was so excited when they agreed to publish my work. They were on board with the idea of a book launch and agreed to split the cost of the catering between us. I suggested holding it at the Civic Centre in Leyland where I worked at South Ribble Borough Council, and they agreed. The publisher kept pushing me to invite more and more guests and I kept him informed of all the arrangements and costs, and we catered for 250 guests. I also organised for a disco and comedy duo, to keep everyone entertained, which left the buffet to be taken care of by the publisher, with my share to be deducted from the book sales. Revealing a story that had never been told before, attracted more people who wanted to come than could be safely accommodated, and I met with him at the venue on the afternoon of the launch for him to check all was in order. I introduced him to the Catering and Bars Manager, and during a conversation with him, he asked if there was any chance of some discount from the bill, but he was told it had already been discounted because I was an employee

The book launch took place on 11 November 1994 and it was hugely successful. My Dad, our Pat & Andy, were there to support me, along with many of my friends and work colleagues, the Mayor of South Ribble, Councillor Tom Hanson, and a plethora of guests from my football family. I also invited former Blackpool and England football legend, Jimmy Armfield, top race horse trainer, Jack Berry, Alex Bruce, Steve Elliott, and several other former PNE football stars, to add an extra sporting flavour to the evening, and the television cameras were there to film the highlights. The Dick, Kerr Ladies were back together in force and they loved being the centre of attention once again. A night like this had never happened before, it was completely unprecedented and attracted a great deal of publicity, and was certainly the talk of the building for some considerable time. The publisher said he had never sold as many books before. I'm sure he never expected such a huge response for a women's football team. But even at the outset, he wasn't honouring the terms of our publishing agreement and failed to make royalty payments for book sales at the end of November. The first payment he did make was by cheque on 23 January 1995, but it was returned to me by the bank. I do still have all documentary evidence to substantiate all of these events.

Part of my job at South Ribble Borough Council at that time, was visiting businesses in the area who hadn't paid an invoice for whatever service the council had provided, the department was called Sundry Debtors. Early in 1995, Pride of Place Publishing came up on the Sundry Debtor list for the book launch and a red bill was issued as a reminder. I was asked to speak to them in the course of my duties, which I did. I visited the premises in Euxton, with a copy of the red invoice. The publisher told me he was having cash flow problems and would be in a position to pay the bill during the first week of February. I reported this to the Sundry Debtor department and the information was recorded on computer records. Time went by and I didn't hear any more so I assumed he had paid the outstanding amount to my employer. During this time, I was still having my own problems with Pride of Place Publishing and I had only received £200 from them despite them having sold over one thousand books. It had cost me in excess of that for the disco and entertainment alone, and the bounced cheque still remained unpaid.

As a result of all the publicity surrounding my book, we were contacted by two guys from London who ran a small film production company and were interested in making a film based on my book. They came up to Preston and we had a meeting in February 1995. They said they saw it as the next big thing, bigger than ABBA winning the Eurovision with their song, *Waterloo*. People could immediately see the full potential of this book. It was at this meeting, when the publisher claimed the copyright of my work was with him; but this was not true. The contract clearly stated: *The copyright of the book contents shall remain the property of the Author*. By this stage, I was losing confidence in the integrity of the publisher and getting rather concerned about my legal position, and contacted a solicitor for advice to clarify my situation. She said this; '*although the film company have approached the publishers about making a film of the book, the publishers have no right as the agreement stands at the moment, to give them permission. Any agreement should be between yourself and the film company.*' The solicitor also said: *There are no formalities needed for copyright to exist. Copyright exists in any work which is written, spoken or sung. Copyright can therefore certainly exist in a factual book. Your copyright in the book will be infringed if anyone copies or adapts it without your permission.* Given all this advice, I contacted the film people and asked them to deal with me directly for any future negotiations. The publisher wasn't best pleased I had spoken with a solicitor to affirm my rights, and our relationship was rather strained from then on, but moving forward, I would deal with the film interest. However, it turned out to be a moot point when the production company folded soon after. But it seems clear that the publisher thought there was money to be made from a film of this book.

In June of 1995, an invoice of £1250.00 from South Ribble Borough Council, landed on my doormat. It was the total amount for the book launch and was now in my name, with no covering letter or any explanation. I was in a state of complete shock and panic. How could they do that, how could they send an invoice to me when it had already been issued in the publisher's name, at least twice, without so much as one word of explanation? I tried to speak to the then Director of Finance to see if he could shed some light, but he refused to see me. Why was this nightmare happening? It wasn't my debt, but no one would speak to me. I was distraught.

I contacted my solicitor, but it didn't resolve the matter. The head of the legal department at South Ribble, responded to my solicitor saying, quote; '*your client had obtained a sizeable financial advantage from her employer seemingly without intending to pay for it.'* How could they possibly question my integrity in such a defamatory way when I handled thousands of pounds of cash for the council on a daily basis collecting rents and council tax, without having any deficit in the balance at the end of the day? If I couldn't be trusted, why was I allowed to continue doing the same job? Why wasn't I suspended and put on 'garden leave'? And also, for clarity, the so called sizeable financial advantage he refers to was by no means a discount. The catering manager agreed to provide a smaller buffet at a cost of £5 per head, reducing the amount of food items from the original buffet priced at £6.25 in the official literature. The buffet was still a competitive price reflecting its content, and any profit margin was still in their favour. There was no financial advantage afforded to me, sizeable or otherwise. They were getting a very good deal, and made a 'sizeable' profit having the event staged there.

This had been going on for some time, it was causing me a great deal of stress and anxiety, and I sought help from the union at Unison head office in Manchester. Experience had taught me, an independent view, rather than in house, might be the best way to go, but was told I first had to go through the union rep at South Ribble. I went to see the branch secretary in the hope he would see the injustice of what was happening and be prepared to help me. He seemed sympathetic at first, but I wasn't coping well with all the worry and had to take some time off work. He came to visit me at home and could see how I anxious I had become, and advised me to go and see the doctor. I took his advice and was immediately signed off with work related stress. The doctors' first comment after I explained the cause of my anxiety was, *'it sounds like someone at South Ribble has got it in for you.'* I was off work for at least six weeks.

The branch secretary later told me of the head of Legal having spoken to him quite forcefully in the office, warning him not to get involved, and saying in a raised voice, within earshot of other staff members, *'it was clear she had organised the event without intending to pay.'* I was also told by the Director of Leisure Services, of the publisher having written to the council stating that as they had nothing in writing from him, he was denying all responsibility for the costs; without having any regard or concern for any repercussions this would have for me. The council were obviously aware they didn't have a leg to stand on because they hadn't provided a booking form, so they decided to make me their target.

In August, I was interviewed by the head of Personnel, presumably to ramp up the pressure. During the grilling, she informed me the head of Legal had told her, *'time was running out for me, and they wouldn't be so lenient if I didn't sort the matter soon.'* After this, I contacted Pride of Place Publishing to let them know exactly what I had been subjected to over last few months, I was close to breaking point and couldn't take much more. Once I had put them in the picture, they said the following: They claimed to be horrified at how I had been treated; said they were astonished how SRBC could send two separate invoices for the same bill; they were at a loss why the council had failed to respond to their last communication on 25 May, and they showed me a short letter signed by the then, assistant director of finance, thanking Pride of Place for their letter and said, *they were dealing with the matter*. They assured me they would take sole responsibility to resolve the issue directly with the council, and when they telephoned the head of Legal to discuss it with him, they experienced a small taste of the same treatment I had received and they were, quote; '*astonished by his tone, manner, abruptness, and the quite unbelievable unhelpfulness he displayed*'.

Despite Pride of Place Publishing contacting SRBC and taking responsibility for the debt in October of 1995, they totally disregarded all of this and sent me a Court Summons, now with added court costs which amounted to £1325.00. My solicitor contacted the publisher by telephone and he told her he was prepared to come to court on my behalf and admit to owing the money, but he wasn't prepared to pay as he felt he could negotiate a discount. (I think that just about sums up his character and integrity). How could it be legal, or indeed lawful, for SRBC to send an invoice to me when they had previously issued it to someone else, and then send me a court summons? Why didn't the original and correct debtor get a court summons after those invoices went unpaid? Could it possibly be something to do with what the Head of Leisure had said to me, *there was no booking form in his name*? But there wasn't one in my name either.

I was completely shattered, and I didn't have the strength to fight anymore. My Dad gave me the £1325.00 from the small lump sum he received from his works pension and said, '*here you are Wacker, get them off your back.*' South Ribble Borough Council were nothing less than heavy handed unscrupulous bullies, they put immense pressure on the one most vulnerable because they knew they wouldn't get any money from the publisher. It is clear to me they knew they had been negligent in not getting a booking form signed by the publisher. Had I been given a booking form, first as an employee, and second as author of the book, I would have taken it to the publisher of said book, for his signature and authorisation. There was nothing legal or lawful in respect of their conduct for the manner in which they treated me. I wish I would have known then what I know now about the workings of councils, and their phoney courts, I would have taken them to the cleaners.

The Regional Officer of Unison came to South Ribble Council to represent me and played a blinder. We had a meeting with the head of Legal and I think he had the wind taken out of his sails; it was good to see him squirming behind his desk when I had someone on my side to stand up to him. He had been very thorough in his investigation and taken into account Pride of Place admitting the debt was theirs, and that the council had no booking form for the book launch in my name. The truth was finally in the open and I was to have something in writing clearing my reputation. In his confirmation letter to me, the head of Legal grudgingly wrote, *'I said I would write this letter confirming that I do accept your assurance that you never intended that the bill should not be paid'.* That was it. No apology for everything they had put me through and questioning my integrity, but there was some cold comfort in knowing they were proven wrong. It was too little too late to be honest, and no money was ever refunded so they had still got what they wanted. I had put my heart and soul into writing that book, it was my life's work, but that edition felt tainted for many years. All the pride I had in the work had been stolen by all those who played a part in everything that happened. Was someone jealous because a female had been successful with a football book, or as the doctor suggested, that someone there had it in for me? To be perfectly honest, in all my working life at SRBC, there was never really anyone to turn to with a problem, they always closed ranks and looked out for each other. I always thought it was an incestuous sort of building.

In December, over a year since my book had been published, I had another meeting with Pride of Place Publishing and they agreed to pay everything they owed me, but it was to be in instalments. A cheque was handed to me on 6 Dec but it was only to be paid into the bank subject to a telephone call to their office the following week, and I was to receive six further cheques over the next six months. At least I had some hope of giving my Dad his money back, albeit eventually. I paid in the first cheque as instructed, and guess what? It was returned to me by the bank. Pride of Place soon went into liquidation and I was never compensated for any loss. But worse than that, after all my efforts in writing my book, all the trauma and stress they put me through, my book was no longer available and I was left with absolutely nothing and nowhere to turn. And I also had to remain working for a bullying corporation who acted unlawfully.

Towards the end of 1996, I was contacted by Sue Lopez, who was writing her book *'Women on the Ball,'* to be published by Scarlett Press in London. She wanted help with information about the Dick, Kerr Ladies, and I was happy to oblige. We had several conversations and written correspondence, and I confided to her my experiences with Pride of Place Publishing, the film interest, and my bitter disappointment how it all concluded. I also told her about a recent contact from Real Life Productions at Yorkshire TV, who were keen to make a documentary about the team. Not long after this, Sue got in touch to say Scarlet Press were interested in re-publishing my book in paperback. I could hardly believe it; I was absolutely thrilled and couldn't believe my luck, it meant I could hopefully put the past behind me. I worked with Scarlet Press with my revised manuscript and they published my book in November 1997. We had a book launch at Preston North End, a much smaller affair than before, but the Dick, Kerr Ladies were all in attendance, and it attracted quite a bit of publicity. BBC Radio 4 came to do a broadcast for their Woman's Hour programme, and as a result, I was contacted by a gentleman purporting to be a friend of a famous actress who was looking to move to the other side of the camera and direct a film. She thought this story was just what she was looking for. Due to all the new publicity about my book, I also received a phone call at work from the former branch secretary of the union at SRBC. He had left the council by this time and was living in Wales. He heard on the radio about this new edition and called to say how pleased he was I'd done it again. He also wanted to apologise for his lack of support when I needed his help, and admitted he '*could have handled it better*.' Unlike his former employer, he seemed to have a conscience and at least had the decency to say sorry.

Anyway, it turns out this famous actress was Rita Tushingham, the BAFTA and Golden Globe winner who had starred in such films as, *A Taste of Honey, Doctor Zhivago,* and *The Girl with Green Eyes.* She called me at home and told me all about her plans and invited me to her Mayfair apartment to discuss things. Bloody hell, this book really was grabbing folk's attention, wasn't it? I said to her, '*I'm just an ordinary lass*,' and she said, '*so am I*,' so I accepted her invitation and got my train ticket to London. I was a bit daunted at the prospect to be honest, and wondered, '*how should I play this*.' I decided the best thing to do was just be myself, and I arrived at her apartment in Mayfair with my flask and my butties in a Kwik Save carrier bag! It was a very relaxed and friendly meeting, and I immediately trusted her. When I was leaving, she said, '*you wouldn't like a Selfridges carrier bag would you?*' I laughed and said, '*no thank you, I came with my Kwik Save bag, I'll go home with my Kwik Save bag,*' and off I went back to Preston and we became good friends from then on. Rita wanted to direct her first movie and had been looking for the right story to come along, and my book about the Dick, Kerr Ladies fitted the bill. We talked often on the phone and I was happy to share everything I knew about the team. Her vision for the film was basically to simply tell it as it is; of course there would have to be room for drama, but she saw the authenticity of the story and realised its importance. She took the idea to her friend Bill Kenwright, and he was keen to support her new venture. By the end of 1999, he took up the option on my book and secured Jeremy Paul to write a script. Jeremy had written for the television drama 'Upstairs, Downstairs,' and it was thought his experience of writing period pieces would make him perfect for the job. I met up with him at Barton Grange Hotel when he was in the area and we had a really good discussion, but unfortunately it didn't work out with his first draft, and the second one fell short too. So, they were on the lookout for another writer.

Rita was the surprised guest on 'This is Your Life' in 1999, and I was invited to be in the studio during the recording of the programme. I didn't have a speaking part but it was such an amazing experience being part of her special night. Before everyone arrived, I was sat on the studio sofa with Angharad Rees and Hugo Speer, and among the guests' giving tributes to Rita were, Spike Milligan, Alun Armstrong, Bill Kenwright, Carla Lane, Dora Bryan, Jean Boht, and Paul Danquah, who she starred with in 'A Taste of Honey'. The after-show party was great fun and Rita introduced me to Alun Armstrong, who she had ear marked to play the DKL team manager, we shook hands and he said he admired my work. I was rather chuffed and told him I admired his work too. More publicity followed about the proposed film with Rita being the director and she was invited on Gloria Hunniford's 'Open House' to discuss it. They also invited me and June Gregson, a former goalkeeper for the team. It was a bit daunting being in front of a live audience for the first time, but I think we did ourselves proud. There was a genuine buzz about the place as everyone was embracing this incredible story.

In 2000 I organised the last ever Lancashire Trophy, as a final reunion to see in the new millennium when we all became pioneers from the last century. I invited Rita to come and present the trophies, and it gave her the opportunity to meet more of the ladies from the DKL football team. We were putting on an exhibition match before the final, made up of former DKL players, and a few younger legs, versus a team calling themselves Dick, Kerr's Kids. Rita showed what a good sport she was by playing in the DK team, and we all had a great time celebrating these incredible legends. It was wonderful to play on the same pitch as them. What a spectacle it was, all that history.

Back row: Rita Tushingham, Yvonne Hamer, June Gregson, Barbara Widdows, Sheila Parker, Cath Brindle
Front row: Nancy Thomson, Lynn Arstall, Edna Broughton, Joan (Titch) Burke, me

The lady who owned Scarlet Press informed me she was going to live in Spain to run a Bed & Breakfast business. Realistically, this meant she wouldn't be publishing books anymore, just selling what remaining stock there was, and it also meant I was tied to a contract without any proper representation; it wasn't ideal. For International Women's Day 2003, I was helping the National Football Museum organise a special celebration dinner to honour the Dick, Kerr Ladies. The museum was housed at Preston North End back then, and I had loaned them numerous rare objects passed on to me by the players and as part of the evening, guests were to have a private tour of the museum to view them. I contacted Scarlet Press in Spain and asked them to organise some books to be delivered to the museum in time for the dinner, but arrangements were never made for them to arrive. I was very disappointed, but the event was still a huge success and Rita Tushingham was there to support us.

Rita Tushingham second left with me and some work colleagues; Wendy, Gail, me, Anne, Allyson

There had been several attempts to get another writer on board for the film, but nothing seemed to work out. Potential investors also seemed reluctant to come on board because Rita would be a first-time director and no one was prepared to give her the chance. And because it was a period drama, the cost of the production budget would be significantly higher and perhaps not worth the risk. It could also have been the view that women's football wasn't particularly relevant. With all these things in the way, Bill Kenwright let the option lapse. He was busy with his efforts to take over Everton FC, and that was his priority.

It was around this time when a fictional account of the Dick, Kerr Ladies was published, but all the publicity for it was just like reading about my own work. The information and playing record I had uncovered was the same, but it was interspersed with fictional stories which have sadly come to be mistaken for fact. It was clear what had happened, and I was absolutely devastated. It's too long to go into here, but signed statements do exist to substantiate my points, and it has always been obvious to me when people use my work because I was the one who first compiled it. I received no support whatsoever from Scarlet Press throughout this period and I was at a loss for what to do. I contacted the Writers Guild for some support, and after paying a £150 membership fee, they weren't much help at all, so to all intents and purposes, I was on my own; again. Scarlet Press wanted to keep me stuck in a contract with no end date, even though they were no longer publishing books, or giving me any proper representation. What could possibly have been their motives? I was left with no option but to engage a solicitor to help me. His charges back then were £250 per hour + vat. I was living alone with a mortgage to pay and I told him I could only afford two hours of his time, and I lived on a diet of spam and beans to make ends meet. It didn't resolve the issues with Scarlet Press totally, but our relationship had completely broken down and I informed them I wanted nothing more to do with them. I had mentioned to the solicitor about the other book, and he kindly suggested speaking to a barrister friend of his in London who offered to take a look at the situation on a no win, no fee basis. This was around the time of the controversy over the Dan Brown book, *The Da Vinci Code*. He looked over everything and concluded the author had sailed very close to the wind, been very clever, just enough so it couldn't be taken any further. I was bitterly disappointed.

Rita was still on the case to get a film made of my book. One of her daughters was working at a film company close to Los Angeles. They did a lot of work making commercials and were responsible for the Coca Cola adds. They were very interested in the story and were the second film company to actually take up the option. Ali Pennells, who had previously won awards writing scripts for Emmerdale, was on board now, and in 2005, Ali and I were invited to LA to work on a timeline for the proposed film. We were flown out to Los Angeles and stayed at a hotel in Santa Monica, very close to the beach, and within walking distance of their offices. They were talking a budget of $30+ million to make the movie, and we were out there for a week. They were a small company with a lovely family feel and it was a wonderful experience spending time with them. We also got to meet the guy who wrote the screenplay for '*Robin Hood, Prince of Thieves*', who very kindly gave some of his time and advice on screenplay writing. He said to me, '*you have a great story here.*' It was a wonderful privilege to be among people of such pedigree and know they believed in my work. We did get a day off from working on the storyline, and spent it in Hollywood, seeing the Walk of Fame and visiting the cinema where the Oscars took place. I also managed to tick something off my bucket list. I had long been a fan of Judy Garland, and always dreamed of going to the place in Hollywood where she put her hands in the cement, so that I could put mine there too. It was an unforgettable day.

Dream come true in Hollywood

Sadly, the euphoria didn't last long with the film company in LA. They went broke and a film was put on the back burner once more. Another disappointment to add to the ever-growing list. Rita and I were still in contact and she continued to try to find someone to take it on. In 2008, I was approached by another small film company in London, who said they were interested in making a film based on my book. A lady came to visit me at my home, we talked for some time, and on the surface, she appeared to be quite nice. But experience has taught me, they all do when they want something. She ran this company with another guy, both had angelic names, and I was soon to discover they were anything but. All was going well in the first instance. I introduced them to Rita and they took us took to lunch at BAFTA in London, but it was all a bit strange, it was like an information pumping exercise. To cut a long story short, they wanted me to sell my soul to them for £250. Gave me the sob story about how difficult these things were, they were only a small company, didn't have much money, blah, blah, blah. I told them I wasn't prepared to let them have the rights to all my work for as little as their initial offer and they weren't prepared to increase it. The lady with the angelic name was not at all happy with my refusal and told me in no uncertain terms, that they didn't really need me and were going to go ahead on their own. And go ahead they tried to do. I heard they received some funding amounting to £40k, but karma did her job and they failed get their project off the ground. There are other stories like this from over the years, too many to go into detail, but this has been a recurring pattern and lots of wasted time and a great deal of upset. Rita did tell me at the beginning how people in this industry would sell their own grandmother to get what they wanted, and boy, was she right. I have been shafted so many times. But it's not just in the film business, as I have also found to my cost.

When my book was initially published in 1994, it was the first book of its kind to document a history of a women's football team. The story had never been told before, and it showed how women's football does have a wonderful history, not just something that began as recently as the early 1970s, and it obviously inspired others to begin doing research of their own. As a result of all the publicity about my book, I was contacted by many people who were keen to know more about the Dick, Kerr Ladies, and view the precious mementos I had been fortunate to accumulate. Students doing dissertations, journalists, television reporters; the list goes on, and I was always eager to help, share my knowledge and enthusiasm, and show them my collection. But it wasn't long before my work began appearing on the new internet, not in articles written by me, but others who took it upon themselves to use my work. (Remember what it says at the beginning of this chapter about copyright) Serious question now, when does my work become someone else's? Some of my images were also used without permission, appearing in other articles and books, or cropped to try to disguise their origin. I started to become less trustful, far more cynical about the intentions of others, and more protective of the Dick, Kerr Ladies and my own work. Some years down the line, I was looking for some assistance with an issue I needed resolving. I contacted one of the first students I welcomed into my home to help with their studies, who I hoped would now be able to help me in return. However, when I approached them for their cooperation, I was met with a refusal. I was definitely learning the hard way. It seemed to be all take, take, and take some more.

It wasn't until 2011, I finally learned that Scarlet Press had been dissolved, and was no longer registered at Companies House. After two disastrous and soul-destroying associations with publishers, at last I was free to do what I wanted with my own work. Finally having no one to answer to, I self-published a revised and updated edition of my book in 2014. I had uncovered much more information about the team, and individual achievements of some of the players, which needed to be documented. I decided to have a book launch at Bamber Bridge FC, returning to where my Dick, Kerr Ladies journey began with Brenda Eastwood. Were it not for meeting Brenda, none of this would ever have happened and it just seemed to be the perfect place. She had been a great supporter of Bamber Bridge FC for many years and they still have a tribute plaque in her memory behind the bar. The BBC came along to film a live outside broadcast, to record former goalkeeper Margaret Goodinson being reunited with her old team mates for the first time in over fifty years, and guests from women's football included, Sylvia Gore MBE, Gill Coulthard, Natasha Dowie and Becky Easton. Among the many other guests who came along to celebrate with me, was Tom Pilkington, former manager and supporter of Preston Rangers. He reminded me of his comment at the Emgals tournament in 1983, when he said he thought I was the best left back in the country. I told him I remembered. He said it was true, and his opinion hadn't changed even after all this time. Thank you, Tom.

Towards the end of 2014, I was contacted by a lady at the London offices of Sony. She told me they were interested in the Dick, Kerr Ladies story and invited me to London for a meeting. It was all a bit strange really as she said they wanted to have a third party involved. I didn't really understand, Sony are a huge company who you would expect to be in a position to finance such a project, and this went on for a couple of months. In early 2015, she introduced me to Sue Horth and Kate Ambler, who had been working on their own project of the DKL story. They already had a script and some promotional material ready to go. To cut a long story short, Sony backed out and I started working with Sue and Kate. After lots of discussions took place, and many reassurances given, the option to make a film/drama based on my book was taken up by them and we worked together for several years. However, Sue has now moved on to other projects and Emily Morgan, Christine Gernon, and Emma Strain, are now on board with Kate and we are all working together to try to get this over the finish line. Very recently, two writers have been commissioned to write the script, Beth Kilcoyne and her sister Emma Kilcoyne, and I am keeping everything crossed that this project can finally get across the goal line.

Given everything that has happened to me regarding the Dick, Kerr Ladies, hopefully there will be a happy ending. I am now very cautious and far more careful with what I say and what I share, especially when it comes to rare and valuable images. I am but a product of what has been done over the years, and trust doesn't come easy. A lot of damage has also been done due to all the misinformation and I am still doing my best to tell the true story of the team. I have also taken precautions to protect their name and logo which are now Registered Trademarks with the Intellectual Property Office. I don't know what the future holds, but let's hope a film will finally be produced and the Dick, Kerr Ladies can be immortalised on the big screen forever.

SEARCHING FOR UNCLE JOE

I was always aware my Dad was named after his Uncle Joe who was killed during the First World War, but when I was younger, I never really gave it a great deal of thought. I knew my Dad was very interested in the history of both World Wars and I remember watching '*All our Yesterdays*' with him on the tele, with that big pendulum swinging on a clock in the opening credits. I'm ashamed to say, due to the folly of youth, I didn't pay much attention to my Grandad either, he was Uncle Joe's older brother and I believe he fought at Gallipoli during the same conflict. He was 'just an old man' to me then, who often sang the same old war songs. I don't really know anything of Grandads service, but I do know he was gassed during the war, and had to go to hospital. He is pictured below, recovering with some of his injured comrades, and I would give anything to listen to his stories today.

Grandad, LCpl Robert Matthew Newsham, 1st left front row cross legged

Dad was always very proud to be named after Uncle Joe and he inherited a treasured picture postcard sent by him to his only sister Edi, (Emily Edith Newsham) and we are lucky to still have it as a family keepsake. There is no known grave for Uncle Joe but he is named on the Thiepval Memorial in tribute to the missing.

12453 LCpl Joe Newsham Loyal North Lancashire Regiment

In 2013, I had the crazy idea of going to France to see if we could find him. I knew he was killed in action during the Battle of the Somme on 23 July 1916, but that was pretty much the sum total of my knowledge of him. The centenary of the start of the Great War was approaching, and I suggested the trip to Lenore. I didn't really have a clue where to look, or what to look for, but we booked a camp site in San Quentin in the Somme region. I had no idea how big the area was, but at least it was a start. We soon learned it was a good forty-five minute drive from the campsite to where many of the War Cemeteries were located, but we made the most of our daily excursions and enjoyed the countryside. We must have walked by tens and tens of thousands of graves that week looking for any clue that might lead us to Uncle Joe. We were completely in the wrong area, but it was all very enlightening. Weather wise it was a miserable rainy week in a damp tent, and I was so grateful to Lenore for all her support, I couldn't have done any of it without her. Towards the end of our stay, we eventually found our way to Flat Iron Copse Cemetery, close to the village of Bazentin and Mametz Wood. There were some Loyal North Lancashire Regiment soldiers buried there who were killed on the same day as Uncle Joe, but some of the graves had the inscription, 'Believed to be' a particular soldiers name, and others that said, 'Believed to be Buried in this Cemetery'. I started to think, perhaps if I could find out where Uncle Joe might be buried, maybe the Commonwealth War Graves Commission (CWGC) would let me pay to have a headstone for him. Flat Iron Copse was the last cemetery we visited before heading for home, and my initial thoughts were he might be in there. But little did we realise just how close we were to where he actually fell.

I did more research and contacted the Infantry Museum at Fulwood Barracks in Preston, to see if they had any records of where Uncle Joe may have been killed. They were very helpful and sent me a map of the area where D Company, 7th Battalion Loyal North Lancashire Regiment, were engaged in battle on 23 July 1916. At least I knew where to look the next time we went back. It was a strange, yet comforting feeling. I'd gone to France looking for my Dad's Uncle, but in my heart, I brought home my Uncle, and I wanted to do everything I could to honour his memory and make my Dad proud

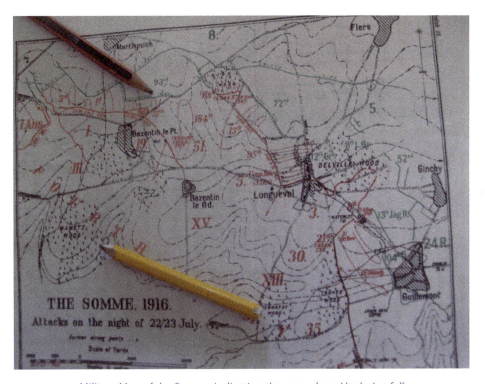

Military Map of the Somme indicating the area where Uncle Joe fell

As the centenary anniversary of the start of the Great War approached in 2014, we made plans to return to the area to see what other information I could glean. I'd looked through the war diaries and was armed with more details of the battalions movements for July 1916, and we found a campsite closer to the area where we needed to be. We had a new inflatable tent for this trip, but it was a bit of a mistake and turned out to be too heavy for us and this was our only stay in it. I'd had a memorial cross made for Uncle Joe, and wanted to leave it in the area around Bazentin on the anniversary of his death, the 23rd July. I didn't want to come home thinking I may have left it in the wrong place and wishing I had placed it somewhere more appropriate, so I asked for a 'sign' to help me find the best possible location. There are several War Grave Cemeteries in the immediate surrounding area of the village of Bazentin. Flat Iron Copse, Thistle Dump, Bazentin le Petit, High Wood, and London Cemetery and Extension. We searched in all of these cemeteries to see if there was any indication of Uncle Joe being there, and we both agreed there was nothing to suggest he was in any of those mentioned. And then we went to Caterpillar Valley Cemetery. There are over 5,500 lads buried there and we started wandering around, looking for the Loyal North Lancashire Regiment badge on the headstones. During all the research I had done regarding the battalions movements, I came across this extract from the War Diaries where it notes some of the officers from D Company 7th Battalion LNLR, who also lost their lives on 23 July 1916.

> At 8.50 p.m. the Battalion was relieved and went back to dug-outs in Mametz Wood, having during the last four days had eleven officers and 290 other ranks killed, wounded and missing. Of these eleven officers the following were killed : Lieutenant W. A. Dawson, 2nd Lieutenants H. J. R. Hosking, H. Hoyle, R. W. Jardine and McK. F. Turpie.

We could see quite a number of LNLR badges dotted about and we hadn't been there very long when I was given the 'sign' I had asked for. Among the many LNLR lads buried in Caterpillar Valley Cemetery, I discovered the resting place of Lieutenant W A Dawson, and 2nd Lieutenant H Hoyle, who are mentioned above in the war diaries. Both were killed on 23 July 1916 and are buried side by side and I could hardly believe I had found them. They were a Pals Battalion, and Pals Battalions fought and died together didn't they, so it would be a fair assumption that the other soldiers who lost their lives on that fateful morning, were in here among the other men, whether named or not. I felt certain this was the place where Uncle Joe would be and so this is where I left the memorial cross for him on 23 July 2014, with love from his family. It was a very emotional day.

Uncle Joe's cross

WHERE POPPIES GROW

There was a man I never knew, who lost his life in War
He answered our nations call to arms like we'd never seen before
As part of Kitchener's Army he signed up to fight the foe
Full of anticipation, he couldn't wait to go.
Off to defend our liberty, although he did not know
He would ne'er return, from the land where poppies grow.
A patriotic fever had swept right throughout our land
As young men in their thousands joined, united they did stand
Singing as they marched away they waved a fond goodbye
With eager hearts, their spirits high, and victory was their cry
'We'll all be home by Christmas, we'll have Gerry on the run'
It seemed a big adventure; they thought it would be fun.
As a Pals Battalion, they went to fight this bloody War

They little knew the horrors of just what lay in store
They could ne'er imagine what sights from hell they'd see
Nor the fear that would engulf them, 'will the next to die be me'?
Young men in their thousands, some of them just boys,
Were soon to learn at first-hand how quickly War destroys.
In trenches full of rats and mud, their flesh infested with lice
Then came the order, 'over the top', to face the ultimate sacrifice
The smell of rotting corpses, the bodies piled so high
Praying that God would help them, they didn't want to die.
Bombs and bullets everywhere and carnage all around
The cries of dying comrades were a constant harrowing sound
What terror must have gripped them, we will never know
But now they rest together in a land where poppies grow.
And this young man I never knew was my great Uncle Joe,
A soldier of Kitchener's Army, he couldn't wait to go.
He was a Lewis gunner, fighting to take High Wood
Trying to make a difference for the greater good
Uncle Joe fought bravely; but it was his fate to die,
And he perished on the Somme on the 23rd of July
Was it really worth it, just what does history show?
Row upon row of white headstones, in a land where poppies grow.
One hundred years have passed us by since that awful War began
And it still remains the bloodiest fight ever known to man
A poppy is a symbol now to show that we remember
And we commemorate their sacrifice every 11th of November
For saving our tomorrow they gave us their today
Our freedom and our life, a debt we can't hope to repay.
But I'm sad I never knew him, my brave great Uncle Joe,
Who is resting somewhere with his Pals, in the land where poppies grow.

Gail J Newsham 2014

Uncle Joe

When we got home, I did a great deal more research about the battle he was involved in and I felt more confident he was in Caterpillar Valley Cemetery. I contacted the CWGC and shared what I had discovered and hoped I could have a gravestone for Uncle Joe with the words, '*Believed to Be Buried in this Cemetery*.' Rightly or wrongly, I thought they would be delighted to honour another young lad who gave his life fighting for his country. Here is a quote from a book about the Somme: *The Battle of the Somme which opened on 1 July is now recognised as one of the bloodiest in Britian's long military record. What began as attrition, developed into prolonged mutual destruction and is now chiefly remembered for its tragic and unprecedented, even pointless, loss of life. Bitterly contested and dominating the Bazentin Ridge, High Wood was the focal point of the battle area. The wood finally fell to the British in September, but the successful divisional commander was dismissed for 'lack of push' and a 'wanton waste of men.'*

This article copied below, was printed in the *Preston Herald* on 26 September 1916, by a LNLR soldier who actually took part in the same offensive as Uncle Joe. A graphic story from a Chum, he shares what the Preston Pals went through on the morning of 23ʳᵈ July 1916. *"I wish to tell you all I know and what exactly happened in the attack that morning. After being out for a rest behind Albert, orders came through suddenly on the night of the 19ᵗʰ and we moved up to the trenches, straight into the support trenches the same night. We had been heavily shelled and it had been a long march up the valley, but we had a few casualties and pushed forward through the remains of Bazentin le Petit and dug in about 400 yards in front of the village between two roads, with a ridge between us and the Huns rising to the right, and High Wood on the right flank.*

We had some men sniped while we were digging in, then we held the shallow trench for three days in very hot sun, with little water and no chance of making any tea, and no communications only over the top. On the first day we saw one of our planes bring an Alleymayne (sic) plane down after a hard fight nearly over our heads and very near the floor. Our plane drew slightly away and our rifle and machine gun fire finished the Bosche, one of the greatest sights we have seen.

(War Diary extract below regarding above account. Uncle Joe was a Lewis Gunner)

7-00pm   Our lewis guns brought down a German aeroplane just in front of our front line, it burst into flames and both men were burnt to death.

On the night of the 22nd, the artillery on both sides were very active and the Huns sent a lot of high shrapnel over our trench, and the machine guns played incessantly. There were the lights and noise of a big strafe going on in High Wood and about 1 o'clock we were reinforced by our other two companies coming over the top from support just in front of the village. In about ten minutes, the word came down, "B and D Companies prepare to mount the parapet" (Uncle Joe in D Company) and we saw our Captian (Thompson) and the Sergeant Major getting over on the right. The boys went over and troops (regular and otherwise) never went over in better spirit in the face of heavy shrapnel and machine gun fire. Things were not so bad till we got to the ridge, and we had kept in line and direction as well as possible in the dark.

When we got over the ridge, we were met by a strong enfilade fire from the right, which mowed us down in rows like corn, and in a few minutes before we could get a footing in the trench, all our Officers were gone, and very few men left, and after two rushes to try and get into the trench on the right we had to withdraw and try to get back to our own trench. Clive, Cyril and I all used to 'grub' together and we had just divided our rations out between us when I was sent for by the Captain, along with another of the scouts and we had pushed down the trench near to where the Captian was when the word came down "stand fast" and the supports started coming into the trench; then the word came to advance, so that when we went over I was separated from Clive and Cyril, and did not see them again. It was impossible to tell who was next to you only by shouting. The bullets tore up the ground and tinkled as they hit the steel helmets, and a lot of the chaps who got back had bullet holes through their canteens, or their clothes ripped. When we got back as dawn was breaking, there were very few men in the trench, and the Sergeants who were left were afraid the Huns would counter-attack and so we who were left had to "stand to" and be ready to repel the attack if it came.

There were very few of our platoon left, and they told me that Cyril had gone down to the dressing station, but I could hear nothing of Clive (Whittle) or anyone who had seen him. We were relieved early that evening by another Regiment, and went back into the reserve trench in the wood behind the village (Mametz Wood). During the day we were only able to get the chaps in who were wounded near our line, but plenty crawled in from further out. Sergeant Rawcliffe, one of our boys, crawled in during the evening, badly wounded in the groin, and he told us that he had passed both 13071 Ronald Charles Targett and Clive (Whittle) near the top of the ridge, and that Clive had been hit through the body and must have died instantly. Rawcliffe, I am sorry to say, died in hospital a few days later.

We remained in the reserve trench a week, and I have never spent a more miserable week, for most of the old faces were gone, and the Bosche continued to shell us day and night with "coal boxes". The first day in the reserve trench we lost 20 by the shelling. I made enquiries and a Sergeant in A Company said Clive was slightly behind him when he saw him fall, and went to him, but that he was dead when he got there. I am in an unfortunate position, because I never saw Clive, and have only these fellows word for it. You cannot tell how I felt about it and it is idle for me to try and sympathise, because sympathy is not shown by mere words or writing; but he was my pal since joining the Army and always kept the section in roars of laughter and was one of the most popular chaps in the Battalion as well as the Company. But a lot of us will be with him before long, and you really get that you don't mind dying if they would get it over quickly. We made it up that if anything happened, whoever was left would send all private things of any importance home that we had in our valises, but when we came out, the wounded and missing men's kits had been gone through and savaged, which gives you and idea of the Army system.

To explain what happened with the fallen soldiers, here is a diary extract of Pte Macpherson 9th Royal Scots (154 Brigade) who writes about the same attack on High Wood, the battle where Uncle Joe fell, and it is highly likely he was with the reinforcements mentioned in the eye witness account above. 'The survivors of the two attacking companies were marched off and we were left to 'clean up'. The dead had to be stripped of valuables (pocket books, rings, watches,etc) to send home later, and then were carried in waterproof sheets, placed in shell holes and covered with loose earth. This makeshift burial performed, rude crosses made of pieces of ration boxes with the name, number and regiment of the dead soldier, were erected to mark the place. Though the burial was carried out without any service or spoken prayer, nevertheless the uncertainty of life will be more strongly felt in such circumstances than with all the pomp and ritual of a Church Service. When the burial party know that they may, any minute, follow the path of the comrade they are burying, there must be an earnestness in their attentions, however rude makeshift they may be, often lacking in such ceremonies in normal times'.

Front Line Bazentin le Petit where the Preston Pals fell – High Wood in the distance

After the War, it was decided by the powers that be, for all soldiers who fought and died in France and buried in this manner, to be exhumed and placed in the collective cemeteries we see today. Uncle Joe and his comrades lay buried in the fields of Bazentin le Petit (above) for six years, from 1916 until the exhumations took place in 1922, when they were placed in Caterpillar Valley Cemetery. Given the conditions described in the eye witness account of how quickly they were buried where they fell, and the battle for High Wood contining until September 1916, months after the soldiers of 7th Battalion LNLR had lay dead in these fields, it is nothing short of a miracle for any memorial crosses to have survived while the battle still raged around them, let alone for six years. The fact there are so many unidentified soldiers, Known unto God, in all of the cemeteries bears testament to that.

I can't begin to count how many letters went backwards and forwards to the CWGC, and how many 'reasons' they gave for not letting me have a headstone for Uncle Joe. I researched all their 'reasons' and proved each of them wrong. I researched the military records of all the lads who had a grave in Caterpillar Valley Cemetery, downloaded all their paperwork and compared their records to those of Uncle Joe, and in the majority of cases, his paperwork was far more conclusive than those who had been granted a memorial headstone. The battalion commanders knew he had been killed in action, he was never reported missing, as were some of his comrades, he was immediately documented as killed

266

in action on 23 July 1916, all his personal effects had been sent home, so there must have been a body to take them from. One of the first reasons the CWGC gave for not approving a headstone was because, on the Military History Sheet for where Uncle Joe was killed, was written, *place not stated*,' and they therefore concluded, quote; '*the service authority (Army) was not aware of a specific location where he died.*' But in actual fact, '*place not stated*' was also written on the military records of many of those soldiers who died along with him. On closer inspection of the form, printed on the top right corner, it clearly states, *the country only to be shown – it is not necessary to show separately the service in different stations of the same country.* And that is the reason why place of death was not stated; it was not required. The CWGC also gave examples of other LNLR soldiers buried in other cemeteries. Research proved these men to be either from different battalions and not involved in the same offensive or, as in the case of SGT W Rawcliffe, the eye witness report tells of him being badly wounded but managed to crawl back over the line some five hours later. He was taken to a field hospital dressing station where he died of his wounds a few days later and buried in a cemetery near the hospital where he passed away, and not the battle field where the wounds occurred.

Uncle Joe was promoted to Lance Corporal on 15 July 1916, and you can clearly see the stripe on his arm in the photo over the page. Eight days after his promotion, he was killed in action, so this is probably the last ever picture taken of all of these men. I suspect it was taken in Albert, where the battalion was resting after action at La Boiselle, until the order came to mobilize on 19 July. One soldier who died along with Uncle Joe was 13141 LCpl Frank Wilcock. The soldier on the front row with the little girl on his knee bears an uncanny resemblance to Frank Wilcock who was reported missing on 23 July 1916, and can be seen in the newpaper article below. He has a memorial headstone in Caterpillar Valley Cemetery, along with Clive Whittle, who is mentioned in the eye witness account, with the words, '*Known to be Buried in this Cemetery*'. In this case, Known to be buried in this cemetery, could possibly indicate there were no definitive remains to identify, other than a name. He had been officially reported as 'missing'.

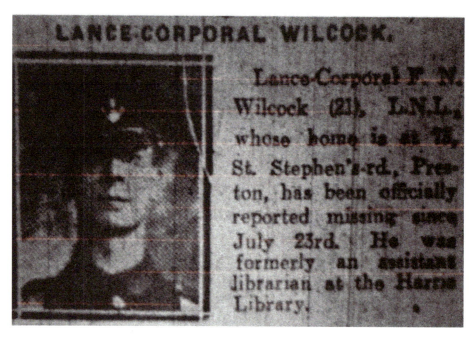

LANCE-CORPORAL WILCOCK.

Lance-Corporal F. N. Wilcock (21), L.N.L., whose home is at 75, St. Stephen's-rd., Preston, has been officially reported missing since July 23rd. He was formerly an assistant librarian at the Harris Library.

Lance Corporal William Broad, (opposite) looks to me as though he could also be with Uncle Joe on the picture above, and he too was reported missing and has a grave in Caterpillar Valley Cemetery. I will leave you, dear reader, to draw your own conclusions.

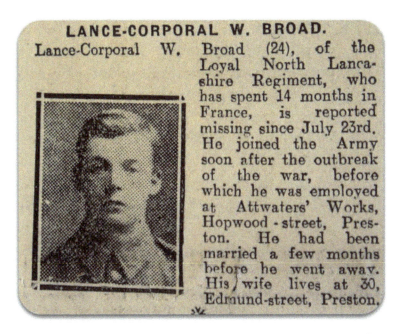

LANCE-CORPORAL W. BROAD.

Lance-Corporal W. Broad (24), of the Loyal North Lancashire Regiment, who has spent 14 months in France, is reported missing since July 23rd. He joined the Army soon after the outbreak of the war, before which he was employed at Attwaters' Works, Hopwood - street, Preston. He had been married a few months before he went away. His wife lives at 30, Edmund-street, Preston.

In the same cemetery, there is a headstone in a memorial plot for Pte Ben Southern, South Lancashire Regiment, who has the inscription, '*Believed to be buried in this Cemetery*'. The Casualty Form entry, lists him as *wounded in the field on 22/23 July 1916,* then it later documents him as wounded and missing, but he wasn't actually declared as killed in action until 4 November 1916, which rather suggests his remains were never found. The Burial Return form for Pte Southern at the time of exhumation states, '*No bodies were found. After a most diligent search, digging down 7 feet, no trace of any bodies for the above cross were found.*' For there to be no remains of Pte Southern being discovered, it may suggest a makeshift memorial cross being left by his comrades in tribute to a lost pal.

There are other memorial headstones in Caterpillar Valley Cemetery, for three soldiers killed in action near Flers, whose graves were destroyed in later battles. They each have a memorial headstone and are remembered with the words, '*Their Glory Shall Not Be Blotted Out.*' Just a short distance away, in Bernafay Wood Cemetery, there is a grave for 2Lt Ellicott, who was killed on 9 July 1916. The inscription on his headstone reads '*Believed to be buried in Bernafay Wood, or in an adjoining wood, but the actual site of a grave is unknown.*' I didn't think it unreasonable to ask the CWGC for the same consideration to be given to Uncle Joe, as was clearly shown for 2Lt Ellicot and those men killed in action near Flers. There is no doubt that Uncle Joe died along side his comrades in Bazentin-le-Petit on 23 July 1916, he certainly never came home. I believe it was simply an unfortunate case of bad luck for his memorial cross to not survive the six years from 1916-1922. Irrespective of all that, he died serving his country, and in my opionon the very least he deserves for his ultimate sacrifice is a headstone in the same cemetery with his pals. The table below relates to my own research of the grid references from where some of the LNLR soldiers where exhumed. The second image is a close up of the final tally of soldiers exhumed from just one of the squares in this grid, directly in front of the front line, where 286 men were found.

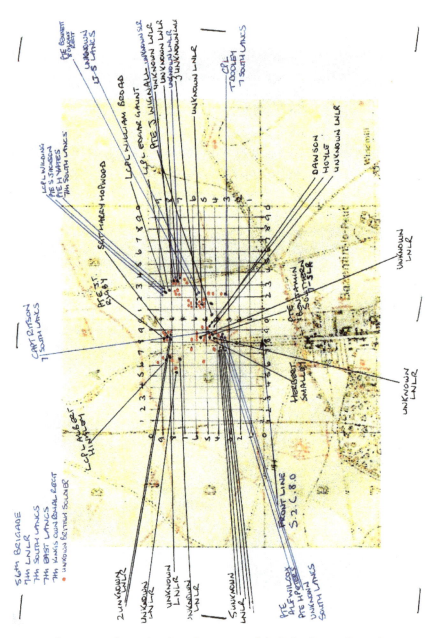

Army map of area showing where some of the lads where exhumed

270

Actual numbers of men exhumed. Square 2 is close up of area in previous image – 286 men

While CWGC admitted, *it is highly probable that LCpl Newsham was serving with his battalion and regiment at the time of his death,* they were still steadfast in their refusal to grant him a memorial headstone. After I had provided them with eye witness accounts, all the information of the other soldiers, and complained to them of the injustice of their refusal, they actaully said, '*I am sorry that you feel an injustice has been done. The Commission could not agree that this is the case, as to do so would devalue the commemoration of the 757,750 Commonwealth war casualties, with no known grave, commemorated on Memorials to the Missing.* I was absolutely flabbergasted and disgusted at such a statement. In other words, by granting a headstone to Uncle Joe, a man who gave his life fighting for our freedom, it would devalue every other soldier whose name was listed on Thiepval, or any other memorial to the missing. What a load of utter rubbish. I honestly cannot comprehend that kind of logic and it rather seems to me, that those charged with the gruesome task of exhuming the graves of dead soldiers, and treating their remains with the dignity, reverence, and respect they deserved, had a far greater grasp of compassion than what I encountered during my dealings with CWCG.

Throughout all my efforts to get a headstone for Uncle Joe, I wrote to David Cameron, who passed it on to MOD. I wrote to the Queen who couldn't get involved. I wrote to Prince Harry who also couldn't get involved, and I wrote to a reporter at the Daily Mail who had written an article about Theipval, who didn't even have the courtesy to reply, and I went to the top and wrote to the

271

Director General of the CWGC, but none of it made a scrap of difference. I came to the sad conclusion that for all of those people, the whole thing is just a show, a complete charade, Remembrance Sunday, the lot. Not by the veterans who genuinely care and faithfully gather to remember the fallen and have actually taken part in these bloody and futile wars, but those in so called positions of power, the warmongers themselves, the ones who actually create and fund all these conflicts in the first place, who only pretend to care about the dead when the cameras are rolling, like the current and former politicians we see at the Cenotaph in London every year. The line up on Remembrance Sunday in 2023 illustrated that very point. In my humble opinion, they couldn't give an effin toss. They are a disgrace.

After having no support whatsoever from CWGC or anyone else, I had another memorial cross made for Uncle Joe, and we went back to Bazentin le Petit in time for the 100th anniversary of his death on 23 July 2016 and we had upgraded to a trailer tent for this visit. I decided to leave the cross at Crucifix Corner, situated at the bottom right flank of the area where the battle for High Wood took place. The cross was much bigger than the one we placed in Caterpillar Valley Cemetery in 2014, and I was concerned, given all my dealings with CWGC, if we placed it within their grounds, it might be removed. Crucifix Corner has the orignal Crucifux from 1916 and still bears bullet hole scars from the War. I thought Uncle Joe may even have seen it during his battalions march to the area. Other small memorials had been left there and it seemed a safe and respected place to leave it. It was very emotional placing it in the ground paying tribute to a young man who had lost his life not too far from that very spot, exactly one hundred years ago. The poppy on the cross came from Dads wreath when he passed away. I think he would have been pleased with that.

Crucifix Corner 2016

Uncle Joe's Cross 23 July 2016

After we had placed the cross, we went to Caterpillar Valley Cemetery and walked by every single one of the 5,500 graves to make sure we were as close to Uncle Joe as possible. It took over two and a half hours, but it was worth it. Later in the day, we were walking through Delville Wood when we came across an English guy who lived in the area. We got chatting and I told him about the cross and he said he would look after it. I felt comforted. This was perhaps the most rewarding of all our visits and we went home feeling we had done the very best we could.

We returned to France in 2018 for the centenary of the end of the First World War, but this time we had upgraded from the trailer tent to a lovely retro Eriba caravan. We were happy to revisit the same campsite in Feuilleres, we had become familiar with the area and knew where the supermarket was for all our supplies, it was just like going home.

Home from home

It was really hot for the two weeks we were there and it always makes me think about the soldiers in the trenches and how hard it must have been for them in those conditions. When we returned to Crucifix Corner, we were sad to discover Uncle Joe's cross was no longer there. I tried not to get too upset about it, even though it felt a bit like 'grave robbing', and hoped it wouldn't have brought any joy to whoever took it. I had done what I set out to do, to honour Uncle Joe, and I think that he, Grandad, and my Dad, would be immensley proud of all our efforts to find him. I did have some replica medals made for Uncle Joe and I keep them next to my Dad's. I've often wondered if Grandad had his original medals passed on to him by his Dad, and if they met the same fate when Hughie destroyed them, but I don't like to dwell on it.

It has become something of an annual pilgrimage for us as we returned again in 2019 to pay tribute to the fallen. Several friends had asked us to leave crosses for their relatives, and we have added them to our ever growing list. I had reconnected with one of my childhood friends, Tina Ward; we lost touch in the 1960s when she moved away from Fleetwood Street and now lives in Nashville, Tennessee. She told me about her great Uncle, Michael Connolly, who was serving with the Lancashire Fusiliers and was killed on the first day of the Battle of the Somme. He is buried in Connaught Cemetery, very close to the Ulster Memorial Tower, and Thiepval Wood where he fell. We visit him every year and place a memorial cross on his grave and send a photo to Tina. I know it means a great deal to her family. It isn't a sombre trip, it's very rewarding knowing that in many cases, we will probably have been the only people to have visited their graves and placed a cross of remembrance for them. They have become like friends now, we know where they all are, and I feel sad when we're leaving them to come home. After all they did for their country, it's the least we can do to show we care.

Lenore and I made our first visit back to Bazentin le Petit after the lockdowns in 2022 and I am delighted to say that the cross we placed for Uncle Joe in Caterpillar Valley Cemetery in 2014, was still there. It looks a bit worse for wear now, but at least he is still commemorated with his comrades. After all the support Lenore has given me in my search for Uncle Joe over the past ten years, she recently discovered she too has a great Uncle who died during the First World War. He lost his life close to Thiepval Wood, and thankfully, there is a grave for him. 19131 Rifleman Alan Edgar Mahood, 13th Battalion, Royal Irish Rifles, Killed in Action on the first day of the Battle of the Somme, 1 July 1916, aged 18. We now visit him in Serre Road Cemetery and honour his memory along with all the other young lads on our visiting list.

We returned again in 2023, armed with over fifty crosses given to us by some of our friends. It enabled us to leave one on the grave of every soldier from the Loyal North Lancashire Regiment in Caterpillar Valley Cemetery, whether named or unidentified. It was a privilege to be able to honour so many in this way. There is a memorial plaque on Preston Railway Station to the Preston Pals, these are the very lads we visit. It's wonderful to know how these brave souls are commemorated so respectfully in their home town. It's a great honour to know where they are resting, and be so familiar with their names and their stories. I like to think they are pleased when we visit, and we'll be returning again in 2024. We will remember them.

The Preston Pals – Uncle Joe's Regiment

N.B. Just as my Dad was proud to be named after Uncle Joe, I too am proud to have Josephine as my middle name, in honour of them both.

SISTERS IN ARMS

I was living on Kiln Croft in the late 1990s, when Captain Erskine, my Staff Captain from Dusseldorf, got in touch to let me know she would be coming to the North West. Her unit was taking part in an exercise in the Merseyside area and we made arrangements for her to visit me on her way back up the road to Scotland. I hadn't seen her since I left the Army but we had kept in contact, and every year we would send Christmas cards and an annual letter sharing our news. When she got married, she even sent me a piece of her wedding cake. She was Lieutenant Colonel Helen Homewood now, and arrived at the house in combat gear. It was so lovely to see her after all those years, and I instinctively wanted to stand to attention and salute when she came in. We had a brew and a good catch up and I was absolutely thrilled she made the time to come and see me. Her support meant the world to me when we first came back to Preston and we are still in touch to this very day.

Thanks to social media, in 2013 I was contacted by my old Army buddy, Sue Scott, who I did my basic training with back in 1974. She was living near Peterborough, having met and married a soldier, and I soon made plans to visit her and husband Pete, for a weekend of catching up. Sue had kept up her military connections and was a staunch member of the WRAC Association, which has local branches up and down the country where ex-servicewomen can meet and keep in touch, and she suggested I consider joining. She was also a member of the WRAC Dinner Club, an annual function held every year over a weekend, and said what a great time they all have and asked if I would like to come along. I wasn't keen on being involved with either of them and declined her kind invitations. After my experience in Dusseldorf, I didn't want to have to explain myself to anyone ever again, or answer any questions about why I left the Army. She assured me it wasn't like that anymore, but I wasn't convinced and didn't want to put myself through what I saw as any unnecessary scrutiny and upset.

In 2014, Sue pointed out it was forty years since we had joined up together and she asked me again about coming to the Dinner Club later that year. She explained because I was ex forces, I could just go as a guest, which meant I wouldn't have to fill in any forms or answer any questions, so that was reassuring. Forty years was a bit of a milestone and I thought it might be nice to celebrate this special anniversary with Sue, and that was the only reason I decided I would give it a go. But I am so glad I did. What a fantastic time I had, I bloody loved it, and it was wonderful to be part of an Army community again. We entered the room to the WRAC Regimental March, The Lass of Richmond Hill, and everyone clapped and sang along until each guest had taken their seat, it was amazing. Sue was right, the other stuff simply didn't matter anymore. Well, it didn't matter to anyone else, it mattered to me, I still felt like a bit of an outsider, and it was only through going there I realised just how much 'stuff' I had carried with me since 1977. I did feel as though I wasn't as good as the others, because of what had happened to me, and I still felt that sense of rejection, but it really was one of the best nights I'd had. There was even one of our platoon Corporals there, who both of us hadn't seen since we left Guildford. I was on such a high, I could hardly sleep.

WRAC Dinner Club 2014. Sue and me seated far right.

Following on from my first ever visit to the Dinner Club, I immediately joined and became a fully-fledged member. I also joined the WRAC Association with no questions to answer, they just wanted to know my Army number, rank, and when I served. That was it, easy peasy. To top it all off, I also learned that being a former member of the Armed Forces, I was eligible to apply for a Veterans Badge. How bloody chuffed was I. I just wish my Dad would have been here to see it.

Armed Forces Veteran's Badge

The WRAC Association holds a Grand Reunion every three years and the next one was taking place in Harrogate in March of 2015. I made arrangements with Sue to attend the dinner on the Saturday night and it was yet another wonderful evening. Among others, we managed to meet up with Denise Bird from our basic training days, who I had actually shared a room with. How truly wonderful to meet up with these people again after all those years. We also met up with RSM Agnes Doig at another Dinner Club event. Agnes was RSM when we were in trade training at Blackdown and she always seemed very strict and scary to us back then. It was lovely to meet her again, she was actually quite a pussycat and was surprised to hear we had been scared of her, but I bet she knew really.

Sue, Denise, Me

Being a member of the WRAC Association gives you the opportunity to take part in parades at various official functions. The next big date in the calendar was Armed Forces Day in June 2015, and it was taking place in Guildford, the spiritual home of the WRAC. I put my name down, but being the new kid on the block, I never really thought I would be accepted and wasn't surprised at not being given a place after the applications went in. Then one day, I received a phone call from Association HQ, someone had dropped out and they were offering me a place in the parade. I was really nervous and asked could I think about it first. It was such a big occasion, I felt quite apprehensive, but I didn't want to pass up on this wonderful opportunity and called back to accept. I am so glad I did. I spent ages bulling my new parade shoes getting ready for the big day, and given it had been forty years since I'd done it, they didn't look half bad.

Shoes bulled for the parade

Words could never express how I felt to actually have the opportunity to take part in Armed Forces Day with the WRAC Association. To be marching up Guildford High Street, with large crowds clapping and cheering as we paraded through the town, was more than I could ever have wished for. The icing on the cake was being able to march wearing my Dad's medals. I am sure he would have been just as proud as I was.

Guildford High Street – we started at the bottom

The Parade

Marching in Guildford 2015

Me and Sue back together in Guildford

Lenore came with me, we decided to make a holiday of it and stayed at a camp site in East Horsley. The campsite was in a great location and I was able to visit where the WRAC Training Centre used to be, and saw the pub I was in on the night of the IRA bombings in 1974. There was also a memorial garden in Guildford to all those who were killed on that fateful night. It was heart-warming to see that the two young WRAC recruits who had their lives cut so tragically short, will never be forgotten. We had a fantastic week; the sun shone every day and I even got to go back to Camberley again. It was wonderful to re-live some special memories and walk once more in the footsteps of a very younger me. It was absolutely priceless. The WRAC College was no longer there, sadly it is yet another housing estate, but it has the same access road as the entrance to the camp, which is just a bit further down the road on the left in the photo opposite. The trees were still there though, and I said hello to the trees because we had met many times before. I will treasure the memories of that very special week for the rest of my life.

Our Camplet Trailer Tent

Portsmouth Road Camberley

Remains of the entrance to the WRAC College

There are no official WRAC branches in my area, the nearest ones to me are Bury and Liverpool, and I thought it would be a good idea to have some kind of informal meeting venue closer by. The best place seemed to be just off the M6/ M61/M65 which would be central for anyone travelling from either motorway, so I put something on one of the social media pages to see if anyone was interested. It turned out to be quite successful and our informal lunch group was born in 2015. It's wonderful for us all to meet up every six weeks or so and we have all become very good friends. We are very lucky to have such a special group.

WRAC – ladies wot lunch

Thanks again to social media, I was able to meet up with the girls I shared a room with at Camberley after saying goodbye to them at the beginning of 1976 when I was posted to Dusseldorf. Bailey lives in the South East, Karen lives in Australia, and Sue lives in Nottingham. We met up in the run up to Christmas 2015, at Salford Quays in Manchester when Karen was home visiting family. It was wonderful to see them all again and the years just melted away, it was like we'd never been apart. A lot of catching up was done, it really was incredible. Another wonderful memory to treasure.

Me, Bailey, Karen and Sue

Being a member of the WRAC Association gave me the opportunity to go in the ballot to take part in the Remembrance Day Parade at the Cenotaph in London. Fresh from my wonderful experience in Guildford, I really wanted to be able to march in London in 2016 to commemorate the centenary of Uncle Joe being killed in action on the Somme, and of course honour my Dad and Grandad. I could hardly believe it when I was accepted to take part in something so special and so very important to the nation. We managed to get on the television as well and I have no photographs of the actual parade other than this one over the page taken from the tele, just as we are about to march past the Cenotaph. I can't put into words exactly how much this meant to me, and I know my Dad would have been absolutely bursting with pride, and probably marching right by my side, his heart would have been full. After all the times we had watched it together, to finally be there was a fairy tale ending.

Remembrance Day Parade London 2016

As an Armed Forces Veteran, I was able to become a member of the Union Jack Club in London. It's a wonderful place where serving, and ex-service personnel, can stay for official gatherings, or just for visits to the capital. When I first stayed there with my new Army friends from the Dinner Club, I felt like I didn't really deserve to be there. But I am happy to say I do now feel comfortable whenever I visit. I've even stayed on my own if I've been down to London for some football related matters, it's such a safe place to be and the location is perfect, directly opposite Waterloo train station and just a few minutes' walk from the South Bank.

Another WRAC group was an annual gathering at Fort William in Scotland. It was a weekend packed full of fun and games, trips out, a formal dinner on the Saturday night and a remembrance service at the Commando Memorial at Spean Bridge before heading for home. I had two memorable trips, had loads of laughs and made many new friends.

Commando Memorial Spean Bridge 2016

Tartan themed Dinner 2017

Commando Memorial Remembrance Service 2017

At the Dinner Club in 2017, I met up with Major Heath for the first time since I left Camberley in 1976. She was the OC who made me feel valued, I had never forgotten her words and it was lovely to see her again. I think she was chuffed I had remembered, even if she didn't. Coincidentally, she moved to Poulton le Fylde the following year and came to our WRAC lunch group. It was wonderful to have lunch with my former OC and I couldn't wait to introduce her to the others. Isn't it amazing how things work out? As my Dad would have said, '*who'd have thowt*.'

Me and former OC Major Norma Heath

It's been a long journey finally finding reconciliation, and a feeling that actually, I do deserve to belong. I was a good soldier. I am proud of my service, and proud to be a Veteran, and I will always be eternally grateful to Sue for not giving up on me and giving me the strength to come back. I have been so truly blessed to have had the opportunity to catch up with old friends and make many new ones and it is wonderful to be part of the WRAC community again. And I will always be immensely proud to wear my Dad's medals.

Armistice Day 2023

Back row: Christine Hardman, Ann Butcher, Alice Masters
Front line: Lee Telford, Colette Watson, Betty Hair, Marilyn Bainbridge, Jane Barmer, me

MY FAMILY ACROSS THE POND

After a blaze of publicity in 1999 regarding a film being made based on my book about the Dick, Kerr Ladies, I was contacted by Winnie Bourque from Massachusetts in USA. One of her nieces had been on holiday in Wales where she saw some of the newspaper reports and told her aunt all about it. Winnie's mother, Alice Mills, had played for the team in 1921 and she was keen to hear more about her Mom, and if she would be featured in the film. We became kind of pen friends at first and would also speak on the phone quite regularly and I kept her up to date with any developments.

Alice Mills was born on Marsh Lane in Preston in 1904, and as a child going to school, every day I would pass by the very house where she had lived. I was also christened at the same church as Alice, and both our names are in the same book in the church register. Alice travelled with the Dick, Kerr Ladies on the tour to USA in 1922, and she loved the country so much, she wanted to return to make a new life. She was determined to pursue the American Dream, and began making plans as soon as she arrived home. Less than twelve months later, Alice left her home town of Preston for ever. She soon met, and fell in love with, J Aime Lambert and they were married in November 1925. The newlyweds worked hard and saved enough money to bring the out rest of her family to live in America; her widowed mother, Mary Ann, and siblings, Elizabeth Ann, Mary, Winnie and Joe, and it wasn't long before they all became proud American citizens. Alice went on to give birth to six daughters, Irene, Louise, Winnie, Terry, Frankie and Rose.

Winnie and I talked often and she shared stories of her Mom and the rest of the family, and it was lovely for me to get to know so much about them. Alice played for the team during their most successful period and Winnie would send me old newspaper clippings and things her Mom had written before she died. I felt very privileged to be able to call her. I was telling Winnie about a dinner I was involved in organising with the National Football Museum on International Women's Day 2003, to honour the Dick, Kerr Ladies. Winnie expressed an interest in coming, along with two of her sisters who were to fly over with her. I was thrilled they wanted to travel so far to share in the night with us. A few days later, I got a call from Winnie to tell me that all six of them were going to come, I could hardly believe it. They had never been to Preston before, but here they all were ready to cross the Atlantic to honour the memory of their Mom at Preston North End. It was an incredible night, but it was the Lambert girls who really stole the show.

Irene, Louise, Rose, Frankie, Terry, Winnie

We still kept in touch over the next few years and Winnie was keen for me to come out and stay with her for a holiday. I didn't have the funds available to make the trip at that time and Winnie insisted she wanted to pay for my flight. So off I went to the USA at the end of June 2008, and what a fantastic time I had. When I arrived, Winnie had arranged a party in her back yard to introduce me to all her family, and I was there for the 4th July celebrations. They took me to Plymouth Rock and on a replica of the Mayflower. To the Tennis Museum at Newport, Rhode Island, where Billie Jean King had some exhibits on display from her Battle of the Sexes match against Bobby Riggs, and to her sister Rose's house at Cape Cod. She took me to see the house where they all grew up together and to some places where the Dick, Kerr Ladies had played in 1922. Winnie also took me to Newport Creamery, her favourite place to get an ice cream, and it was delicious. We also had a day in Boston and went on the Boston Duck tour on the water. Everyone made me feel so welcome and I had the most wonderful time. I can't believe how lucky I was.

Marquee in Winnie's back yard for the welcome party

A bit different from our back yard at Whittingham Street

Terry, Winnie and Frankie outside their childhood home

The following year, Lenore and I flew over to stay with Winnie and see everyone again. Winnie's granddaughter Jennifer, daughter of her sister Rose, arranged tickets for us to watch the Boston Breakers play at Harvard, with Kelly Smith and Alex Scott in the line-up. We went to Fenway Park to see the Boston Redsox play baseball, and even brought home a brick from the old stadium before it was rebuilt. Another trip to Cape Cod to see Rose and John and lunch at Winnie's with all of her sisters, absolutely priceless.

Me, Lenore, Winnie, Frankie, Rose at Cape Cod

Winnie's home was built at the edge of a Golf Club, owned by her son Glenn, who also lives close by, and the club is named Chemawa. I was intrigued by the name and asked Winnie what it meant. She told me it is Native Indian, for *Our Happy Home*. I liked that, I thought it was a lovely sentiment. In 2010, Winnie, Rose and Jennifer came to stay with us for five days and we surprised them with the name we had called our home. They loved it.

Winnie, Jennifer and Rose outside our happy home

During their visit, we took them to Hoghton Tower to see where the Loin of Beef was knighted by King James I. It wasn't yet open for visitors but we were given a private tour of the house by my friend Anne Swarbrick who worked there, and kindly took us round. They were very impressed. We took them to Marsh Lane to see where Alice was born, to St Walburges Church to see the font where she was christened and to Lancashire Archives to do some family research. We went to Ashton Park where Alice had played football with the Dick, Kerr Ladies, and showed them the factory where the team had been formed. We also had a trip to the Lake District and finally to a local restaurant for dinner. Then it was over all too quickly.

Jennifer, Rose and Winnie at the table where King James I knighted Sirloin of Beef

Lenore and I flew out to stay with Winnie again in 2012, but this was just for a visit to spend time with her and not gallivanting all over the place. It was lovely to have some quiet time and see everyone, perhaps for the last time. She was very poorly early in 2021, and we thought we were going to lose her, but after a few scary months, she pulled through and is doing really well. Sadly, she lost two of her sisters within the space of six weeks later that year. Irene who was the eldest, and Terry who was born after Winnie. They had both been unwell and it was all very sad. I'm just so glad I had the opportunity to meet them all. Winnie celebrated her 92nd birthday in January 2024 and she really enjoyed this milestone. She is still as bright as a button and we remain in touch talking often on the phone. We also keep in contact with Jennifer on facetime and WhatsApp and it is such a joy to have them all in our lives, our family across the pond. All thanks to Alice Mills playing football for the Dick, Kerr Ladies over one hundred years ago.

EPILOGUE

I couldn't finish these memoirs without mentioning Sooty, my teddy bear. He has been the one constant in my life who I have loved since I was a babe in arms. My Mum's brother Phil bought him for me when I was about three months old, and throughout my life he has never been far from my side. I can't put into words how much I have loved that little bear. He represents my childhood as being my comforter, my soother, my companion, my friend, and the memories I have of my Mum making that wonderful squeaky little voice for him, will always be treasured. I have so many emotions invested in Sooty, I just love him with all my heart. He is so much more than just a stuffed toy. And now that Mum, Dad and our Pat are no longer here, Sooty is my last link to them and our home at 42. When I was a kid, I was running along the top end of Pedder Street, just near the Maudland pub, when I tripped over my cowboy pants and hit my head with a mighty thud on the pavement. I ran home crying my eyes out with a big lump on my forehead, and the start of the biggest black eye you have ever seen. Mum put me to bed, but we couldn't find Sooty anywhere, and I had to have a doll for comfort as Mum nursed the swelling on my forehead. The doll was nowhere near as comforting as my faithful teddy, and I sobbed my heart out. I remember holding her, she was called Jacqueline, and talking to her between sobs, *'don't worry, Jacqueline, I'll be alright.'* Thankfully, Sooty was eventually found to help me on the road to recovery.

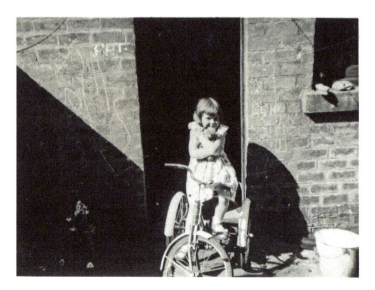

Me aged 4, and Sooty – back yard Whittingham Street

After a lifetime of being loved, Sooty was becoming quite frail and I had known for some considerable time he needed some serious attention, but I just couldn't bear the thought of leaving him somewhere for any restoration to be performed. I can't put into words the very real worry and concern I felt about entrusting his care to someone else. What if something went wrong? It might sound daft, but the thought of him not being with me, literally brought me to tears, I just couldn't do it. He'd had some minor repairs over the years, my Mum once stitched the seam on his throat a long time ago, and other attempts at keeping him together were tried, but he was literally starting to fall apart and had become too fragile to even hold, so I had to resort to putting him in a drawer where he would be safe.

Sooty

In 2014, I came across someone on a social media site who restored teddy bears. I contacted him and explained all my fears about being parted from Sooty, but deep down I knew I had to find the courage to let him have the chance of a new lease of life. I was really concerned about his personality being changed by any restoration, and I stressed this to the guy doing the repair. I told him I wasn't sure if I wanted Sooty to have eyes, he had been without them for so long, I didn't want him to look different than the Sooty I had shared my life with. He said something that completely melted my heart. *'But what if he wants to see his Mum again.'* This was the final push I needed to let him go. If he could say something so thoughtful, maybe it would be ok. I sent him off special delivery to ensure he didn't get lost in the post and he arrived safely the next day. I was kept informed of how things were going, and he reassured me Sooty was well and making new friends. He sent the photo below of Sooty with one of his new friends when he was on his way home.

Sooty and his new friend

When he finally arrived, I have to admit I was quite disappointed, he didn't look like Sooty to me anymore. His nose was too big and his features had been changed. I was happy to have him back home with me, but for quite some time, I just left him sat on my desk and didn't interact with him much at all. But I finally came to my senses when I thought about how he must have been feeling, being left sitting there not being properly loved. I felt really sad for him. After all we had been through together, he was still Sooty, he just looked a bit different. I didn't stop loving my Mum when she looked different, so there was no excuse for not treating him with the same devotion. Sooty is no longer sat on my desk, but he is back where he belongs and sleeps with me every night. But I'm sorry to say he is looking like he is soon going to need some more attention. Unlike the Teddy Bear Ladies on *The Repair Shop*, Sooty wasn't given a lining to strengthen him and some holes are starting to appear on his tummy and a couple of other places, so I might soon be facing the same dilemma all over again. I wish the Teddy Bear Ladies had been around for his first repair. But I feel so lucky to have had such a special little bear in my life. Through all my ups and downs, Sooty has always been there and I love him more than words can say.

Lenore and I returned to Cyprus for a holiday in 2015. We first visited the island in 2005 and really enjoyed our stay at the Ledra Beach, an all-inclusive 4 star hotel in Paphos, and we decided to book to go there again. We loved everything about the holiday and returned year after year for our annual September fortnight in the sun, a special treat after being away camping, which we always loved and had some wonderful adventures, but it is hard work and we enjoyed being pampered for a change. We met some lovely people who we became very good friends with and always met up with Kath and Tom Reece from Leicester. Lovely people and equally lovely memories.

Lenore, Tom, Kath, me

Thoughts of my Mum and Dad are never far away and I still try to do things to make them proud. Dad never forgot baby June, the sister between me and our Pat, who was born in 1947. They couldn't afford to pay for a grave for her, so she was buried in a family plot along with Dad's Auntie Edi. Coincidentally, it came to pass that this grave wasn't far from where Grandma, Grandad, and Kash were eventually buried, and whenever I was at the cemetery with Dad he would always point to the direction of where June was in relation to where his Mum, Dad and sister were. There was no headstone on June's grave, so we never knew its exact location, but he always kept a note of the grave number. He had written it on a piece of card and gave it to me not long before he passed away. I kept it safe and knew that when I could, I would do what Dad had wanted, and with Lenore's help, we got it sorted. I know he would be proud. I have taken a wreath for Kash every Christmas since she passed away in 1989, apart from when I had my appendix out, and now I can take one for our June at the same time.

Our Junes grave 2016

In 2019 I was made an Honorary Fellow of the University of Central Lancashire, in recognition of my work in the promotion of women's football over the years. I was completely overwhelmed when I was first informed of the honour, and then to learn the nomination actually came from David Taylor CBE DL, Vice Chairman of Preston North End, I was completely blown away. It was a very proud day indeed for this lass from Whittingham Street, and as Joe would have said, '*who'd 'ave thowt.*'

Honorary Fellow 2019

We had lunch before the Graduation Ceremony took place, in the newly finished building on the corner of Fylde Road and Maudland Road, which was my playground when I was young, and not far from where my Dad grew up on Bedford Street. It was on the site of where the Star Cinema used to be and very close to the Miley Tunnel. When we were all sat down to eat, I was sharing stories of my adventures down there all those years ago. Work was still ongoing in the area as part of the university expansion programme and they very kindly arranged for me to be taken down to revisit the tunnel a few weeks later. This was the first time I had been down there legitimately, not having to sneak past any signal boxes, or look out for railway men. There was only the first part of the tunnel accessible now, but it didn't half bring back some wonderful memories. What a great thrill it was, and isn't it amazing how things work out.

Start of the Miley Tunnel – no lights when we were kids, and one of the alcoves 2019

In August of 2020, we were deeply saddened to hear of the passing of our Scottish cousin Andy McCabe. He was always the life and soul of the party and the last one on the dance floor; Andy would walk five hundred miles, and then he'd walk five hundred more, and he always gave the biggest of hugs whenever we met at family gatherings. He had been battling cancer for some time and was taken far too soon. His 60th birthday was celebrated in the hospice just before he passed away. In March of 2022 his brother, and our cousin Michael also passed away, he was just fifty-nine years old. Michael was immortalised on video at Mum and Dads Golden Wedding, when he sportingly joined in dancing with one of Mum's friends, to Tina Turner's *Simply the Best*. It certainly was a show stopper with everyone joining in clapping the performance. And it even got a mention at his funeral.

Both Andy and Michael were pall bearers at Mum's funeral. We have shared many weddings, anniversaries and funerals, on both sides of the border over the years, and despite the distance, the family love is such a special gift. The McCabe's have always been so supportive to us Newsham's over the years. Whatever gatherings we've had, happy or sad, they have always been there for us. They have never let us down.

The McCabe's – our Scottish family

The boys: Michael, Andy, Patrick, John
The girls: Julia, Agnes, Kathleen, Margaret, Theresa

I had been doing some family history research on Ancestry after our Pat passed away and decided to take a DNA test to see if it could help uncover more ancestors. I'd grown up all my life believing I was half Scottish because of Mum, and I knew there was some Irish there too because of Dad's Mum. But I never expected to discover that Mum has more Irish blood than Scottish. I don't know what she would make of it. It was a bit of a surprise for me to discover I am 57% Irish, 36% Scottish and only 7% English. I wish our Pat was still here so that we could talk about it, I'll bet she would have been as surprised as I was. It's one of the reasons why I decided to write this book. Maybe in a hundred years, my future family might want to know a bit about who we were and what life was like for us. I hope my tales might survive somewhere for them to discover who that bloody Gail Newsham was.

I reached the grand old age of seventy in July 2023, and after the sadness and loss over the last few years, I decided to have a party to celebrate this mile-stone. We gathered at Bamber Bridge Football Club for some corned beef hash and some welcome bubbles, to share some memories of our younger days. There

305

were people from every chapter of my life, some I hadn't seen in over forty years, it was an absolutely wonderful night. I feel truly blessed to have such special people still part of my life. Clive who I played football with, Julie my friend from school, Wendy and Mal who have been part of my life for the longest time. Mal was a midwife throughout her working life, and she delivered over 10,000 babies during her career. Also there was Steve Shaw from our Whittingham Street days. Steve served in the Royal Marines and is a veteran of the Falklands War. Sometime after this conflict, he was on exercise with his unit in the Lake District and was returning to camp late one night when he fell through a railway bridge and broke his back. It was a bitter cold November night, and he lay on the rocks all night, unable to move until he was found the next morning. Had he not been wearing a big thick jacket, he may not have survived the cold. But Steve is made of strong stuff and he didn't let this life changing injury get the better of him. He came to live in Bamber Bridge for a while, and I'd see him when I was working in the council office there, but he soon went to live in Spain. He took up lots of different sports that took him all over the world, he was and is incredible. One of the sports he did extremely well at was Sit Ski, and he competed in the 1998 Winter Paralympics in Nagano, Japan. He has returned to live in Preston now and I am delighted we are back in touch again.

Clive, Linda, Julie, Wendy, Mal, Billy, Steve, Tracey

My Scottish cousins – Theresa McCabe, me Una, Margaret & Agnes McCabe

My Peter Craig family: Angela, Jennifer, Margaret, Mandy, Janet, Pauline, Lesley

For our Pat's birthday on 12 February 2024, Lenore and I went to the Villa at Wrea Green, to raise a glass to her. It was the first time I had been there since she took me for my eighteenth birthday in 1971. We had a lovely table next to a window and the food was delicious. Our Pat is in my thoughts every day, and it was lovely to walk down memory lane to celebrate her heavenly birthday in that special place, I am sure she would have approved. She was still very much on my mind as we approached the 2nd anniversary of her passing on 9th May, and when I woke up that morning and looked at the clock, it was 6.07am, the exact same time as the incident in ICU.

When I look back at what I have done in my life, things that might have made a difference, I feel my efforts in saving the Dick, Kerr Ladies history is probably my greatest achievement. Leaving school at fifteen without any academic qualifications and working in a shoe factory, I had no training, or knowledge of the skills required for writing and researching. It was just a passion that came from within and I know I had a lot of spiritual guidance, I always knew I wasn't alone and I genuinely believe they chose me as the one to tell their story. I grew up in the same area as many of them, we have walked the same streets, and I loved football from a very early age, I believe it was just one of those things that was meant to be. I know how much joy they felt, and how much it meant to them, being brought back into the limelight after being forgotten for so long, but they have enriched my life in equal measures. The friendships and bonds I made with these amazing women is something I will always treasure. We did many things together over the years, promoting women's football and telling their story. As I watched them all get older, I helped some of them claim Attendance Allowance when they needed more help and care, and I attended their funerals when their time came. There are very few left now. I was particularly close to Joan Whalley, we genuinely were great pals and I feel truly blessed to have had the opportunity to get to know her as I did. I love being able to share their stories and keep their memory alive.

Me and my special pal, Joan Whalley

Now looking forward with what is left of my own family, the ranks are thinning out and soon the batton will be passed on to the next generation. Some of them are coming up to the age I was when I set off hitch hiking to Italy. I wonder what life adventures await them? I don't know what they will make of their maternal Great Grandma and Grandad, but there is a little bit of Sadie and Joe in all of them. They are all grown up now and doing really well, all being good scholars and going to university. I hope they might read about us all someday and be proud of our side of their roots.

Sophi, Sarah, Ian

Life is a short but very precious gift, and an incredible journey filled with a wealth of experiences and emotions; joy and sadness, love and loss, elation and despair, success and failure, and learning all life's wondrous lessons. We are here to learn and I really do believe the universe has a plan for us, and we sometimes have to suffer injustice, pain and sorrow to get us on the right path to where we are meant to be, and although we can't always see it at the time, things do have a

309

way of working out. My belief of everything happening for a reason is mirrored in my experiences. I have come to the conclusion that all the upset of leaving the Army was to get me home to take care of Mum when she was so ill, and I would do it all again in a heartbeat. I know I could never have coped being so far away when she was going through so much suffering, and someone had to be there to enable Dad to go to work and keep a roof over their heads. The same with Fairways Garage, as despicable as their treatment was, I once again needed to be there for Mum; no contest really and everything worked out for the best. I think I also had to leave Preston Rangers for a while, otherwise the Lancashire Trophy may never have happened because there would have been no void to fill. That very special tournament brought a great deal of pleasure to so many people over the years and everything worked out in the end with Preston Rangers. I haven't worked out the reason for the South Ribble Council episode yet, but my book turned out to be successful in the end in spite of them.

I believe life has brought me to where I am now meant to be, things have turned out pretty well and I have no complaints. I have been fortunate to do most of the things I ever dreamed of doing, and lucky to meet some of the people I always wanted to meet. I am happy and content and truly grateful for the life I have been given and the good health I enjoy, I genuinely count my blessings on a daily basis. They say life is made up of two dates and a dash, in my case 1953 - 20??. I hope I have made the most of the dash. But of course, I have made mistakes along the way, there are things I wish I hadn't done and some things I wish I had, but hopefully I have learned the lessons from it all, and I am genuinely sorry for any hurt my actions may have caused others.

I consider myself a very lucky lass and I am truly grateful to everyone who has touched my life. Thank you Lenore for your love, wisdom and unwavering support, the wind beneath my wings. Thank you for being part of my journey. Thank you everyone for your love and friendship. I hope your lives have been as blessed as mine. I will always miss my Mum, Dad, and our Pat; my life will never be the same without them and the love I feel for them could never be expressed in words. I miss being a daughter and I miss being a sister, but I am so grateful to have had them as my family, and everything we shared together. I wouldn't swap them for a gold clock and I will carry them in my heart always.

One thing is for sure, wherever I've been, whatever I've done, I have never forgotten where I came from and I wear it as a badge of honour. It has undoubtedly been a huge part of making me who I am and I wouldn't change a single thing. You can take the girl out of Whittingham Street, but you'll never take Whittingham Street out of this girl.

POSTSCRIPT

DAWN

The dawn breaks through
The sun comes up to start the day anew
And in the quiet peace
As I watch you sleeping
For a moment, all is well
But reality dawns
There's a journey to make
Across the sea to say goodbye
Another loved one
Their time is done
And we are left to wonder why
So much grief and pain for those who remain
Only time will heal the scars
It's so hard to part and all we can do
Is keep them close within our heart
With a sad goodbye and a tear in our eye
We turn to walk away
But deep in our heart their memory will stay
For we will be together
One day
But life and death go hand in hand
And we all come to discover
As on this journey we undertake
There's never one without the other
For every autumn there is a spring
As life returns anew
And those we love
We'll see once more
And our faith will see us through

Gail J Newsham